EDITH WHARTON

Modern Critical Views

Henry Adams
Edward Albee
A. R. Ammons
Matthew Arnold
John Ashbery
W. H. Auden
Jane Austen
James Baldwin
Charles Baudelaire
Samuel Beckett
Saul Bellow
The Bible
Elizabeth Bishop
William Blake
Jorge Luis Borges
Elizabeth Bowen
Bertolt Brecht
The Brontës
Robert Browning
Anthony Burgess
George Gordon, Lord
  Byron
Thomas Carlyle
Lewis Carroll
Willa Cather
Cervantes
Geoffrey Chaucer
Kate Chopin
Samuel Taylor Coleridge
Joseph Conrad
Contemporary Poets
Hart Crane
Stephen Crane
Dante
Charles Dickens
Emily Dickinson
John Donne & the Seven-
  teenth-Century Meta-
  physical Poets
Elizabethan Dramatists
Theodore Dreiser
John Dryden
George Eliot
T. S. Eliot
Ralph Ellison
Ralph Waldo Emerson
William Faulkner
Henry Fielding
F. Scott Fitzgerald
Gustave Flaubert
E. M. Forster
Sigmund Freud
Robert Frost

Robert Graves
Graham Greene
Thomas Hardy
Nathaniel Hawthorne
William Hazlitt
Seamus Heaney
Ernest Hemingway
Geoffrey Hill
Friedrich Hölderlin
Homer
Gerard Manley Hopkins
William Dean Howells
Zora Neale Hurston
Henry James
Samuel Johnson and
  James Boswell
Ben Jonson
James Joyce
Franz Kafka
John Keats
Rudyard Kipling
D. H. Lawrence
John Le Carré
Ursula K. Le Guin
Doris Lessing
Sinclair Lewis
Robert Lowell
Norman Mailer
Bernard Malamud
Thomas Mann
Christopher Marlowe
Carson McCullers
Herman Melville
James Merrill
Arthur Miller
John Milton
Eugenio Montale
Marianne Moore
Iris Murdoch
Vladimir Nabokov
Joyce Carol Oates
Sean O'Casey
Flannery O'Connor
Eugene O'Neill
George Orwell
Cynthia Ozick
Walter Pater
Walker Percy
Harold Pinter
Plato
Edgar Allan Poe
Poets of Sensibility & the
  Sublime

Alexander Pope
Katherine Ann Porter
Ezra Pound
Pre-Raphaelite Poets
Marcel Proust
Thomas Pynchon
Arthur Rimbaud
Theodore Roethke
Philip Roth
John Ruskin
J. D. Salinger
Gershom Scholem
William Shakespeare
  (3 vols.)
  Histories & Poems
  Comedies
  Tragedies
George Bernard Shaw
Mary Wollstonecraft
  Shelley
Percy Bysshe Shelley
Edmund Spenser
Gertrude Stein
John Steinbeck
Laurence Sterne
Wallace Stevens
Tom Stoppard
Jonathan Swift
Alfred, Lord Tennyson
William Makepeace
  Thackeray
Henry David Thoreau
Leo Tolstoi
Anthony Trollope
Mark Twain
John Updike
Gore Vidal
Virgil
Robert Penn Warren
Evelyn Waugh
Eudora Welty
Nathanael West
Edith Wharton
Walt Whitman
Oscar Wilde
Tennessee Williams
William Carlos Williams
Thomas Wolfe
Virginia Woolf
William Wordsworth
Richard Wright
William Butler Yeats

These and other titles in preparation

Modern Critical Views

EDITH WHARTON

Edited and with an introduction by
Harold Bloom
Sterling Professor of the Humanities
Yale University

CHELSEA HOUSE PUBLISHERS ◊ 1986
New York ◊ New Haven ◊ Philadelphia

© 1986 by Chelsea House Publishers, a division of Chelsea
House Educational Communications, Inc.
  133 Christopher Street, New York, NY 10014
  345 Whitney Avenue, New Haven, CT 06511
  5014 West Chester Pike, Edgemont, PA 19028

Introduction © 1986 by Harold Bloom

Printed and bound in the United States of America

∞ The paper used in this publication meets the minimum
requirements of the American National Standard for Permanence
of Paper for Printed Library Materials, Z39.48–1984.

Library of Congress Cataloging-in-Publication Data
Edith Wharton.
  (Modern critical views)
  Bibliography: p.
  Includes index.
  1. Wharton, Edith, 1862–1937—Criticism and
interpretation. I. Bloom, Harold. II. Series.
PS3545.H16Z645 1986   813'.52   86–9696
ISBN 0–87754–699–1

Contents

Editor's Note   vii

Introduction   1
    Harold Bloom

A Writer of Short Stories   9
    R. W. B. Lewis

Undine   29
    Richard H. Lawson

Fairy-Tale Love and *The Reef*   39
    Elizabeth Ammons

Hudson River Bracketed and *The Gods Arrive*   51
    Margaret B. McDowell

Ethan Frome: "This Vision of His Story"   65
    Cynthia Griffin Wolff

Edith Wharton and the Ghost Story   89
    Allan Gardner Smith

Purity and Power in *The Age of Innocence*   99
    Judith Fryer

The Divided Conflict of Edith Wharton's
Summer   117
    Carol Wershoven

Debasing Exchange: Edith Wharton's *The House
of Mirth*   123
    Wai-chee Dimock

The Death of the Lady (Novelist): Wharton's *House of Mirth*   139
    Elaine Showalter

Chronology   155

Contributors   159

Bibliography   161

Acknowledgments   165

Index   167

Editor's Note

This book gathers together a representative selection of the best criticism so far published upon the fiction of Edith Wharton, arranged in the chronological order of its original publication. I am grateful to Chantal McCoy for her erudition and judgment in helping to edit this volume.

The editor's introduction addresses the complex issue of Wharton's social and psychological reductiveness, with particular emphasis upon *The Custom of the Country* and *Ethan Frome*. R. W. B. Lewis, Wharton's biographer and best critic, begins the chronological sequence of criticism with the introductory essay to his massive edition of her short stories, the strongest of which he accurately ranks with her most eminent achievements.

Undine Spragg, the fascinating monster who is the protagonist of *The Custom of the Country*, is analyzed by Richard H. Lawson, who traces Wharton's indebtedness to Fouqué's *Undine*. *The Reef*, a Jamesian mythic novel, is read by Elizabeth Ammons as Wharton's subtle protest against the male vision of the salvation of women through men.

Margaret B. McDowell attempts to rescue *Hudson River Bracketed* and *The Gods Arrive* from comparative neglect, finding in them Wharton's portrait of Americans caught up in the first phase of the Great Depression (1929–32). A very different perspective, psychological rather than social, is employed by Cynthia Griffin Wolff in her analysis of *Ethan Frome*.

Wharton's remarkable ghost stories, outstanding in the genre though rather neglected, are judged as being quasi-feminist in an overview by Allan Gardner Smith. The justly celebrated, rather Jamesian, *The Age of Innocence*, in a reading by Judith Fryer becomes the sadly ironic parable of Newland Archer's inevitable surrender to an idea of order, minimal and fading, that he nevertheless authentically incarnates. Carol Wershoven, examining the passionate portrayal of Lawyer Royall in *Summer*, finds in Royall's marriage to his ward Charity an act of expiation for the usual paternal pattern that informs male dominance of women.

This volume concludes with two advanced readings of *The House of Mirth,* by Wai-chee Dimock and Elaine Showalter. Dimock subtly analyzes the book as an instance of the economics of exchange, a study in social and personal morality. Showalter, one of our leading feminist critics, maps in *The House of Mirth* the outlines of a new image of the woman as novelist, a precursor of "a literary history of female mastery and growth."

Introduction

The most formidable figure in all Wallace Stevens's marvelous roster of fabulistic caricatures is that grand reductionist, "Mrs. Alfred Uruguay":

> So what said the others and the sun went down
> And, in the brown blues of evening, the lady said,
> In the donkey's ear, "I fear that elegance
> Must struggle like the rest." She climbed until
> The moonlight in her lap, mewing her velvet,
> And her dress were one and she said, "I have said no
> To everything, in order to get at myself.
> I have wiped away moonlight like mud. Your innocent ear
> And I, if I rode naked, are what remain."

Not for a moment do I suggest that this is an imaginary portrait of the formidable novelist Mrs. Edith Wharton, for Edith Wharton was more than a reductionist. Rather, Stevens's Mrs. Uruguay is a fierce reductionist out of old New York society as Wharton herself might have represented such a personage, and sometimes did. By "reductionist" I mean an adept in practicing what might be called "the reductive fallacy," which is the incessant translation of: "Tell me what she or he is *really* like," as: "Tell me the very worst thing you can, about her or him, which is in any way true or accurate."

Wharton's most savage portrait of such a reductionist is Undine Spragg in *The Custom of the Country,* which is likely to seem, some day, Wharton's strongest achievement, though I find it rather an unpleasant novel to reread. Undine Spragg (marvelous name! but then, Wharton's names are always superb) is not quite of the eminence of Thackeray's Becky Sharp, but she has an antithetical greatness about her that R. W. B. Lewis, Wharton's biographer, shrewdly traces to Wharton's dialectical self-knowledge:

> But the most of Edith Wharton is revealed, quite startlingly, in the characterization of Undine Spragg. No one (except possibly Ethan Frome) would at first glance seem more remote from Edith Wharton than Undine: a crude, unlettered, humorless, artificial, but exceedingly beautiful creature, with the most minimal moral intuitions and virtually no talent whatever for normal human affection. Undine did, undoubtedly, stand for everything in the new American female that Edith despised and recoiled from. But the matter, as it turns out, is much more interesting than that.
>
> There are smaller and larger telltale similarities. As a child Undine, like Edith, enjoyed dressing up in her mother's best finery and "playing lady" before a mirror. Moffatt addresses her by Edith's youthful nickname, "Puss." Edith's long yearning for psychological freedom is queerly reflected in Undine's discovery that each of her marriages is no more than another mode of imprisonment; and Undine's creator allows more than a hint that the young woman is as much a victim as an aggressor amid the assorted snobberies, tedium, and fossilized rules of conduct of American and, even more, French high society. Above all, Undine suggests what Edith Wharton might have been like if, by some dreadful miracle, all her best and most lovable and redeeming features had been suddenly cut away.
>
> So imagined, we see in Undine Spragg how Edith sometimes appeared to the view of the harried and aging Henry James: demanding, imperious, devastating, resolutely indifferent to the needs of others; something like an irresistible force of nature. James's image of Edith as a cyclone is borrowed (Minnie Cadwalader Jones probably showed her the letter) to describe the uproar Undine caused on one occasion, when "everything had gone down before her, as towns and villages went down before one of the tornadoes of her native state." Marvell thinks of his young bride as an eagle, and one has the decided impression of a number of men carried off seriatim, "struggling in her talons." No character Edith Wharton ever invented more closely resembles that bird of prey by which James, Sturgis, and others so often, and only half-jokingly, portrayed Edith herself. Undine Spragg is, so to say, a dark Angel of Devastation: Edith Wharton's anti-

self; and like all anti-selves, a figure that explains much about its opposite.

To Lewis's fine characterization of Undine Spragg and Edith Wharton as "demanding, imperious, devastating . . . an irresistible force of nature" (all qualities also of Mrs. Alfred Uruguay) I would add only "darkly reductive" for Undine and (sometimes) "ironically reductive" for Wharton. That ironic reductiveness can mar her strength at representation, as it does in the concluding vision of Undine in *The Custom of the Country*:

> There was a noise of motors backing and advancing in the court, and she heard the first voices on the stairs. She turned to give herself a last look in the glass, saw the blaze of her rubies, the glitter of her hair, and remembered the brilliant names on her list.
>
> But under all the dazzle a tiny black cloud remained. She had learned that there was something she could never get, something that neither beauty nor influence nor millions could ever buy for her. She could never be an Ambassador's wife; and as she advanced to welcome her first guests she said to herself that it was the one part she was really made for.

Undine has just been told by her first, fourth, and final husband, Elmer Moffatt, a Kansas billionaire, that he could not have become Ambassador to England, because: "They won't have divorced Ambassadresses." To Undine, it is "as if the rule had been invented to humiliate her." In some curious sense, Wharton revenges herself upon her antithetical self, Undine, in a mode more reductive than even the formidable Undine deserves. We hear the voice of old New York speaking through Wharton's satisfaction that there was something Undine could never buy, and we remember Mrs. Uruguay's satisfaction in having wiped away moonlight like mud. Not that Undine is other than a false moonlight, but rather that she has force, drive, and desire, and a cold splendor, and our imaginations wish to hear her final note as a grand villain should be heard, holding on in wicked glory.

II

In 1911, two years before *The Custom of the Country* was published, Wharton brought out the short novel that seems her most American story, the New England tragedy *Ethan Frome*. I would guess that it is now her most widely read book, and is likely to remain so. Certainly *Ethan Frome* is Wharton's only fiction to have become part of the American mythology, though it is hardly an early-twentieth-century *Scarlet Letter.* Relentless and stripped, *Ethan Frome* is tragedy not as Hawthorne wrote it, but in the mode of pain and of a reductive moral sadism, akin perhaps to Robert Penn Warren's harshness toward his protagonists, particularly in *World Enough and Time.* The book's aesthetic fascination, for me, centers in Wharton's audacity in touching the limits of a reader's capacity at absorbing really extreme suffering, when that suffering is bleak, intolerable, and in a clear sense unnecessary. Wharton's astonishing authority here is to render such pain with purity and economy, while making it seem inevitable, as much in the nature of things and of psyches as in the social customs of its place and time.

R. W. B. Lewis praises *Ethan Frome* as "a classic of the realistic genre"; doubtless it is, and yet literary "realism" is itself intensely metaphorical, as Lewis keenly knows. *Ethan Frome* is so charged in its representation of reality as to be frequently phantasmagoric in effect. Its terrible vividness estranges it subtly from mere naturalism, and makes its pain just bearable. Presumably Edith Wharton would not have said: "Ethan Frome—that is myself," and yet he is more his author than Undine Spragg was to be. Like Wharton, Ethan has an immense capacity for suffering, and an overwhelming sense of reality; indeed like Edith Wharton, he has too strong a sense of what was to be the Freudian reality principle.

Though an exact contemporary of Freud, Edith Wharton showed no interest in him, but she became an emphatic Nietzschean, and *Ethan Frome* manifests both a Nietzschean perspectivism, and an ascetic intensity that I suspect goes back to a reading of Schopenhauer, Nietzsche's precursor. What fails in Ethan, and in his beloved Mattie, is precisely what Schopenhauer urged us to overcome: the Will to Live, though suicide was hardly a Schopenhauerian solution. In her introduction to *Ethan Frome,* Wharton states a narrative principle that sounds more like Balzac, Browning, or James, but that actually reflects the Nietzsche of *The Genealogy of Morals*:

> Each of my chroniclers contributes to the narrative *just so much as he or she is capable of understanding* of what, to them, is a complicated and mysterious case; and only the narrator of the tale has scope enough to see it all, to resolve it back into simplicity, and to put it in its rightful place among his larger categories.

But does Wharton's narrator have scope enough to see all of the tale that is *Ethan Frome*? Why is the narrator's view more than only another view, and a simplifying one at that? Wharton's introduction memorably calls her protagonists "these figures, my *granite outcroppings*; but half-emerged from the soil, and scarcely more articulate." Yet her narrator (whatever her intentions) lacks the imagination to empathize with granite outcroppings who are also men and women:

> Though Harmon Gow developed the tale as far as his mental and moral reach permitted there were perceptible gaps between his facts, and I had the sense that the deeper meaning of the story was in the gaps. But one phrase stuck in my memory and served as the nucleus about which I grouped my subsequent inferences: "Guess he's been in Starkfield too many winters."
>
> Before my own time there was up I had learned to know what that meant. Yet I had come in the degenerate day of trolley, bicycle and rural delivery, when communication was easy between the scattered mountain villages, and the bigger towns in the valleys, such as Bettsbridge and Shadd's Falls, had libraries, theatres and Y.M.C.A. halls to which the youth of the hills could descend for recreation. But when winter shut down on Starkfield, and the village lay under a sheet of snow perpetually renewed from the pale skies, I began to see what life there—or rather its negation— must have been in Ethan Frome's young manhood.
>
> I had been sent up by my employers on a job connected with the big power-house at Corbury Junction, and a long-drawn carpenters' strike had so delayed the work that I found myself anchored at Starkfield—the nearest habitable spot—for the best part of the winter. I chafed at first, and then, under the hypnotising effect of routine, gradually began to find a grim satisfaction in the life. During the early part of my stay I had been struck by the contrast between the vitality of the climate and the deadness of the community. Day by day, after the December snows were over, a blazing blue sky poured down torrents of light and air on the white landscape, which gave them back in an intenser glitter. One would have supposed that such an atmosphere must quicken the emotions as well as the blood; but it seemed to produce no change except that of retarding still more the sluggish pulse of Starkfield. When I had been there a little longer, and had seen this phase of crystal clearness followed by long stretches of sunless cold; when the storms of February had pitched their white tents about the devoted village and the wild cavalry of March winds

had charged down to their support; I began to understand why Starkfield emerged from its six months' siege like a starved garrison capitulating without quarter. Twenty years earlier the means of resistance must have been far fewer, and the enemy in command of almost all the lines of access between the beleaguered villages; and, considering these things, I felt the sinister force of Harmon's phrase: "Most of the smart ones get away." But if that were the case, how could any combination of obstacles have hindered the flight of a man like Ethan Frome?

The narrator's "mental and moral reach" is not in question, but his vision has acute limitations. Winter indeed is the cultural issue, but *Ethan Frome* is not exactly Ursula K. LeGuin's *The Left Hand of Darkness*. It is not a "combination of obstacles" that hindered the flight of Ethan Frome, but a terrible fatalism which is a crucial part of Edith Wharton's Emersonian heritage. Certainly the narrator is right to express the contrast between the winter sublimity of: "a blazing blue sky poured down torrents of light and air on the white landscape, which gave them back in an intenser glitter," and the inability of the local population to give back more than sunken apathy. But Frome, as the narrator says on the novel's first page, is himself a ruined version of the American Sublime: "the most striking figure in Starkfield . . . his great height . . . the careless powerful look he had . . . something bleak and unapproachable in his face." Ethan Frome is an Ahab who lacks Moby-Dick, self-lamed rather than wounded by the white whale, and by the whiteness of the whale. Not the whiteness of Starkfield but an inner whiteness or blankness has crippled Ethan Frome, perhaps the whiteness that goes through American tradition "from Edwards to Emerson" and on through Wharton to Wallace Stevens contemplating the beach world lit by the glare of the Northern Lights in "The Auroras of Autumn":

> Here, being visible is being white,
> Is being of the solid of white, the accomplishment
> Of an extremist in an exercise . . .
>
> The season changes. A cold wind chills the beach.
> The long lines of it grow longer, emptier,
> A darkness gathers though it does not fall
>
> And the whiteness grows less vivid on the wall.
> The man who is walking turns blankly on the sand.
> He observes how the north is always enlarging the change,

With its frigid brilliances, its blue-red sweeps
And gusts of great enkindlings, its polar green,
The color of ice and fire and solitude.

That, though with a more sublime eloquence, is the visionary world of *Ethan Frome,* a world where the will is impotent, and tragedy is always circumstantial. The experiential puzzle of *Ethan Frome* is ultimately also its aesthetic strength: we do not question the joint decision of Ethan and Mattie to immolate themselves, even though it is pragmatically outrageous and psychologically quite impossible. But the novel's apparent realism is a mask for its actual fatalistic mode, and truly it is a northern romance, akin even to *Wuthering Heights.* A visionary ethos dominates Ethan and Mattie, and would have dominated Edith Wharton herself, had she not battled against it with her powerful gift for social reductiveness. We can wonder whether even *The Age of Innocence,* with its Jamesian renunciations in the mode of *The Portrait of a Lady,* compensates us for what Wharton might have written, had she gone on with her own version of the American romance tradition of Hawthorne and Melville.

R. W. B. LEWIS

A Writer of Short Stories

Edith Wharton began as a writer of short stories and, in a sense, she finished as one. Her first publications (apart from the poems that appeared anonymously in the New York *World* and the *Atlantic Monthly,* and were privately printed as *Verses* in 1878) were a series of stories brought out by *Scribner's,* starting with the issue of July, 1891, when Mrs. Wharton was in her thirtieth year. By the time she completed her first novel, *The Valley of Decision,* in 1902, two volumes of her shorter works had appeared, volumes which included such fine and remarkably varied stories as "A Journey," "The Pelican," "Souls Belated" and "The Recovery." And while she wrote no unquestionably first-rate full-length novel after *The Age of Innocence* in 1920—*The Buccaneers,* had she lived to finish and revise it, might have proved the gratifying exception—the four collections of stories in those later years contained items as distinguished as "A Bottle of Perrier," "After Holbein," "Roman Fever" and "All Souls'," the latter composed apparently within a year or so of her death in 1937. Mrs. Wharton produced eighty-six stories in all, leaving behind in addition several promising but tantalizingly fragmentary manuscripts; and of this impressive number, eighteen or twenty strike this reader as very good indeed, many more as displaying an at least occasional excellence (the description of an Italian garden, the disclosure of a moral quirk, a flash of wit), and no one of them as totally bereft of interest.

From *The Collected Short Stories of Edith Wharton,* vol. 1. © 1968 by Charles Scribner's Sons. Originally entitled "Introduction."

What does distinguish the best of them must be specified with some care. It cannot be said, for example, that Mrs. Wharton significantly modified the genre itself—as during her lifetime, James Joyce and D. H. Lawrence and Ernest Hemingway were so differently doing. On the formal side, she was, to borrow a phrase from Louis Auchincloss, "a caretaker." She was the dedicated preserver of classical form in narrative, of the orderly progression in time and the carefully managed emphasis which, she reminds us in "Telling a Short Story," the French writers of *contes* had derived from the Latin tradition and the English in turn had taken over from the French. In "Telling a Short Story" (the second chapter of her book, *The Writing of Fiction*, 1925), Mrs. Wharton says much that is engrossing and valid, but virtually nothing that is new, at least to a reader of late Victorian literature. Perhaps the one surprising element—I shall come back to this—is her special admiration for the ghost story, "the peculiar category of the eerie" to which she turns her attention at once, even before getting down to questions about subject matter, characterization and the proper degree of economy in the short story proper. Elsewhere, she talks sensibly about "unity of vision," the strategically chosen "register" or point of view by which the experience is to be seen and by which it is to be shaped, with due acknowledgment to Henry James for first establishing the primacy of this fictional resource. She observes that the development and exploration of character is not the business of the short story, but rather that of the novel. And she lays it down that "situation is the main concern of the short story," so that "the effect produced by the short story depends entirely on its form, or presentation."

Such critical language does not sound very demanding, and in story after story Mrs. Wharton remained faithful to the principles announced. An old lady's view of the grubby yards adjacent to her boardinghouse—her one consolation in life—is about to be cut off; a young woman returning from Colorado to New York with her desperately sick husband, finds that he is lying dead in his sleeping-car berth and that she may be put off the train, with his corpse, in the midst of nowhere; a married woman has fled to Italy with her lover; a young man who is about to be exposed as an embezzler prepares to escape to Canada—in each case, we are introduced at once to a "situation." And yet in practice, Edith Wharton was often subtler, and both her ambition and her imaginative achievement greater, than her common-sense critical remarks might lead one to expect.

Early stories like "That Good May Come" and "A Cup of Cold Water" do in fact consist in the *working out* of a given situation, the active resolution, happily or unhappily, of some moral dilemma. But in the best of her stories—in "Souls Belated," "The Other Two," "The Eyes," "Autres

Temps . . . ," "A Bottle of Perrier" and others—it is rather that the situation itself is gradually revealed in all its complexity and finality. What we know at the end, in these "crucial instances," is not so much how some problem got resolved, but the full nature, usually the insurmountable nature, of the problem itself. It is then that Mrs. Wharton's stories gain the stature she attributed to the finest stories everywhere—those, in her account, which combined French form with Russian profundity: they become "a shaft driven straight into the heart of experience." It is then too that they comprise what she felt all so rightly any work of fiction should seek to comprise: a judgment on life, an appraisal of its limits, an assessment of the options—if options there be—that life has to offer. The immediate human situation has, in short, become a paradigm of the human condition.

II

The situations she chose so to treat and to enlarge upon are not, at first glance, very original or unusual ones. In "Telling a Short Story," Mrs. Wharton quotes with approval Goethe's contention that "those who remain imprisoned in the false notion of their own originality will always fall short of what they might have accomplished." Mrs. Wharton, who entertained no such false notion, was content with the received forms and conventions of the short story; and she did not attempt to apply the art of storytelling to any hitherto unheard-of subject. There was, however, one area of experience which she was perhaps the first *American* writer to make almost exclusively her own: even more, I dare say, than Henry James, who would in any event be her only rival in this respect. This is what . . . I call the marriage question. . . .

To point to so persistent a concern may seem only to stress the resolutely traditional cast of Mrs. Wharton's imagination; for while American fiction in the nineteenth century (before Howells and James) had not much focused on the marriage question, that question had provided the theme of themes for a whole galaxy of English, French, and Russian writers. A generation for whom the marriage question tends to be sporadic and peripheral is likely to forget its former centrality, and to suppose that for Jane Austen, for Trollope, for Stendhal, for Tolstoi, the question was *merely* the occasion for some far more arresting human drama. And a generation that does so may find it difficult to appreciate how much Mrs. Wharton, examining the question over the years, managed to make of it.

She made, one might say, almost everything of it. It is not only that she explored so many phases and dimensions of the question: the very grounds for marrying, and premarital maneuvering, in "The Quicksand," "The Dilettante," "The Introducers" and others; the stresses and strains, the withering hopes and forced adjustments of the marital relation in "The Fullness of Life," "The Lamp of Psyche," "The Letters," "Diagnosis" and elsewhere; the intricate issue of divorce in "The Last Asset," "The Other Two," "Autres Temps . . ."; the emotional and psychological challenge of adultery in "Souls Belated," "Atrophy," "The Long Run," and so on; the phenomenon of illegitimacy in "Her Son," "Roman Fever" and with gentle mockery in "His Father's Son"; the ambiguous value of children in the piercingly satirical "The Mission of Jane." It is not only that her treatment of the question, in these multiple phases, displays so broad a range of tone and perspective, and so keen an eye for the dissolving and emergent structures of historical institutional and social life with which the question was enmeshed. It is that the question, as Mrs. Wharton reflected on it, dragged with it all the questions about human nature and conduct to which her generous imagination was responsive.

There are of course urgent biographical reasons for Edith Wharton's near obsession with the perplexities of marriage, though, as I shall suggest, her deeper and more private passions found covert expression in ghost stories and romances. The chief cluster of stories bearing upon marriage, divorce and adultery were written during the years (up to 1913) when her personal problems in those regards were most pressing: when, among other things, her own marriage was becoming unbearable to her, when her husband Edward Robbins ("Teddy") Wharton was succumbing to mental illness and given ever more frequently to bouts of disjointed irascibility, and when her relation to Walter Berry (the international lawyer who was her mentor and romantic idol) arrived at one peak of intensity. But whatever the immediate causes, the whole domain of the marriage question was the domain in which Edith Wharton sought the truth of human experience; it was where she tested the limits of human freedom and found the terms to define the human mystery.

"Souls Belated" is an excellent case in point. The situation there is that of Mrs. Lydia Tillotson, who has abandoned her husband and come to Europe with her lover Ralph Gannett to spend a year wandering through Italy and then to settle for a time, registered as man and wife, at a resort hotel on one of the Italian lakes. Her divorce decree is at this moment granted, and the lovers are free to marry; but Lydia, to Gannett's astonishment, is passionately opposed to remarrying. She is appalled at the thought of yielding to that conventional necessity, of returning to the social fold and eventually of being received by the very people she had hoped to escape. "You judge things too theoretically," Gannett tells her. "Life is made up of compromises." "The life we ran away from—yes!" she replies. To this Gannett remarks with a smile: "I didn't know that we ran away to found a new system of ethics. I supposed it was because we loved each other." One of the merits of "Souls Belated" is the author's delicate division of sympathy between Lydia's anguished impulse to escape and Gannett's readiness to compromise (just as one of this early story's minor flaws is a certain shiftiness in point of view); but it is evident that on this occasion Gannett speaks for Edith Wharton. The impossibility of founding a new ethic—of a man and woman arranging their life together on a new and socially unconventional basis—was one of Mrs. Wharton's most somber convictions, and a conviction all the stronger because (partly out of her own anguish) she tested it again and again in her stories.

Edith Wharton's moral imagination, as it exercised itself on this fundamental theme, may be usefully contrasted with that of D. H. Lawrence. Writing about Anna Karenina and Vronsky (in his posthumously published *Study of Thomas Hardy*), Lawrence argued that, in effect, Tolstoi had let his characters down; that "their real tragedy is that they are unfaithful to the greater unwritten morality" (greater, that is, than conventional social morality), "which would have bidden Anna be patient and wait until she, by virtue of greater right, could take what she needed from society; would have bidden Vronsky detach himself from the system, become an individual, creating a new colony of morality with Anna." In *Women in Love* and *Lady Chatterley's Lover,* Lawrence presents us with couples who do detach themselves from the system and do seek to create just such a new colony. Neither Birkin and Ursula nor Connie Chatterley and Mellors meet with much success; the site of the new colony is not located within the bounds of the two novels. But given Lawrence's apocalyptic view of modern industrial society, and his intense belief that no genuine human relation can be consummated within it, it is the continuing search that Lawrence espoused.

For Edith Wharton, the effort was utterly doomed from the start; society, crushing as it might be, was all there was. "I want to get away with you," Newland Archer tells Ellen Olenska in *The Age of Innocence,* "into a world . . . where we shall be simply two human beings who love each other, who are the whole of life to each other." Mme. Olenska's reply is poignant and final. "Oh my dear—where is that country? Have you ever been there?" So it is in "Souls Belated": Lydia tries to leave Gannett, but she knows she has literally no place to go; she comes wearily back to him, and at the story's end they are heading for Paris and the ceremony which will marry them back into respectable society.

The relation between man and woman—whether marital or extramarital—was, in Mrs. Wharton's sense of it, beset by the most painful contradictions. "I begin to see what marriage is for," Lydia Tillotson says in "Souls Belated." "It's to keep people away from each other. Sometimes I think that two people who love each other can be saved from madness only by the things that come between them—children, duties, visits, bores, relations. . . . Our sin," she ends up, is that "we've seen the nakedness of each other's souls." But such dire proximity, such exposed nakedness—which Mrs. Wharton seems to have ardently desired and fearfully shrunk from—could occur within marriage as well.

Her consciousness of the dilemma was made evident in the exchange that took place a good many years after the writing of "Souls Belated" between Mrs. Wharton and Charles Du Bos, the gifted French essayist and student of French and English literature, who had known her since 1905, when he undertook to translate *The House of Mirth*. On an afternoon in the summer of 1912, driving through the French countryside, the two of them had been comparing their favorite literary treatments of married life. In fiction, they agreed upon George Eliot's *Middlemarch,* and Du Bos quoted the words of the heroine, Dorothea Brooke, that "marriage is so unlike anything else—there is something even awful in the nearness it brings." But if Mrs. Wharton assented to that, she also—after an interval, during which they selected Browning's "By the Fireside" and his "Any Wife to Any Husband" as the best poetic examples—went on to exclaim, with a kind of desolation, "Ah, the poverty, the miserable poverty, of any love that lies outside of marriage, of any love that is not a living together, a sharing of all!"

It is because of some such principle that Halston Merrick, in "The Long Run" (a story written a few months before the exchange just quoted), sends away his mistress Paulina Trant, when the latter offers to abandon her dreary husband and run off with him. In the course of their dialogue about the risks and sacrifices that might be in store for them, Paulina had observed with sad irony that "one way of finding out whether a risk is worth taking is *not* to take it, and then to see what one becomes in the long run, and draw one's inferences." What becomes of Halston and Paulina, as they retreat into the conventional, is in its well-cushioned manner not much less dreadful than what becomes of Ethan Frome and Mattie Silver. (One notes in passing that more often than not Edith Wharton's destroyed characters survive to take the full measure of their destruction.) Halston, who once had serious inclinations to literature, turns into a joyless bachelor, the manager of his father's iron foundry. Paulina, after her husband's death, marries "a large glossy man with . . . a red face," and is seen regularly at dinner parties, listening to the banal conversations with "a small unvarying smile which might have been pinned on with her ornaments," ready at the proper moment to respond with the proper sentiment. This superb and gruesome story adds to the impression that, for Edith Wharton, if the individual is offered any real choice in life, it is usually a choice between modes of defeat.

Of course, the human condition envisaged is not always so bleak in Edith Wharton's short stories, nor the alternatives so desperate; she was not so driven by a theory of life that she remained blind to variety both in experience and in narrative. In "The Letters," when Lizzie Deering discovers that her husband had not even opened the tender letters she had written him years before during the time of their courtship, she does not yield to her first impulse—to take their child and to leave him. She is stricken by the deception and by all that it implies, but she slowly adjusts "to the new image of her husband as he was." He was not, she realizes, "the hero of her dreams, but he was the man she loved, and who had loved her." The situation she now takes in and accepts—in a "last wide flash of pity and initiation"—is that "out of mean mixed substances" there had, after all, been "fashioned a love that will bear the stress of life." And in an altogether different mood, there is "The Mission of Jane," wherein Mrs. Lethbury (a woman "like a dried sponge put in water; she expanded, but she did not change her shape") and her elegant, helplessly embarrassed husband adopt a baby girl. This unspeakable child, as she grows up, assumes as her mission the relentless reform of the entire household. She fulfills that mission at last, and after hair-raising hesitation, by marrying and departing—thus allowing her parents to come together on the common ground of enormous relief, joining in fact and spirit as they had never done in two decades of marriage.

One of the seeming options for the domestically harried and entrapped, under the circumstances of modern American life, was, needless to say, the act of divorce; and it is not surprising that Mrs. Wharton (whose decree was granted in 1913) dealt with this alternative a number of times. For some years before Mrs. Wharton began writing, divorce had been "an enormous fact . . . in American life," as William Dean Howells had remarked when he was writing *A Modern Instance* (1882), a novel of which "the question of divorce" was to be "the moving principle." Howells complained that "it has never been treated seriously"; but following his lead, Edith Wharton did so in some of her most successful stories—among them, "The Reckoning," "The Last Asset," "Autres Temps . . ." and "The Other Two." She caught at the subject during the period when divorce was changing from the scandalous to the acceptable and even the commonplace; and it is just the shifting,

uncertain *status* of the act on which Mrs. Wharton so knowingly concentrated. In her treatment, it was not so much the grounds for divorce that
interested her (though she could be both amusing and bitter on this score),
and much less the technicalities involved. It was the process by which an
individual might be forced to confront the fact itself—especially in its psychological and social consequences—as something irreversible and yet sometimes wickedly paradoxical. (The contemporary reader, for whom, again,
divorce may seem little more than tangential to the main business of the
personal life, can enjoy a shock of recognition in reading the stories cited.)
Divorce, thus considered, was also the source of a revelation: about manners
and the stubborn attitudes they may equally express or conceal; about the
essential nature of the sexual relation; about the lingering injuries to the
psyche that divorce, given certain social pressures and prejudices, may inflict
on all concerned.

It is all those things that Julia Westall is driven to understand in "The
Reckoning." Julia had been a young woman with "her own views on the
immorality of marriage"; she had been a leading practitioner, in New York
Bohemia, of "the new dispensation . . . *Thou shalt not be unfaithful—to
thyself.*" She had only acted on her own foolishly selfish ideas when she
brusquely demanded release from her first husband; now she is reduced to
hysteria and almost to madness when her second husband, who had been
her disciple in these matters, makes the same demand of her. "The Reckoning" is somewhat overwritten, and it is uneven in tone; it is an anecdote,
really, about the biter bit, though by no means unmoving. A richer and more
convincingly   terrible   story   is   "Autres   Temps . . .,"   the   account   of
Mrs. Lidcote's forced return from a dream of freedom to "the grim edges
of reality," a reality here constituted by the social mores, at once cheerfully
relaxing and cruelly fixed, about divorce. Years before (the story was written
in 1916), Mrs. Lidcote had suffered disgrace and exile because she had been
divorced and remarried. Now it appears that times must have changed, for
her daughter has done the very same thing without arousing the faintest
social disapproval. Mrs. Lidcote dares to return to America; but after two
experiences of profoundest humiliation, she learns that for her the times and
the mores will never change. Few moments in Edith Wharton's short stories
are as telling in their exquisite agony as those in which first Mrs. Lidcote's
daughter and then her kindly would-be lover acknowledge by a slow, irre-
pressible, and all-devouring blush the truth of *her* situation. Those moments
have the more expansiveness of meaning, because few of Edith Wharton's
heroines accept the grim reality with greater courage or compassion for their
destroyers. And in few stories are the radical ironies of social change more
powerfully handled.

"The Other Two" is a yet more brilliant dissection of the mannered life, and it is very likely the best story Mrs. Wharton ever wrote. It can stand as the measure of her achievement in the short story form; for it has scarcely any plot—it has no real arrangement of incidents, there being too few incidents to arrange—but consists almost entirely in the leisurely, coolly comic process by which a situation is revealed to those involved in it. It is revealed in particular to Waythorn, his wife's third husband, who discovers himself in mysterious but indissoluble league with "the other two," as exceedingly different in background or in style as all three are from one another. Waythorn comes by degrees to perceive that the wife he adores, and who had seemed to him so vivid and above all so unique a personality, is in fact (and in a disconcertingly appropriate figure) "'as easy as an old shoe'—a shoe that too many feet had worn. . . . Alice Haskett—Alice Varick—Alice Waythorn—she had been each in turn, and had left hanging to each name a little of her privacy, a little of her personality, a little of the inmost self where the unknown god abides.'"

Those last echoing phrases add up to a splendid formulation, and they contain a good deal of Edith Wharton's basic psychology. But for the most part, the rhetoric of "The Other Two" does not need or attempt to rise to such overt and summary statement. Everything is communicated, rather, by the exact notation of manners—of dress and gesture and expression: of Haskett's "made-up tie attached with an elastic," and Waythorn's uneasy distaste for it; of Varick sitting by Mrs. Waythorn at a ball and failing to rise when Waythorn strolls by; of Mrs. Waythorn absentmindedly giving her husband cognac with his coffee. The story's last sentence brings an exemplary little comedy of manners (which could serve as a model in any effort to define the genre) to a perfect conclusion. The three husbands are together for the first time, in the Waythorn drawing room. Mrs. Waythorn enters and suggests brightly, easily, that everyone must want a cup of tea.

> The two visitors, as if drawn by her smile, advanced to receive the cups she held out.
> She glanced about for Waythorn, and he took the third cup with a laugh.

III

Edith Wharton declared her affection for the supernatural tale in both *The Writing of Fiction* and the preface to *Ghosts*; and though, like the historical romances, her ghost stories are a provocatively mixed lot, she displayed her skill in this category often enough to be ranked among its modern masters. For an addict like the present commentator, "Kerfol," "Mr. Jones," "Pomegranate Seed," and "All Souls'" are thoroughly beguiling and rereadable; while "The Eyes" verges on the extraordinary and contains something of "the appalling moral significance" Mrs. Wharton discerned in *The Turn of the Screw*, that novella of Henry James for which she had a sort of absolute admiration.

Most of these stories deal, as I have said, with the marriage question, but they deal with it in an atmosphere which is a curious and artful blend of the passionate and violent with the muted and remote. In "Kerfol," an American visitor to Brittany encounters what turn out to be the ghosts of a pack of dogs, spectral survivors of a seventeenth-century domestic drama of sadism, revenge, and madness. In "Mr. Jones," the ghost of a majordomo who a century earlier had served as jailer to an unfortunate lady, the deaf-and-dumb wife of his villainous master, endures to commit a contemporary murder. In "Pomegranate Seed," Kenneth Ashby, widowed and remarried, vanishes after receiving a series of letters written in a hand so faint as to be almost illegible; his second wife is left with the belated and blood-chilling knowledge of their source. The genre of the supernatural, Mrs. Wharton conjectures in "Telling a Short Story," did not derive from French or Russian writing, but "seems to have come from mysterious Germanic and Armorican" (i.e. Breton) "forests, from lands of long twilight and wailing winds." She might have added that it seems to derive also from recesses of the imagination other and perhaps deeper than those which give rise to realistic fiction. But this may be one part of what she had in mind when, in the preface to *Ghosts*, she contended that "the teller" of ghost stories "should be well frightened in the telling."

With the ghostly tales of Mrs. Wharton, in any event, one is inevitably interested not only in what happens in the plot, but in what happens in the telling of it. "Pomegranate Seed" offers one kind of clue. In the preface to *Ghosts*, while lamenting a decline in the practice and enjoyment of ghost stories, Mrs. Wharton speaks of the many inquiries she had received about the title of "Pomegranate Seed," and refers a bit cryptically to the deplorable contemporary ignorance of "classical fairy lore." The reference is no doubt to the legend of Persephone (in the Latin version), who was abducted by Pluto, god of the underworld, and who would have been entirely liberated by Jupiter if she had not broken her vow to Pluto—of total abstinence from food—by eating some pomegranate seeds; whereafter she was required to spend the dark winter months of each year in the underworld, returning to earth only with the arrival of spring.

The connection with Mrs. Wharton's tale is superficially slender, especially since the Persephone story is usually interpreted as a seasonal myth—the annual return of winter darkness and sterility, the annual rebirth of nature in the spring. But theorists of a Freudian or, alternately, a Jungian persuasion, have made out a strong sexual motif in most ancient mythology, and find the sources of myth as much in sexual struggles and yearnings as in the cycle of nature. The story of Persephone yields quickly to such an interpretation, and so obviously does "Pomegranate Seed." Edith Wharton, in this view, has taken a familiar story of sexual combat—two women battling over one man, and the man himself divided between conflicting erotic leanings—and turned it into a ghost story: which is then cast into a dimly mythic pattern, and carefully labeled for our guidance. It is thus the dead wife Elsie who has assumed the role of Pluto and has summoned her spouse to leave his earthly existence and cohabit with her in the land of the dead—Ashby having broken *his* vow of constancy by remarrying.

In this and other tales, in short, Mrs. Wharton's imagination was moving in the direction of the mythic, but arriving only at the way station of the ghostly and fantastic. This, for Mrs. Wharton, was far enough; for she was doing no more than adopting the Victorian habit (itself a gesture toward the mythic) of "distancing" the most intense and private sexual feelings by projecting them in the various forms of fantasy. It is notable, for example, that the ghostly context permits a more direct acknowledgment of sexual experience than we normally find in the dramas of manners and the social life. In "The Lady's Maid's Bell," the action turns on the brutish physical demands made by one Brympton upon his fastidious wife: "I turned sick," says the narrator, the English-born maid Hartley, "to think what some ladies have to endure and hold their tongues about." Nor is there much mystery about the nature of Farmer Rutledge's bewitchment by the ghost of Ora Brand in "Bewitched," an artificial yarn which strives for effect by converting the figurative into the literal. But the expertly harrowing "All Souls'" indicates how erotic material could be transmuted into the terrifying without losing either its essential nature or its power.

On the last day of October, Sara Clayburn encounters a strange woman who has come to see one of the maidservants on the large staff of her Connecticut home. Later, Mrs. Clayburn sprains her ankle and is forced to her bed. The maidservant fails to appear next morning, and Mrs. Clayburn hobbles through the house in great pain, searching for help. The house is empty, the electricity cut off, the fire dead. She spends a day and night in panic-stricken solitude. When she awakens again, the servants are at their appointed tasks, all of them insisting that there had been no such passage of time, and the entire episode simply a bad dream. Exactly a year later,

Mrs. Clayburn sees the same strange woman approaching the house, and she flees in hysterics to her cousin in New York. Together, they speculate that the woman must have been a "fetch," who had come to escort the maid and the other servants to a nearby "coven." The story is a fine and highly original narrative study of steadily increasing fear; and I am sure that what one remembers is Mrs. Clayburn's painful progress through the empty house. But the full force of "All Souls'" comes from the retrospective juxtaposition of Mrs. Clayburn's experience and the gathering which is the cause of it. Edith Wharton knew well enough that a coven was an exercise in witchcraft which usually led to the wildest erotic activities. And to put it in a ruinously oversimplified manner, Mrs. Clayburn's terrors—her sense of physically trapped solitude, the loss of her grip on reality, her later hysteria—are in fact her intuitive moral and psychological *reaction* to the coven.

To what extent, in the stories under discussion, was Edith Wharton's imagination working with her own private passions, impulses and fears? To what extent was she "distancing" elements in her personal life by converting them into the eerie or setting them in a far-gone age, or both (as in "Kerfol")? To a very considerable extent, I should suppose. It is easy enough—so easy that I did not pause to say so—to find reflections of Mrs. Wharton's experience of marriage with Teddy Wharton in the stories examined earlier: for example, in "The Letters"; to which we could add "The Lamp of Psyche," in which Delia Corbett's attitude to her husband, after she has detected his basic flaw, changes from "passionate worship" to "tolerant affection"; and the first of the little fables in "The Valley of Childish Things," where the female figure matures after going out into the great world (i.e., Europe) and coming back home, but the male on his return simply reverts to the childish. With the ghostly tales, and with those of the historical romances which can be helpfully included here, the problem is usually more complex, and exactly because the elements being converted were so much more deeply rooted, so much a matter of obscure or wayward or almost inexpressible emotions— and perhaps so alien to Edith Wharton's temperament, as the latter has normally been understood. But even in "Kerfol" (to take an apparently extreme instance), one can, by making a number of substitutions, come upon a fantasy of savage personal revenge, a violent but purely imagined repayment for a series of psychological cruelties.

There the translation from life into story is complete; "Kerfol" needs no biographical interpretation to give it interest. Sometimes, however, Mrs. Wharton's imagination was overcome by her personal feeling, and she failed to make the full translation: which explains, I believe, the unevenness mentioned at the start of this section. "The Hermit and the Wild Woman"—

which can stand for several of the romances (including "The Duchess at Prayer" and "Dieu d'Amour")—is instructive, for it is just such a failure; *its* interest is almost entirely biographical. This story, which takes place in late medieval Italy, is told in a somewhat pretentious style founded on that of the lives of the saints. A so-called Wild Woman has escaped from a convent because she was forbidden to bathe herself; she wanders the mountains till she meets with a Hermit of singular austerity; she performs many miraculous cures, but she is constantly chided by the holy man for her continuing desire to clean and refresh her body in the mountain lake; finally she drowns in the water, and the Hermit realizes too late that her nature was yet more saintly and devout than his own. It is a tedious and contrived piece of work; and one is at a loss to understand why Mrs. Wharton wrote it—until it dawns on one that this is Mrs. Wharton's effort to make a story out of a deeply troubled period in her life, while retaining her privacy by placing the experience in the far temporal distance and the most remote possible atmosphere. It becomes uncomfortably clear that the relation between the Wild Woman and the Hermit is an elementary version, at several kinds of remove, of the relation between Edith Wharton and Walter Berry, during the period when she was escaping or trying to escape from her own convent, her marriage.

The story was written in 1906, and it is fundamentally an account of what was transpiring between the two at that very time. Something of this was made public a few years ago by Wayne Andrews in his introduction to *The Best Short Stories of Edith Wharton,* where he quoted several passages from Mrs. Wharton's "diary" for 1907. It seems in fact not to have been a diary, properly speaking, but a fragment of autobiographical narrative written in diary form. In it, Mrs. Wharton recorded her burning desire (she speaks of a "flame" of feeling) for total intimacy with Walter Berry, along with her tormented meditations on the sinfulness or lack of it of the extramarital physical relation. She indicated her own belief in, as it were, the holiness of the sensuous life: "I feel that all the mysticism in me—and the transcendentalism that in other women turns to religion—were poured into my feeling for you."

So her Wild Woman's exalted spirituality found paradoxical but persuasive expression in her ineradicable need to "sleep under the free heaven and wash the dust from my body in cool water." But Berry, like the Hermit, evidently recoiled in some dismay at these revealed longings, though Mrs. Wharton, discreet even in privacy, only hinted at his tendency to smash their most precious moments together. "It was as if there stood between us . . . the frailest of glass cups, filled with a rare and colorless wine—and with a gesture you broke the glass and spilled the drops." The end of "The Hermit and the Wild Woman" thus appears as an only too familiar act of self-consoling prophecy: too late, her sometime lover would appreciate the true value of what he had missed.

"The Eyes," written in 1910, springs from the same cluster of longings and resentments, but it is an immeasurably superior story; the author's personal feelings have here been perfectly translated into a nearly seamless work of art. Andrew Culwin's reminiscence of his two acts of seemingly spontaneous generosity—the proposal of marriage to his cousin Alice Nowell, his pretense of admiration for the literary talent of young Noyes—and of the two ugly red sneering eyes which appeared after both incidents to glare at him derisively through the night: this is all of a piece. Gilbert Noyes, the godlike youth who turns up suddenly in Rome, is also a cousin of Alice Nowell's, and Culwin's fear of wounding him by making plain his literary ineptness is confused by some vague sense of remorse over abandoning Alice three years before. But the turn of the screw in *this* story is the fact that Frenham, one of the two men listening to Culwin's hideous and shockingly unconscious self-disclosure, is another attractive young neophyte, Noyes's most recent successor. He is the latest proof of the "ogreish metaphor" of one of Culwin's friends, that the old man "liked 'em juicy." To the climax of Culwin's reminiscence, there is added the climax of the tale itself, when Frenham sits transfixed with horror. In the face of his mentor, the very shaper of his own life and personality, Frenham has seen what Culwin remembered seeing: eyes that reminded him "of vampires with a taste for young flesh."

It is not only that the eyes represent Culwin's real self, the egotistical and gradually evil self that (like that of Lavington in "The Triumph of Night") lies hidden behind his "cold and drafty" intelligence, his utter detachment, his occasional moral contentment. It is also that, on the two occasions of generosity, his good conscience—his "glow of self-righteous-ness"—*is* the glare of the eyes. For a character like Culwin's, the generous gesture is a necessary concession to the ego; it is a feeding of the ego on the tenderness of flesh and spirit; and a part of him knows it. Like Henry James, Edith Wharton was alert to the sinister impulses that can sometimes take the form of moral self-satisfaction. But the implications of this astonishing story go beyond that, and open up almost endlessly to thoughtful scrutiny.

Culwin's treatment of Alice Nowell is more than paralleled by his treatment of Noyes. It is explained by it; and all the carefully chosen (and as the manuscript shows, painstakingly revised) details about the old man, about his habits and tastes, his manner of speech and way of life, combine to give a chilling portrait of a dilettantish, devouringly selfish homosexual. The two victims coalesce; indeed, Miss Nowell's Christian name was originally Grace, before Mrs. Wharton (as it appears) decided that it would be too schematic to provide both victims with the same initials. Nevertheless, when we put together the young woman with her unreproachful grief (still unreproachful, one surmises, after Culwin had fled from her) and the aspiring young writer of fiction, we begin to identify a single and very real personality, and to identify "The Eyes" as the projection by Mrs. Wharton of her most buried feelings about Walter Berry. It is, as Louis Auchincloss has pointed out, the Walter Berry as seen in the resentful perspective of Percy Lubbock: "a dogmatic, snobbish egotist and the evil genius of Edith Wharton's life." But the perspective on this occasion at least was also Mrs. Wharton's—though her imagination was in such firm control of her materials that it is unlikely she ever quite knew what she had accomplished. Yet surely, as this beautifully composed story took shape, Mrs. Wharton must have been, however obscurely, more than a little frightened in the telling. (Ironically but tellingly, Berry liked the story, and Mrs. Wharton was pleased that he did. "The ghost story . . . *is* good," she wrote a friend; "even Walter says so!")

IV

One of Edith Wharton's closest friends once addressed her, in a letter, as "Cher ami." She was much amused by the masculine form, and was willing to admit its propriety. The same friend, however, wrote some time after Mrs. Wharton's death that she had been "a great woman" as well as "a great lady." It is perhaps underscoring the obvious to say that in her fiction, too, she was a great woman: or anyhow that, to the degree that she was great at all, she was great *as* a woman, with a distinctively feminine sensibility. We recognize it in the sometimes excessive concern with the details of female dress, and her minute observation of interior *décor* (rooms and the furnishings of rooms are also her chief source of metaphor in the short stories). We see it even more in her subtle apprehension of the many "live filaments" that, Merrick remarks in "The Long Run," individuals throw out to one another when a relationship is forming; of "the thousand imperceptible signs," according to Mrs. Anerton in "The Muse's Tragedy," "by which one gropes one's way through the labyrinth of human nature"; of character and motive and the human relation as comprising delicate clusters of vibrations (to use one of her favorite words). At the same time, everyone who knew her has commented on a certain masculinity in her makeup; in her devotion to the orderly, in the vigorous play of her mind—and in her energetic sense of the satirical. It was, one might say, her friend's "cher ami" who wrote such splendid little satires as "The Pelican," "The Descent of Man" and "Xingu."

These are the best of the many stories that touch upon the cultural scene. Among the others, little need be said about the stories of art and artists, since, as Blake Nevius has observed, they are not really about the artistic life as such, or the drama of the imaginative struggle, but about the human foibles and limitations and disappointments looked at, in these instances, within an artistic context. "The House of the Dead Hand" and "The Daunt Diana," for example, deal with the melodramatic or bizarre obsessions here attributed to art lovers. Others focus on the purely *human* nature, usually the quite unsatisfactory nature, of the great artist or writer: as in "The Muse's Tragedy," which, with its idealistic and frustrated married woman, her shadowy "ridiculous" husband, and the dryly intellectual and apparently sexless poet, seems to be one more reflection of the triangle composed of Edith and Teddy Wharton and Walter Berry. In the more complicated but also more light-spirited story, "The Temperate Zone," Mrs. Wharton, through the eyes of a young American critic, inspects the improbable human sources of creative inspiration: the artlessly greedy and tasteless widow of a distinguished painter, and her present husband, the slack and ingenuous onetime lover of a lady poet of genius. "The Recovery" alone enacts a genuine and important aesthetic experience, and does so most effectively: the confrontation by the skilled but provincial American painter of the European masters, "the big fellows," as Keniston calls them in the story. It is a very real experience which (as one has had occasion to notice) continues to be reenacted in the halls of the Louvre and the Uffizi. But even in "The Recovery," for all its valid implications about American cultural history, the impact of the event is felt mainly from without, by the painter's worried and watchful wife, for whom the confrontation has as much to do with their happiness together as with the nature of artistic achievement.

Keniston's integrity is impressive; and so is that of Dodge in "The Debt," and of Pellerin in "The Legend." But when dealing with integrity, Edith Wharton was not much more than competent. It was the opposite—the loss or total absence or the pretense of intellectual seriousness—that engaged Mrs. Wharton's larger talent: that summoned into play the virile wit, trenchant but falling just short of the merciless, characteristic of the stories set in the New England university town sometimes called Hillbridge (which seems to be Cambridge, Massachusetts, displaced a little way toward Amherst). These—in particular, "The Pelican," "The Descent of Man" and "Xingu"—are the finely wrought predecessors of the many recent fictional anatomies of cultural snobbery and the academic world, a genre which, among American writers, Edith Wharton collaborated with Henry James in inventing.

The language of these stories has the air of taking a rational delight in itself, as it cuts sharply into folly and hypocrisy, drawing blood which only increases the attacker's appetite. But there is an air of tolerance, too, if not always of compassion, and especially in "The Pelican." Here we meet the bemused and humorless but oddly touching Mrs. Amyot, who lectures on everything, everywhere, to pay the various needs of her "baby" son, and does so for a decade after he has grown up, graduated from college and paid his mother back in full. Despite himself, the narrator helps Mrs. Amyot work up a lecture on Plato: "If she wanted to lecture on Plato she should!—Plato must take his chance like the rest of us." Later, Mrs. Wharton sums up a whole range of spurious pedantry when she explains that Mrs. Amyot's lectures on literary "influences" (in the manner popularized by Matthew Arnold) were no longer successful, since "her too-sophisticated audiences . . . now demanded either that the influence or the influenced should be quite unknown, or that there should be no perceptible connection between the two." But with all her capacity for inexhaustible inanity, Mrs. Amyot remains appealing—to the narrator, to Mrs. Wharton and to us—because, as the narrator says, she was "full of those dear contradictions and irrelevancies that will always make flesh and blood prevail against a syllogism."

Mrs. Wharton is harder on Professor Lynyard, Hillbridge's eminent philosopher of science, in "The Descent of Man," a story which begins as a satire on the massive gullibility of the reading public and the cultivated idiocy of publishers, and goes on to portray the corruption of the intellectual by enormous popular success. "Xingu" is an elaborate joke (the entity named in the title being in actual fact what, to the dazed consternation of the ladies involved, it is discovered to be in the story); but in the course of telling it, Mrs. Wharton's masculine wit flexes itself happily to expose the silly snobberies and the fuzzy puritanical idealism of literary clubs. Whether she was or was not a social snob, Edith Wharton (who was learned in the literatures and philosophies of several countries and epochs) was not a snob of the intellectual variety, and could not abide that quality in others. But as we listen to her dismantling it in a story like "Xingu," we hear that sound of full-throated laughter which her friends so well remember.

V

"The people of the old and vanished New York set were not exceptional," the narrator of "The Long Run" tells us. "They were mostly cut on the same conventional and unobtrusive pattern; but they were often exceedingly 'nice.'" It may be surprising how few of Edith Wharton's short stories have to do in any depth with that "old New York" she explored with such balanced sympathies in several novels and in the four novellas collected under the phrase itself. There are in fact only two (apart from that passing recollection, "The Long Run" is concerned with other matters): "Autres Temps . . ." and "After Holbein." But these two are, in a sense, versions of each other, and they suggest the most and the best that could be done with the theme, within the frame of the short story. And this was to deal, not with old New York proper (as in *The Age of Innocence*), but with symptoms of its baleful or ghostly persistence, as a sort of continuing "situation."

The former story testifies gradually to the simultaneous accuracy and pathetic inaccuracy of Mrs. Lidcote's remark to Franklin Ide: "Everything's changed. . . . There's no old New York left, it seems." What *is* left are the phantoms of the destructive old moral clichés and attitudes, at least as regards those already once damaged by them. In "After Holbein," it is two human figures who persist: the incessant diner-out, Anson Warley, who suffers a brainstorm and goes to attend what he believes to be a dinner party given by the former *grande dame* of New York society, Mrs. Jaspar; and Mrs. Jaspar herself, now senile and broken, who holds such imaginary dinners every evening. The title refers to *The Dance of Death* (or *Totentanz*), a set of fifty-seven engravings by Hans Holbein the Younger based on the medieval theme of Death as a dancing skeleton, ceremoniously escorting all humanity, high and low alike, to their graves. There is, in the story, a weirdly ritualistic quality, as the two advance—"at the end of a ghostly cortège" of imaginary guests—to take their places at the long dinner table, as they bow to one another and touch glasses, engaging in little bursts of incoherent conversation. Blake Nevius calls the story a "heartlessly bad and rather theatrical joke." But it may, I think, work to a somewhat different effect if it is considered along with Mrs. Wharton's ghost stories; for at the time of the action, the two main characters are no more than living ghosts, clutching crazily at a long-gone era in which they had been truly alive, participating in an awful parody of the old social rituals. Thus old New York performs its own dance of death, in the persons of Mrs. Jaspar and Anson Warley; and the latter, leaving the house after the ceremony is concluded, has a stroke on the doorstep and dies.

"Roman Fever" might also be called a story about old New York. The two middle-aged ladies who sit together "on the air-washed height" above the Palatine in Rome, slowly squeezing out a long buried truth, once lived across the way from one another on East 73rd Street, some twenty-five years before. It is Mrs. Slade's opinion that her companion and the late Mr. Ansley had been "museum specimens of old New York." But not only did the chief event of the past, like the sporadic conversation in the present, take place in Rome. The situation being quietly revealed has to do, not with a former social milieu, but with the erotic fever of the young, with illicit love and illegitimacy.

"Roman Fever" is the third of Mrs. Wharton's short stories addressed to the theme of illegitimacy (which is also central to *Summer* and *The Old Maid*), the others being "His Father's Son" and "Her Son," written in 1909 and 1932 respectively. The dates of those stories may turn out to be as interesting as their content. Part of the mystery that still hangs over Edith Wharton's birth is a question about the exact moment when she first heard that she might herself be illegitimate—the daughter not of George Frederic Jones, but of a young Englishman who had served as tutor to Edith Wharton's older brothers. Some time after her death, Mrs. Elisina Tyler, who had perhaps been Mrs. Wharton's closest friend for twenty years, told a correspondent enigmatically that the main interest in the rumor about Mrs. Wharton's "irregular birth" was not the rumor itself, but the circumstances under which it reached her. If the stories are any guide (and it is not yet clear that they are), Mrs. Wharton learned of the possibility around 1908 or 1909—that is, during the most emotionally restive period of her life. But in that case, her initial response, as represented by "His Father's Son," was that of many others who have pondered about the rumor: namely, that it was just the kind of false rumor which could appeal to the romantic young person—a person like Ronald Grew, for example, who nourishes the groundless belief that he must be the child of a great artist rather than a commonplace manufacturer of suspender buckles.

If so, the possibility must have edged its way into Mrs. Wharton's mind over the years that followed, gathering conviction. In "Her Son," illegitimacy is a fact, though the parents of the child are later able to marry, and this rather bizarre and long-drawn-out story (with which Mrs. Wharton, as Sir Kenneth Clark recalls, was very much pleased) goes on to raise and then to dismiss a hint of incest, and to conclude in a personal struggle between two women. But shortly before her death, Mrs. Wharton came back to the subject to give it, in "Roman Fever," its most forthright and at the same time most typically furtive treatment. The success of the story lies in the leisurely, almost hesitant, manner of both the narrative and the dialogue, and in the abundance of echoes from past to present. But it lies even more in the fact that the point of view throughout is so largely that of Mrs. Slade. Her companion's nearly inaudible but resolute response in the story's last sentence comes out of a consciousness we have only been allowed to guess at until that moment. The situation of Grace Ansley's whole lifetime is revealed in a single phrase, and just possibly, with all obliqueness, one phase of Edith Wharton's situation as well.

RICHARD H. LAWSON

Undine

If, as Edith Wharton tells it, Anna Bahlmann [her governess] "fed [her fancy] with all the wealth of German literature, from the Minnesingers to Heine," that 750-year course may well have included in its penultimate step Friedrich de La Motte-Fouqué (1777–1843). Fouqué's masterpiece, indeed the only work he wrote which remained popular after his lifetime, was the fairy-tale novella of a water nymph turned human, *Undine* (1811). Four or five years later Fouqué cast the same material, with minimal changes, into a libretto; E. T. A. Hoffmann, versatile genius and author of romantic tales in his own right, wrote the music for this *Undine,* and the opera had its premiere August 3, 1816. After Fouqué's death his *Undine* material was adapted by Albert Lortzing, who also wrote new music for it, and this new operatic *Undine* was first performed April 21, 1845.

It is by no means out of the question that Edith Wharton as an adult was familiar with Lortzing's opera, but what indications we have suggest more strongly the likelihood of her earlier acquaintance with Fouqué's novella. This likelihood is reinforced by the apparent solution of the mystery surrounding her misidentification of the phrase "Hütten bauen [to build huts]," which she wanted to attribute to the New Testament from which she had learned her first German. It is more likely that a subsequent pleasant memory—that of reading Fouqué's *Undine*—had supervened upon a much older pleasant memory—that of learning to read German as an eight-year-old at Bad Wildbad.

From *Edith Wharton and German Literature.* © 1974 by Bouvier Verlag Herbert Grundmann. Translations provided by editor.

In the first paragraph of the fifth chapter of *Undine,* Wie der Ritter auf der Seespitze lebte [The chevalier lived on the point of land]," Fouqué quite obviously paraphrases the Biblical text of Matt. 17:4, Mark 9:5, or Luke 9:33. The sentence as given in Matt. 17:4 will serve as a representative of all three Gospel versions, for we recall that the inter-Gospel variations were not relevant to Edith Wharton's variation. Matt. 17:4: "Herr, hie ist gut sein, willst du, so wollen wir hie drei Hütten machen [Lord, it is good for us to be here: if thou wilt, let us make here three tabernacles]." Edith Wharton, however, remembered it as "Hütten bauen." Fouqué, addressing his readers, describes the point of land, now become an island, on which live the erstwhile water nymph Undine and her foster-parents: "Du meintest . . . hier müsse gut Wohnen und Hütten bauen sein [You might think that it would be good to live here and build huts]." It seems to me that Edith Wharton's memory of this unique German phraseology, coupled with the obvious identity of names: Undine in *Undine* and Undine Spragg in *The Custom of the Country,* as well as a parallelism in theme: social alienation as the price of leaving one's element—all combine to suggest that she had indeed read Fouqué's *Undine* and that her retention of the tale played a role in the composition of *The Custom of the Country.*

Fouqué's Undine, after assuming human form, and a human soul as well, falls in love with and marries the knight Huldbrand (her name means "belonging to the waves," and his means "to pay homage to the seething of the waves"). In her human role Undine is concerned to forestall the malevolent designs of her uncle, the water spirit Kühleborn ("the spring of coolness") on human beings, especially on those she loves—including her human rival for her husband's love, the Lady Bertalda. When the three take an ill-advised boat trip down the Danube, Undine impresses on Huldbrand that he must not express the slightest displeasure against her here on the water, where her kindred spirits are most powerful. At his failure to heed her warning, Undine returns to her native element, her human role no longer bearable. Shortly afterward, Huldbrand, at the point of marrying Bertalda, dies.

The most obvious indication—other than her memory for the phrase "Hütten bauen"—that Edith Wharton was familiar with Fouqué's *Undine* lies in her use of the given name for her redoubtable heroine Undine Spragg in *The Custom of the Country.* It is not such an everyday name that one may dismiss its recurrence in Edith Wharton's novel as mere coincidence. Above all we are struck by her use of the German/English form Undine rather than, say, the French form Ondine. And of course this melodic, allusive first name (cf. New Latin *undina* from Latin *unda* 'wave') in tandem with the harsh monosyllabic last name, Spragg, already introduces an atmosphere of disharmony, not to say irony. Where on earth did the Spraggs of Apex City, one is left to wonder, come across so unApexian a name as Undine for their daughter?

Not, it is safe to say, from a knowledge of German Romanticism. It may, however, prove fruitful to illuminate the range of allusiveness of this name—and that of its bearer too—by reference to a work of German Romanticism with which Edith Wharton seems to have had some connection: Fouqué's *Undine*. This earlier Undine's human foster-parents—her real parents were water spirits—had, at least theoretically, as much latitude in bestowing a name as did the senior Spraggs. But only theoretically. The water nymph Undine—an assertive model of Edith Wharton's contention that *her* characters always arrived bringing their names as part of themselves and that these names never changed—insisted on her own name in her human role, the name that had been given her by her water-spirit parents. To her foster-father "kam . . . das wie ein heidnischer Name vor, der in Keinem Kalender stehe [This seemed like a pagan name, not to be found in any saints' calendar]." The priest, after first reinforcing the foster-father's doubts, allows himself to be coaxed and finally persuaded by Undine's winsome stubbornness, and finally baptizes her with her "heathenish" name.

The method by which the senior Spraggs invented the name Undine for their daughter is "heathenish" too, from the point of view of the cultural level of the New York which the Spraggs aspire to conquer. Mrs. Spragg tells Ralph Marvell, Undine's husband-to-be, who, "echoes of *divers et ondoyant* [various and wavy] in his brain," thought the name a splendid invention: "'Why, we called her after a hair-waver father [Mrs. Spragg's father] put on the market the week she was born—' and then to explain, as [Ralph] remained struck and silent: 'It's from *un*doolay, you know, the French for crimping; father always thought the name made it take. He was quite a scholar, and had the greatest knack for finding names.'"

Pretty clearly Edith Wharton is inviting us to share an etymological joke by which she denotes the cultural level of the Spraggs. The name Undine may be, at several removes, related to *onduler,* but it can't very well come "from" it. If we have perhaps not seized the initial invitation to participate in her linguistic witticism, Edith Wharton repeats the latter in the course of the wedding trip of Ralph Marvell and the former Undine Spragg; this time it is specifically Undine who fails to grasp the allusiveness of her own name. The newlyweds are relaxing on a ledge just behind their villa in the hills near Siena, shaded from the hot sun by an ilex grove. The first allusion is isolated, a hint: "'You look as cool as a wave,' [Ralph] said." Shortly afterward, the

theme is reintroduced, more substantially: "his eyes softened as they absorbed in a last glance the glimmering submarine light of the ancient grove,
through which Undine's figure wavered nereid-like above him." Thus: a
grove is rather suddenly endowed with underwater light so that Undine's
figure may *waver* nereid-like. Finally, Edith Wharton's alerting becomes
forthright: "'You never looked your name more than you do now,' he said,
kneeling at her side and putting his arm about her. She smiled back a little
vaguely, as if not seizing his allusion." Edith Wharton's philological toying
with the Spraggs, and then with Undine in particular, invites us, I think, to
share with her the knowledge of what the name Undine means—and also
where it comes from. The proximate likely source is Fouqué's water nymph
turned human for a time, Undine.

Undine Spragg's origin is in a sense as watery as that of the nymph.
Not that Apex City was a replica of the other Undine's childhood memories
"von goldnen Schlössern, von kristallen Dächern, und Gott weiß, wovon
noch mehr [of gold castles, crystal roofs, and God knows what else]," all
underwater. It seems rather to have been a Midwestern town of depressing
plainness. A typhoid epidemic had claimed the lives of both of Undine's
siblings. This calamity, "by causing Mr. Spragg to resolve that thereafter
Apex should drink pure water, had led directly to the founding of his fortunes." For he played a leading role in the Pure Water Movement, which
bought some land he had taken over from his father-in-law on a bad debt,
and which caused to be built on this land a reservoir and a water-works.
And thereafter Mr. Spragg grew rich and powerful in Apex.

Now, our attention is of course focused not primarily on this rather
characteristic American commercial maneuver, in which Mr. Spragg did well
by doing good, but rather on the watery basis of his prosperity and thus of
his daughter's emergence in the human world of New York. Undine Spragg's
water-borne emergence depends ultimately on the prior water-caused deaths
of her siblings. The water-borne emergence of Fouqué's Undine and her
adoption into the human world of her foster-parents was preceded immediately and, we infer, conditioned by the water-caused disappearance of the
natural daughter of her foster-parents. This parallel, useful as it is to us, will
not easily bear over-refinement, however. Far from dying of typhoid, the
natural daughter disappeared in the water after trying to catch an image at
which she had been gazing (Undine?). Still, Kühleborn and his malevolent
company of water spirits may well be, in pre-Fouqué embodiment, a folk-
personification of, among other things, water-borne epidemics.

Ralph Marvell's culturally conditioned insistence on forcing his bride
Undine into the role signified by her name is an ill omen of the larger tragedy

of his inability to understand her or to adapt to her—or to her world. It is as though *he* had read Fouqué's *Undine,* as we are rather certain that his author had, and cannot free himself from the romantic concept of the water nymph turned human. But his Undine is by no means a romantic concept; rather, she is an all-too-human young woman of some beauty, of narrow horizon, and of extreme selfishness. For Ralph Marvell to confuse this woman with his own romantic vision of artistic creation is narratively comprehensible by virtue of their widely different origins. But more important, his confusion defines the inevitable alienation to follow, as well as, not quite incidentally, his insufficiency as an artist. For Ralph as an artist is an ineffective dilettante, and he is probably to be regarded as occupying the same role with respect to life—certainly with respect to life played by rules to which he is alien—those of the New York of the Invaders.

Ralph Marvell's pitiable and foredoomed attempt to include the former Undine Spragg in his own romantic vision takes place, or rather would have taken place, had he effected it, beside water in its most romantic form—the effect is highly ironic—a waterfall, in fact a green waterfall. This waterfall that did not materialize for him is as much a warning to Ralph as the materialized waterfall in *Undine* is to Huldbrand. This white waterfall is another guise of Kühleborn and it warns Huldbrand never to cease defending his wife—an injunction that the human knight forgets.

The former Undine Spragg, shortly after her failure in the ilex grove to comprehend Ralph's allusion to the meaning of her name, displays so much resentment at the prospect of staying longer in northern Italy, that Ralph proposes a change of scene to a little place in Switzerland: "we can sit and look at a green water-fall while I lie in wait for adjectives." Adjectives—not verbs! But Undine prefers crowded and lively St. Moritz. "He had a fleeting glimpse of the quiet place with the green water-fall, where he might have made tryst with his vision; then he turned his mind from it." They go off to St. Moritz, to a world he neither understood nor liked. "In the quiet place with the green water-fall Ralph's vision might have kept faith with him." But it never had a chance. The doomed and fragile vision was twofold: of his own creative ability as something it was not, and of his wife Undine as someone she was not. "Poor Undine! She was what the gods had made her— a creature of skin-deep reactions." Of course, as applied to Undine Spragg Marvell, "what the gods had made her" is just a figure of speech by Edith Wharton in Ralph Marvell's mind. But it is interesting to consider that the Undine in Fouqué's novella, of whom she is the namesake, was quite literally "made by the gods."

I have said that the ultimate reason for Undine Spragg's emergence in the world represented by New York lay in the death of her siblings. The more immediate reason is more mundane: as her father puts it, "they had left Apex because Undine was too big for the place." We have no such duality of motive in the translation of Fouqué's Undine. There is a single reason for her emergence in the world represented by her foster-parents' homestead, and that is her father's wish that she become possessed of a human soul. At first it seems fortuitous that prior to receiving such a soul—by marriage to a human being, Huldbrand—she replaces the lost natural daughter of her foster-parents, the Bertalda who becomes her rival for Huldbrand's love. For Bertalda, however, Undine has a deep sympathy, and with her she feels a mysterious bond.

The replacement of the human daughter by a water nymph in human form, despite the favorable auspices of Undine's generous, devoted, loving disposition, ends in tragedy, humanly seen. That is, Undine leaves the human world and returns to her own element:

> Aus dunstgem Tal die Welle,
> Sie rann und sucht' ihr Glück!
> Sie kam ins Meer zur Stelle
> Und rinnt nicht mehr zurück.

> [The wave came out of a hazy valley,
> She flowed and sought her luck!
> She flowed here into the sea
> And doesn't flow back anymore.]

The ostensible and superficial reason for her departure is her husband Huldbrand's failure to observe her reiterated warnings and pleas not to offend the water spirits—principally her uncle Kühleborn—by being unkind to her. The deeper reason is Undine's congenital—she was born a nymph—inability to adapt sufficiently to the human world, to play by rules to which she is alien.

The beginning, as well as the symbol of Undine's difficulty, lies in her receiving a human soul, close upon her marrying Huldbrand: "Es muß etwas Liebes, aber auch etwas höchst Furchtbares um eine Seele sein. Um Gott, . . . wär es nicht besser, man würde ihrer nie teilhaftig [It must be lovely and terrible to have to do with a soul . . . were it not better never to participate in it]?" Formerly she had been a water nymph in human form, carefree and impetuous. Now, freighted with a human soul, she is yet neither nymph nor human. Now her inability to adapt to the human world becomes all too clear—as well as, even more regrettably, the inability of the human world to adapt to her.

It is surely important that the encumbering with a soul is concomitant with Undine's marriage: "Eine Seele aber kann unsersgleichen nur durch den innigsten Verein der Liebe mit einem eures Geschlechtes gewinnen [Types like us can only procure a soul by means of the most sincere conjunction of love with one of your race]." We have to conclude that marriage is to be the microcosm of Undine's inability, despite her good will, to adapt—the microcosm of her misery. And in a way which baffles her husband she senses, even as she revels in love, the likelihood of such misery: "Nun bin ich beseelt, dir dank ich die Seele, o du unaussprechlicher Geliebter, und dir werd ich es danken, wenn du mich nicht mein ganzes Leben hindurch elend machst [Now I have a soul, my soul I owe to you, oh you unspeakable beloved, and it will be due only to you, if you don't make me miserable throughout my whole life]."

Undine's premonition of her inadaptability to human ways and relationships receives powerful confirmation when her pure-hearted attempt to reacquaint Bertalda with her parents—Undine's foster-parents—is met with Bertalda's denunciation and enmity. Undine: "ach Gott, ich wußte von euren törichten Sitten und eurer harten Sinnesweise nichts und werde mich wohl mein lebelang nicht drein finden [Oh God, I didn't know anything of your foolish customs and hardness of feeling and I will probably never understand them]." And in fact, over a period of time, Huldbrand's love for Undine declines; it is transferred to Bertalda, and they both begin to fear Undine as a being of another race: "Das kommt davon, wenn gleich sich nicht zu gleich gesellt [That's what happens when like doesn't join with like]." As Huldbrand's fear grows, so does his ill temper against Undine.

Undine is grieved by his growing hatefulness and by the certainty of retribution against him on the part of her kindred water spirits. She reiterates more pointedly her earlier warning against the expression of displeasure toward her while they are on the water. But in vain. "Huldbrand murmelte feindselig: '. . . so wollt ich, daß die tolle Verwandtschaft—[Huldbrand murmured hostilely . . . 'I wish that the marvelous kinship—']." This utterance nearly—Undine has put her hand over her husband's mouth—fullfills the precondition for her definitive departure from the human world. The crucial instances follow, and since they have rather crucial, if pedestrian parallels in *The Custom of the Country,* it may be worthwhile to note them in some detail.

Bertalda, some days before the tragic boat trip *à trois,* had received as a gift from Huldbrand a gold necklace which he had bought for her. Now she is absentmindedly dangling the necklace over the edge of the boat above the surface of the Danube. Suddenly a huge hand emerges from the river,

seizes the necklace, and vanishes with it beneath the water. Huldbrand for
the second time berates the water spirits, including his wife, more furiously
than before. Undine for the second time entreats him: "Mein Herzlieblicher,
hier schilt mich nicht! Schilt alles, was du willst, aber hier mich nicht! Du
weißt ja [My heart's love, don't scold me here, scold wherever you like, but
not me here! You know that]." She then fishes up from under the waves a
dazzling coral necklace and proffers it to Bertalda to make up for the lost
gold necklace. But Huldbrand rushes between Undine and Bertalda, snatches
the coral necklace out of Undine's hand, throws it back into the river, and
for the third time denounces her: "Bleib bei ihnen in aller Hexen Namen mit
all deinen Geschenken und laß uns Menschen zufrieden, Gauklerin du [Stay
with them in the name of all witches with all your gifts and leave us humans
be, you imposter you]!"

Undine, her hand still extended in a well-meant gesture of reconciliation
with the human race to which she cannot belong, gazes in mute shock at
her furious spouse, then breaks into tears, exclaiming, "'Ach, holder Freund,
ach, lebe wohl! . . . fort muß ich, muß fort auf diese ganze junge Lebenszeit.
O weh, o weh, was hast du angerichtet! O weh, o weh!' Und über den Rand
der Barke schwand sie hinaus [Alas, my darling friend, alas farewell! I must
leave this whole new life. Alas, alas, what have you done! Alas!—and she
disappeared over the side of the boat]," victim of an alienation she could
foretell but not understand. It seems to me that her pitiful plight and her
tragic disappearance from a world which she could not adapt to or understand—and which could not adapt to or understand her—can illuminate the
plight and then the suicide of Ralph Marvell as the only way out of the
incomprehensible and alien world to which his marriage to, and child by,
Undine Spragg had willy-nilly consigned him.

Undine Spragg, in this instance like the Lady Bertalda, is the recipient
of a necklace from the husband of another. Though the disposition of this
pearl necklace is almost as summary as that which befell Bertalda's golden
necklace, the exchange is for cash rather than coral. And the occasion is less
momentous, in that it does not result in climactic tragedy, but only in an
opportunity for Undine Spragg Marvell to see her father in a uniquely forceful
parental role and herself in a position to realize some funds. She had counted
on her father's not noticing the necklace, for he was habitually unobservant
of such matters, and uninquisitive. But this time he did notice: "'Did your
husband give them [the pearls] to you?' 'Ralph!' She could not restrain a
laugh." But her father's order to return them "to the party they belong to"
so unnerves Undine that she actually feels and expresses, for the first time,
a need for her parents: "it was the first time in her life that he had ever

ordered her to do anything." But she doesn't obey his order; instead of returning the necklace to its donor (it is not his first gift), she converts it to cash, a gambit to which her father silently and predictably consents. And her briefly felt need for her parents—Fouqué's Undine has similar scant need of her parents, powerful water princes, who wished her to obtain the human soul which lost her to her own family and race—Undine Spragg Marvell's need for her parents, as companions on her return to Europe, expires by mutual agreement after a few weeks of exposure to their touristic maladroitness.

Ralph Marvell, in his inability to adapt to the society into which *he* married, and his consequent misery and tragedy, is something of a classical, or mythical, Undine himself. The metaphor, or at any rate simile, is suggested not only by the above facts of life and death, but also by the array of water metaphors suffusing a dreamlike trance or fantasy that overcomes Ralph after he receives from Undine, across the Atlantic, a final indication of her intent to part from him. While he retains throughout the fantasy an awareness of self in search of Undine, he is at the same time an Undine in his ambiguous relationship to the water. This is one of Edith Wharton's rare evocations of thoroughly allusive fantasy, its theme pointed and counterpointed intensely and poetically.

Ralph Marvell was trying to reach something by which to pull himself out of bed. "It was like trying to catch at bright short waves"—that is, he was, literally, trying to catch at Undine, or at his vision of her. And, in the perfect symbol of wish fantasy, his fingers find something firm and warm: a hand that returns his pressure. But the hand, instead of receiving and helping his, presses him down again, "down into a dim deep pool of sleep"—into an underwater realm, "a silent blackness far below light and sound." There is a veritable tug of war for him between the Undine-force pressing him down into the alien underwater region and the inherent drive—it would be better in the case of Ralph to call it tendency—to return to his own element. He reenacts the dilemma of Fouqué's Undine between an existence in water and above water, although of course for Fouqué's Undine the water was the natural element and above water the unnatural.

In fantasy Ralph gradually floats to the surface. But pain, cruel hands, thongs, and weights "tried to pull him down with them"—observe the change of directional impetus from "press" to "pull" as the author shifts to an underwater point of view. The pain, the cruel hands, the thongs, and the weights are fantasized versions of Ralph's ties with Undine Spragg and with the Invaders, unnatural ties. "But still he floated, floated, danced on the fiery waves of pain." With this last phrase and the word "waves" we may be inclined to abandon any tentativeness about the equation between the pain and the punishment and the alien environment on the one hand, and Undine Spragg Marvell on the other.

But the pool, the sea—Ralph's dream metaphor for alien environment—is not entirely repulsive. It has features that beguile, and in these beguiling features it sounds very much on the order of Fouqué's Undine's memories of her childhood home, replete with pleasant watery images. The pleasant part of Ralph's fantasy: "Charmed intervals of rest, blue sailings on melodious seas, alternated with the anguish. He became a leaf on the air, a feather on a current, a straw on the tide, the spray of the wave spinning itself to sunshine as the wave toppled over into gulfs of blue."

As Fouqué's Undine ultimately must return to her own element, despite the sometime attractiveness—mixed with anguish—of the alien element, so Ralph Marvell's fantasy ultimately returns him, after anguish and pleasure, to dry land: "He woke on a stony beach. . . . He felt the ecstasy of decreasing pain. . . . The beach was his own bed."

After Ralph Marvell as a youth had engaged in a half-humorous revolt against the restrictions and exclusions of his society, Edith Wharton describes his sudden insight into its hereditary coherency and respectability as "one of the ironic reversions of heredity." That after this insight he should marry Undine Spragg, to his subsequent anguish, is thus doubly ironic. It may strike us that the phrase "ironic reversion of heredity" describes equally nicely the return to the water of Ralph's kindred spirit, of whom his wife is namesake, the water nymph Undine. Since her hereditary reversion, inevitable as we are made to believe it is, occurs after her marriage and its anguish, rather than before, we may choose to think of her marriage to Huldbrand as only a singlefold Romantic irony, available for absorption, retention, and complication in the mind of Edith Wharton.

ELIZABETH AMMONS

Fairy-Tale Love and The Reef

"Exquisite," Henry James christened *The Reef* (1912), and Edith Wharton's fourth full-length novel has remained his godchild ever since. Critics remark the similarity between Wharton's entangled quadrangle of lovers and James's quartet in *The Golden Bowl* (1904), note that her manipulation of point of view compares favorably with his technical mastery, and conclude more often than not by looking for a Jamesian moral at the center of her novel. The last is not easy.

Although one reader declares of *The Reef* that "the moral is unmistakable: passion must be subordinated to duty in a stable society," another maintains the opposite: "Anna's tragedy is that she cannot obey 'the voice of her heart'"; yet "it is doubtful whether her career can be considered a tragedy. . . . The absence of a rich social background to give solidity to the main themes makes us feel that . . . [they] are all rather preposterous." Similarly, Louis Auchincloss admits: "It is a quiet, controlled, beautiful novel, but its theme has always struck me as faintly ridiculous." Most specific is Blake Nevius: "Anna Leath is a Jamesian heroine in a Jamesian predicament" but, whereas James's "tone is seldom ambiguous," "one has to grope . . . for Mrs. Wharton's intention," and the book seems to promote a "dubious morality." Existing readings thus endorse the book's relative obscurity by finding *The Reef* artistically admirable but thematically conservative, somewhat ridiculous, and even morally questionable. In my opinion none of these

From *American Literature* 47, no. 4 (January 1976). © 1976 by Duke University Press. Footnotes from the original article have been omitted.

charges applies, and I think the interpretive confusion results from over-
looking *The Reef*'s fairy-tale complexion, an oversight encouraged no doubt
by James's praise for the book's "Racinian" quality.

At a picture-book French château Wharton interlocks the fates of two
couples: the publicly affianced Anna Leath and George Darrow, and the
secretly pledged Sophy Viner and Owen Leath. Both prospective brides harbor romantic dreams of female salvation through love and marriage. Sophy,
although skeptical about marriage in general, decides to marry Owen Leath
because he can make her dream of comfort and security a reality. The more
conventional Anna never questions the institution of marriage and believes
that in becoming Mrs. George Darrow she will awaken to the full awareness
of life she missed in her first, loveless marriage. But Anna Leath's plan to
marry George Darrow disintegrates when she learns that he and Sophy, the
fiancée of Anna's stepson, Owen, and therefore her future daughter-in-law,
have been lovers; and, because Owen suspects and Anna discovers Sophy's
liaison with Darrow, Sophy breaks her engagement to Owen Leath. This
quadrangle of fiancés and former lovers is complicated. But the outcome is
simple. No marriage takes place, and each woman's dream of deliverance by
a man ends in disillusionment to demonstrate Edith Wharton's central theme.
The Reef exposes deluded female fantasies about love and marriage: false
romantic visions generated and perpetuated by limitations imposed on
women—in Sophy's case, economic dependence; in Anna's sexual repression.

As a girl in Old New York Anna Summers (Leath) was "a model of
ladylike repression." She dutifully repressed the emotions and desires her
elders forbade her even feeling, much less expressing, and she idealized the
passion she subconsciously wanted to experience and understand. Yet long
before the novel opens the girl began to resent her sheltered and restricted
life. "Love, she told herself, would one day release her from this spell of
unreality." Marriage—which she envisions as "passion in action, romance
converted to reality"—will be for her "the magic bridge between West Fifty-
fifth Street and life." Rhetoric signals theme. Anna dreamed of becoming a
"heroine" who would be "transfigured" by the love of "a man" and "when
she said 'a man' she did not really mean George Darrow" or, for that matter,
any man in particular: just "a man"—whose love would "release her" from
a "spell" and with whom marriage would provide the "magic bridge" to
"life," the "eternal theme" of which would be their love. This language
comes from fairy tales because the fantasy itself, not of escaping but of *being*
freed, of *being* saved, of *being* awakened and reborn into life by the love of
a man—the fantasy, in short, of Sleeping Beauty's being awakened by Prince
Charming—comes from fairy tales.

The manuscript of *The Reef* explicitly refers to the fairy tale. In the finished novel, Anna Leath and George Darrow, betrothed, spend together at the château de Givré a "perfect" afternoon and evening, during which they discover on the estate "a little old deserted house, fantastically carved and chimneyed, which lay in a moat under the shade of ancient trees." That pleasure house, in an earlier version of the passage, has a name: "the Sleeping Beauty's lodge." Revisions in Edith Wharton's manuscripts often reveal her wish to avoid the symbolically obtrusive, especially in naming people and places; and *The Reef* is no exception. Her deletion of the direct reference to the Sleeping Beauty, as well as her substitution of the names Givré for "Blincourt" ("blin[d] court"[ship], hence "the reef ") and Darrow for "Caringdon" (in addition to "don[e] caring," too close to "C[h]ar[m]ing Don"?), suggests that Wharton, far from abandoning the Sleeping Beauty motif, wanted to make it more subtle, lest she insult the reader's intelligence or mar the book's delicate weave of fairy-tale associations by including heavy-handed symbols. The published novel, stripped of obvious allusion (like a building that no longer needs scaffolding), depends on inherent patterns of imagery and refined symbolism to communicate the fairy-tale motif and its thematic implications.

In her first husband, prior to the action of *The Reef*, Anna Summers thought she found her Prince Charming, her liberator and hero. She soon realized that the change in her name from Summers to Leath had contrary significance. The summers of her life were chillingly replaced by a lethean existence at his château de Givré: palace of rime, hoar-frost. The French château which "had called up to her youthful fancy a throng of romantic associations, poetic, pictorial, and emotional," the château which was for Anna "a castle of dreams, evoker of fair images and romantic legend," turned into a chamber of horrors where "life, to Mr. Leath, was like a walk through a carefully classified museum. . . . [while] to his wife it was like groping about in a huge dark lumber-room where the exploring ray of curiosity lit up now some shape of breathing beauty and now a mummy's grin." Her husband's kiss, instead of awakening her passionate impulses and desires, "dropped on her like a cold smooth pebble." She and her stepson, Owen, "were like two prisoners who talk to each other by tapping on the wall." In effect, Anna found herself living in a gothicized fairy-tale world, complete with wicked mother-in-law and haunting portrait of a dead first wife—the "exiled consort removed farther and farther from the throne." This was definitely the wrong fairy tale. Anna wanted to be awakened into "contact with the actual business of living"; she wanted to be freed, not imprisoned.

Instead of making Anna Summers, like the young women she envied, "wider awake," married life at Givré with its "ghostly tinge of unreality" only prolonged her nightmare of loneliness, sexual repression, and involuntary subjugation: "the history of Anna Leath appeared to its heroine like some grey shadowy tale that she might have read in an old book, one night as she was falling asleep . . ." (Wharton's ellipsis). However, into this midnight tale of frustrated desires comes a rescuer in *The Reef*. Fraser Leath failed, but his widow blames the man, not the dream, and therefore looks forward to marriage with George Darrow. As she anticipates their reunion at the secluded château, the October sunlight gives the estate such luminescence that Anna

> seemed to be opening her own eyes upon it after a long interval of blindness.
>
> The court was very still, yet full of latent life: the wheeling and rustling of pigeons about the rectangular yews and across the sunny gravel; the sweep of the rooks above the lustrous greyish-purple slates of the roof, and the stir of the tree-tops as they met the breeze which every day, at that [afternoon] hour, came punctually up from the river.
>
> Just such a latent animation glowed in Anna Leath. In every nerve and vein she was conscious of that equipoise of bliss which the fearful human heart scarce dares acknowledge. She was not used to strong or full emotions; but she had always known that she should not be afraid of them. She was not afraid now; but she felt a deep inward stillness.

Anna is ready for Darrow. Gradually awakening out of a lifetime of abnegation—first as a model daughter, then an obedient wife, finally a decorous widow—the woman's sense of impending freedom erupts. Impulsively, she runs across the grounds to Owen like a schoolgirl with "the feeling, which sometimes came to her in dreams, of skimming miraculously over short bright waves."

Anna's running feels dreamlike because, exuberantly uninhibited at last, she does live her dream. The "old vicious distinction between romance and reality" for the moment disappears, and she becomes the heroine of her fairy-tale fantasy. Just as "the slanted lights and moist perfumes of the failing day" transform Givré from "a dull house, an inconvenient house, of which one knew all the defects, the shabbiness, the discomforts" into the splendid château it was meant to be, so the prospect of Darrow's arrival arouses the sensuous, carefree spirit so long dormant within Wharton's Sleeping Beauty.

When he arrives, handsome George Darrow—youthful, cultured,

worldly-wise—not only seems the Prince of Anna's dream; in fact, he shares her romantic view of himself and plans to rescue her from her sleep-walk existence at Givré. Diplomacy, a princely vocation, will soon send him on a mission to South America, a distant and unfamiliar land, and he means to take his bride with him. Even his kiss is perfect. As in a fairy tale, he is masterful, she responsive. "For a long moment they looked at each other without speaking. She saw the dancing spirit in his eyes turn grave and darken to a passionate sternness. He stooped and kissed her, and she sat as if folded in wings." Transported by this kiss into what seems the "silver tangle of an April wood," Anna's "imagination flew back and forth, spinning luminous webs of feeling between herself and the scene about her." "Her feelings were unlike any she had ever known: richer, deeper, more complete. For the first time everything in her, from head to foot, seemed to be feeding the same full current of sensation." Like the Prince in *Sleeping Beauty*, Darrow awakens Anna with a kiss, and her dream finally becomes real.

Out of all keeping with fairy-tale expectations, Anna's Prince Charming turns out to be a liar, a hypocrite, a coward, and a libertine. The discovery shocks her into admitting that

> her life had ended just as she had dreamed it was beginning. . . .
> The man who had driven away from her house in the autumn
> dawn was not the man she had loved; he was a stranger with
> whom she had not a single thought in common. . . . She had
> believed it would be possible to separate the image of the man
> she had thought him from that of the man he was. . . . But now
> she had begun to understand that the two men were really one.
> The Darrow she worshipped was inseparable from the Darrow
> she abhorred; and the inevitable conclusion was that both must
> go.

As the image of Darrow as two men emphasizes, the double standard forms "the reef" on which Anna's dream shatters.

Anna's horror of George Darrow's brief affair with Sophy Viner springs from the realization that the double standard not only justifies careless sexual encounters for men but, worse, deception of and contempt for women as a group. Darrow "had come to her with an open face and a clear conscience—come to her from this [the affair with Sophy]! If his security was the security of falsehood it was horrible; if it meant that he had forgotten, it was worse." This reasoning makes sense. As Anna sees it, either Darrow respects her so little that he can glibly lie to her, or he respects Sophy so little that he can casually forget her. Whichever it is, he reveals contempt for one (if not both) of the women. Anna realizes "with a chill of fear that she would never again know if he were speaking the truth or not," and "the idea that his tact was a kind of professional expertness filled her with repugnance." "No doubt men often had to make such explanations: they had the formulas by heart . . . A leaden lassitude descended on her" (Wharton's ellipsis).

Anna tries but cannot renounce Darrow. He has made her feel physically and emotionally aware for the first time in her life, and she desperately longs to recapture their fairy-tale world of romance and sensuality. To do so, she need only listen to him. "Darrow had said: 'You were made to feel everything'; and to feel was surely better than to judge." Terrified of losing him and her dream, Anna gives in to her feelings, and the result is a new but no less frightening state of bondage, this time caused by her emotions overmastering her will. She conforms entirely to Darrow's wishes even though "her fear of doing or saying what he disliked was tinged by a new instinct of subserviency against which her pride revolted." Her newly developed worry about growing physically unattractive to him also disgusts her. But most degrading, she knows, is her desire to rationalize his deceit "by persuading herself that only through such concessions could women like herself hope to keep what they could not give up." Wharton's heroine, in sum, finds herself the victim of an enslaving passion which makes her subservient, acquiescent, and consciously sophistic.

Anna loathes her transformation. "She pictured [her daughter] Effie growing up under the influence of the woman she saw herself becoming—and she hid her eyes from the humiliation of the picture." Indeed Anna has humiliated herself. But why? Surely, Darrow—a liar and an egotist—does not merit her violating her own character. Partly to blame is biology, more accurately society's perversion of her normal biological needs and desires. Anna has been repressed for so long that her erotic longings for Darrow overwhelm her; she cannot control her awakened impulses and responses even though they produce a feeling of dependency reprehensible to her will. Still, sexual repression explains only one dimension of her problem, which is the romantic dream itself: the hope for deliverance through love, with marriage following as a matter of course. As precious to Anna as it has been to most women trapped in comatose lives, the fairy-tale fantasy of being rescued by a man must, Wharton shows, be outgrown. The fantasy is pernicious. It teaches women to accept lives they despise, and, while purporting to free them from living death, in fact glorifies abnegation. Sleeping Beauty does not awaken to live her own life; she is awakened to serve as the Prince's grateful and loving dependent, as Wharton underscores by describing Anna's ecstasy when her dream of love appears to be coming true: "She felt like a slave, and a goddess, and a girl in her teens . . ." (Wharton's ellipsis). This is the apotheosis of Anna's romantic dream—to feel abased, and etherealized, and immature. The image obviously offends any admirable concept of human self-fulfillment because Anna has not been freed, saved, by her Prince Charming. She has been enthralled, in both senses of the word.

The structure of the novel charts the crash of the woman's romantic fantasy. In contrast to the gloomy weather and dingy urban settings of Book I, Anna's idyllic world of latent animation at the château in Book II does seem a fairy-tale world coming to life. However, the harder she clings to her dream in the face of realities it cannot accommodate, the more inhospitable and enclosed the atmosphere becomes. In Book III she has "the eerie feeling of having been overswept by a shadow which there had been no cloud to cast . . ." (Wharton's ellipsis). The day turns rainy and its two main events are Anna's visit to an injured child and Darrow's secret meeting with Sophy in a decaying summer-house. In Book IV Anna does not leave Givré, where her dream of perfect love is attenuated as she learns the truth about Darrow's character. The dream dissolves altogether in Book V, which, like Book I, takes place mainly in Paris. The atmosphere grows stormy and dark, the action consists of frantic journeys and conferences in hotel rooms, and Anna last appears not at the château but in the bedroom of a strange woman in a shabby Parisian hotel. This last scene is upsetting, even cruel, as critics remark. But it is so for a purpose. Although Anna can no longer delude herself about marrying Darrow, she still clings to her hope of being saved by someone other than herself. She decides "it was Sophy Viner only who could save her—Sophy Viner only who could give her back her lost serenity. She would seek the girl out and tell her that she had given Darrow up; and that step once taken there would be no retracing it, and she would perforce have to go forward alone." If successful, the plan will reanimate her dream: Darrow and Sophy's careless affair will be transformed into a beautiful love-marriage, and Anna will be transfigured into a self-sacrificing heroine. Wharton does not let Anna find Sophy and therefore be saved by her. She has her find herself among strangers in a tawdry hotel love-nest, and there all illusion about fairy-tale love explodes. In the person of the slovenly Mrs. McTarvie-Birch at the Hôtel Chicago we finally see the embodiment of Anna's earlier image of the woman in love as "a slave, and a goddess, and a girl in her teens": a prostitute who is bought and owned like a slave, enthroned on her bed like a goddess, and distracted by her pet poodle like a girl in her teens. That Anna mistakes this woman and her pimp for husband and wife serves as one last grotesque indication of how naive she is about the whole subject of love, sex, and marriage.

Edith Wharton, I want to emphasize, does not mock Anna in *The Reef*. (To be sure, the final scene is ironic; but the irony is sobering, not amusing or contemptuous.) Rather, she develops Anna's story to confute a fairy-tale fantasy cherished by many women because they are taught to believe in it. The target of criticism in *The Reef* is not women but the culture which represses them and encourages them to believe that love and marriage will someday release them into reality. Love and marriage are not a release. Anna's dream cannot even withstand an engagement, let alone marriage which, as her first union demonstrated and her relationship with Darrow suggests, simply delivers a woman from one subservient life into another.

Worldly Sophy Viner knows that. "'Oh, I never mean to marry,'" she tells Darrow early in the novel. "'I'm not so sure that I believe in marriage. You see I'm all for self-development and the chance to live one's life. I'm awfully modern, you know." Her modish rhetoric somewhat undercuts the declaration. But in light of her native candor and the marriages she has seen (plus the proposals she has had from repulsive widowers), Sophy's wish never to marry and her skepticism about the institution in general should be taken as seriously as Lily Bart's fear of marriage in *The House of Mirth* (1905). Sophy faces the dilemma of Lily and all women who were not independently wealthy: freedom for anyone requires economic security; economic security for women required marriage; marriage required loss of freedom for women. Sophy capitulates to the inevitable. As her later admission that she does not love Owen Leath confirms, she decides to marry for financial reasons. In the end, however, she reverses her decision and bravely refuses to sacrifice happiness to necessity by contracting herself to a man she does not love. (The name *Owen* suggests the kind of husband he would be.) The alternative—resuming her unstable life as some socialite's appendage—is detestable. But she has no other choice, which is Wharton's point: a talented, ambitious young woman like Sophy Viner has virtually no control over her own life.

Sophy's plot acquires full significance within the context of the fairy-tale motif in *The Reef*. Literally Sophy serves as a foil for Anna; she is the realist whose experience with life highlights the older woman's naiveté. But symbolically more important than the contrasts between the two women are the similarities and connections. Both love the same man, Darrow. Both are closely attached to another man, Owen—Sophy as his fiancée, Anna as his stepmother. But because they "have always been on odd kind of brother-and-sister terms," Anna thinks of herself as Owen's sister, which makes Sophy more like Anna's future sister than daughter-in-law. Indeed, if Sophy were to marry Owen, Anna and Sophy, like sisters, would share the same mother-figure (Madame de Chantelle) just as they already share the care of the same child (Effie). The intertwining of the two women's identities to imply figurative sisterhood suggests that symbolically Anna Leath and Sophy Viner represent a split heroine, a dichotomous embodiment of one basic identity. That basic identity in *The Reef* is the would-be fairy-tale heroine who is rescued from a miserable life by a Prince Charming hero. For if Anna Leath resembles Sleeping Beauty, waiting for a man's passion to animate her, Sophy Viner in her way recalls the tale of Cinderella—a poor, neglected, down-to-earth girl who is transported to riches by her Prince Charming.

Especially reminiscent of Cinderella in Book I, Sophy Viner appears remarkably cheerful and adaptable in the face of hardship; and for a woman in her middle twenties, she has an unusually fresh, juvenile quality. Her physical appearance and movements often look "boyish" to Darrow, so spontaneous and guileless she seems, while her earthy "naturalness" is so pronounced that she reminds him of "a dryad in a dew-drenched forest" (note also her surname). Like Cinderella setting out for the ball, Sophy emerges dressed for the theater "looking as if she had been plunged into some sparkling element which had curled up all her drooping tendrils and wrapped her in a shimmer of fresh leaves." Her exuberance transfigures her and tricks Darrow into believing her old outfit "some miracle of Parisian dress-making." In fact, her whole adventure in Paris—sightseeing, dining out, attending the theater—seems a fairy tale come true; and George Darrow obviously plays the hero. "'Do you want to know what I feel?'" she asks him and then exclaims: "'That you're giving me the only chance I've ever had!'" Very like Cinderella at the moment of transformation from peasant to princess, Sophy marvels: "'Is it true? Is it really true? Is it really going to happen to *me*?'" The answer is both yes and no.

Sophy Viner gets her adventure, enjoys it, and never regrets it. The dream-come-true, however, evaporates. In contrast to the storybook version, this miraculous adventure does not conclude in her living happily ever after with her Prince Charming, nor with his surrogate, Owen Leath, at his gorgeous château. The moral of Sophy's plot mirrors that of Anna's. Whether the Cinderella myth of economic salvation or the Sleeping Beauty myth of sensual/spiritual salvation, the fairy-tale fantasy of being saved by a man from a life of misery is an illusion which ends in disillusion.

Precisely that happens in *The Reef*. Each woman's dream comes true and, in doing so, results in disillusionment. Both women are rescued by a man only to discover that the rescue brings with it unsuspected disadvantages. George Darrow does awaken Anna Leath's repressed sexuality, and she therefore feels sensuously and emotionally aware for the first time in her life. Owen Leath does propose to Sophy Viner, and she therefore can antic-

ipate economic security and luxury for the first time in her life. The terrible
irony is that, while each rescue is successful, it is at the same time self-
defeating. Anna discovers that sexual expression does not entitle her to express herself fully but requires the suppression of many other emotions and
desires. Her fantasy comes true, but she is still only a partial being. Similarly,
Sophy discovers that luxury and economic security will not entitle her to the
freedom she really wants and that life with Owen Leath will not be plea-
surable. Her dream promises to come true, but she will still be a dependent
and perforce compliant person. Wharton's thematic logic is subtle yet unmistakable. Even as rescue by a man fulfills the letter of the fairy-tale fantasy,
it is false to its supposed spirit. For if a woman looks to a man as her
deliverer, she acquiesces in the dispensation of superior power to men and
consequently must accept as just and moral the subordination of women,
which condones the double standard and the idea of male proprietorship.

In the myth Prince Charming frees or brings to new life his heroine—
Sleeping Beauty or Cinderella—so that she may become his human re-cre-
ation and possession. Likewise, in *The Reef* George Darrow has toward
women "the male instinct of ownership" and a distinct Pygmalion-attitude.
Before he becomes her lover, Sophy reminds Darrow of "a terra-cotta stat-
uette, some young image of grace hardly more than sketched in the clay";
and he regrets not having been able to bring Anna to life when she was
younger. He thinks: "If she had been given to him then he would have put
warmth in her veins and light in her eyes: would have made her a woman
through and through. . . . A love like his might have given her the divine gift
of self-renewal." Magnanimous as it sounds, this Pygmalion-attitude reflects
astounding masculine egoism.

Women for Darrow, a man of "traditional views," fall into two categories, each ordained for his pleasure and patronage.

> George Darrow had had a fairly varied experience of feminine
> types, but the women he had frequented had either been pro-
> nouncedly "ladies" or they had not. Grateful to both for minis-
> tering to the more complex masculine nature, and disposed to
> assume that they had been evolved, if not designed, to that end,
> he had instinctively kept the two groups apart in his mind. . . .
> He liked, above all, people who went as far as they could in their
> own line—liked his "ladies" and their rivals to be equally un-
> ashamed of showing for exactly what they were.

Thus, Sophy Viner, not a "lady" in his opinion, is just "the chance instru-
ment of his lapse," the panacea for "his wounded vanity." Impressed by her

"responsive temperament," he at one juncture entertains "a fleeting desire to make its chords vibrate for his own amusement"; and he disports himself another evening, before he converts fancy to fact, by casually undressing her in his mind's eye: "his imagination continued to follow her to and fro, traced the curve of her slim young arms as she raised them to undo her hair, pictured the sliding down of her dress to the waist and then to the knees, and the whiteness of her feet as she slipped across the floor to bed . . ." (Wharton's ellipsis).

In contrast, Darrow displays little erotic interest in Anna Leath, a "lady." He prizes her like a fine object of art or a spirited horse he plans to own. Looking forward to "the high privilege of possessing her" he exalts: "Pride and passion were in the conflict—magnificent qualities in a wife! . . . Yes! It was worth a great deal to watch that fight between her instinct and her intelligence, and know one's self the object of the struggle." She brings to mind "a picture so hung that it can be seen only at a certain angle: an angle known to no one but its possessor. The thought flattered his sense of possessorship . . ." (Wharton's ellipsis). In this character Wharton exposes the real values implicit in the Prince Charming fantasy. The self-acknowledged savior of women, Darrow believes they exist solely for his pleasure, and he has no difficulty fitting Sophy Viner and Anna Leath into his two categories of women: whores or ladies—which is to say, sexual objects or decorative objects but in neither case autonomous people. Women, in effect, represent human property at his disposal. Wharton's characterization is probably too harsh. (Darrow and Owen are so weak and unsympathetic that one could accuse Wharton of stacking the deck and therefore miss, or dismiss, her criticism of institutionalized fantasies; she comes close to attacking men per se rather than ideas they are taught to have about women and their relation to them.) But her theme is important and clearly developed. The love of this man, or of any man sharing his "traditional views," cannot possibly rescue any woman from a life of involuntary subordination.

Simone de Beauvoir remarks on the male orientation of the Sleeping Beauty and Cinderella myths (which she too considers together): "What would Prince Charming have for occupation if he had not to awaken the Sleeping Beauty? . . . The Cinderella myth . . . flourishes especially in prosperous countries like America. How should the men there spend their surplus money if not upon a woman?" Beauvoir continues: "It is clear that in dreaming of himself as donor, liberator, redeemer, man still desires the subjection of woman; for in order to awaken the Sleeping Beauty, she must have been put to sleep; ogres and dragons must be about if there are to be captive princesses. . . . What he requires in his heart of hearts is that this struggle remain a game for him, while for the woman it involves her very destiny. Man's true victory, whether he is liberator or conqueror, lies just in this: that woman freely recognizes him as her destiny." It is against this concept of female destiny that Edith Wharton argues in *The Reef*, a book highly praised by readers from Henry James to the present for its artistic beauty but nevertheless dismissed because that artistry has not been properly understood as the expert execution of Wharton's argument. The fairy-tale fantasy of deliverance by a man appears to be but is not a dream of freedom for women. It is a glorification of the status quo: a culturally perpetuated myth of female liberation which in reality celebrates masculine dominance, proprietorship, and privilege. That reality, for both of Edith Wharton's heroines, in the end marks "the reef."

MARGARET B. McDOWELL

Hudson River Bracketed
and The Gods Arrive

THE DEVELOPMENT OF THE ARTIST AS A PASSIONATE MAN

Although Edith Wharton did not visit America in the last fifteen years of her life, she recognized in *Hudson River Bracketed* (1929) and in *The Gods Arrive* (1932) the changes wrought by the Great Depression in the everyday living of Americans. Despite the tendency of critics to disregard these novels, they are books of magnitude, interest, and merit. Although they are not among her greatest works, they attain a respectable position in her canon and are novels that round out with distinction a literary career of some forty years. Intellectually, they represent a culmination of many of Edith Wharton's earlier preoccupations; for she dramatizes in these novels the struggle of the artist to find his own voice, his need to establish a meeting-ground between the demands of his integrity and of the marketplace, the relationship of his vocation to his life as a person, the positive effects upon him of feminine interest in his work, and the destructive effects upon him of irresponsible passion. These two novels are in part the outcome of Edith Wharton's extensive but often postponed plans for the never-completed novel, *Literature,* which was begun in 1915 and which was to have traced the development of a writer. These two novels also provide a significant reflection of her views on trends in literature during her later years and are therefore essential to a full understanding of her aesthetic views and practice.

The novels chronicle Vance Weston's emergence as a writer from his

From *Edith Wharton*. © 1976 by G. K. Hall and Co. Twayne Publishers, 1976.

first short story to his successful novels, but they also chronicle the closely related subject of his love life. His first relationship ends in disillusionment with the promiscuous Floss Delaney in Euphoria, Illinois; and this affair is succeeded by a disturbing marriage to lovely and dependent Laura Lou Tracy who dies at the end of the first book. Thereafter, and at the heart of both novels, is his life with Halo Tarrant, who inspires him as a platonic influence in the first book and who becomes his mistress in the second. Throughout the two novels, Mrs. Wharton focuses intensively upon Vance Weston's achievement of identity as a writer and of his growing awareness as a man.

After Vance's abortive relationship with Floss, he leaves the Midwest to live with his distant relatives, the Tracys, in rural New York. He is relatively innocent and has hoped to become a writer by absorbing the sophisticated life of New York City. To his dismay, he is disappointed in all such expectations when he finds himself in a run-down house in a rural area at some distance from the city, an area which, if anything, is more isolated and backward than his home town. His impoverished relatives clean and care for "The Willows," which was described in an 1842 book on architecture as the best example of Hudson River Bracketed, an ornate mode characterized by irregular narrow balconies supported with wooden brackets. But "The Willows" is crucial to Vance's career, though he does not realize it at the time. In the tiny library at "The Willows," he discovers the "Past" and becomes convinced that, through familiarity with the literary tradition which he can gain by perusing the old books there, he will become, like Samuel Taylor Coleridge, a distinguished writer. Halo Spear, a relative of the Tracys, who is a few years older than Vance, eagerly volunteers to be his intellectual guide as he plans to immerse himself in the classics.

Intellectual ambition does not represent for Vance his only fulfillment at the time. His emotional nature demands recognition; and as a result, he persuades the gentle, naive Laura Lou Tracy to break her engagement to the enterprising Bunny Hayes and to elope with him. But their relationship, far from harmonious, is tragic for Laura Lou. Because Vance has to discipline himself in order to write, he ignores her loneliness. A complication supervenes also when Vance retreats to "The Willows" in search of a more relaxing atmosphere for writing each day. Halo begins regularly to meet him to help him with his novel.

Local gossips, particularly Mrs. Tracy, interpret these meetings to Laura Lou as sexual infidelity. Dissension between husband and wife reaches new intensity when Vance takes Laura Lou to the city after his first success. While he makes the rounds of social and literary New York and becomes involved in maneuvering for an important prize, Laura Lou lives a lonely existence in a boarding house. All is not to be smooth for Vance in the city either. Halo Spear's husband, a magazine editor, Lewis Tarrant, hires Vance, exploits him financially, and eventually fires him. Though Vance's first novel sells phenomenally, he receives little money from it.

Toward the end of *Hudson River Bracketed*, Vance and Laura Lou find an abandoned house at the edge of the city and live there in extreme poverty for months. So as not to disturb Vance's frustrating work on another novel, Laura Lou heroically hides the fact that she is hemorrhaging from tuberculosis. In the closing scene of *Hudson River Bracketed*, Halo Spear finds the Westons after much searching, announces to Vance that she has separated from Tarrant, and learns a moment later that Laura Lou has just died. Halo's arrival anticipates the second book, in which Edith Wharton details Halo's life with Vance, particularly as it relates to their troubled personal relationship and to her attempts to shape his work.

Blake Nevius declares that none of the many artists in Edith Wharton's work bears the stamp of authenticity. He overstates the case, however, although Vance's personal problems are often more important and interesting than Mrs. Wharton's presentation of his career as artist. The books center more around the women he loves, his social position, and his constant fight to get money for survival than they do around the mastery of his craft. However, he does provide a voice through which Edith Wharton can express her views, and his activities and struggles as a writer are grim enough. In fact, Mrs. Wharton's involvement with Vance makes him, in some respects, the most believable and interesting artist in her fiction. Granted that she satirized Vance's romanticism as he finds himself inspired by "that celestial Beauty which haunted earth and sky and the deeps of his soul" and that she tended at such times to forget his mundane responsibilities, he emerges as her more authentic spokesman because he is not idealized.

Through Vance, Mrs. Wharton reiterates some principles about literature she held throughout her career, such as the artist's obligation to select detail and his need to reveal a structural sense in his work. In the two books she also voices through him or through his mentor, Halo Spear, her views on the literature of the 1920s and 1930s. When either Vance or Halo expresses sensible views on the nature of literature, a loquacious writer or editor advances opposing ideas. The result is a further exposition of some of Vance's or Halo's principles in the form of a literary dialogue with spirited antagonists. Vance and Halo denounce the superficiality of young writers who are commercially ambitious, the pessimism of Naturalist authors, and the fragmentation of personality which Edith Wharton felt was induced in a character by the use of the stream-of-consciousness technique. Vance certainly speaks for her whenever he discusses writing, especially when he tries to analyze his problems as a writer of fiction. In her description through Vance of the creative process, Edith Wharton resembles Henry James with his idea of the *donnée* from which all else is derived. The imagination builds upon a single fragment of fact—a single kernel which the author separates from all others and plants in his mind to grow independently.

The artist must learn to observe economy both in his personal life and in his art, for they depend on each other. This principle of moderation in all things Vance learns as he leaves "The Willows" after his first visit at the beginning of *Hudson River Bracketed*. Edith Wharton relates this principle to the action at several points in *The Gods Arrive* since Halo's failure to understand it precipitates the rift between her and Vance and causes some of Vance's problems and misfortunes. Too much intense experience upsets Vance; his abnormally keen sensibility can only accommodate a certain amount of stimulation if he is to do his best work: "When the impressions were too abundant and powerful, they benumbed him" (*Gods*). In Spain, for instance, Vance grows lazy; and he seems to have lost even his desire to store his sensations for use in his future work, precisely because they are too abundant here for him to value correctly. We suspect that Edith Wharton suffered from a similar surfeit of experience during the World War I period when she postponed indefinitely the actual composition of *Literature* and other novels and when she could not write *A Son at the Front* until she was further removed in time from her war experience.

When Vance visits Chartres, he suspects that he may have already heard too much about its alleged sublimity. He is not surprised that his reactions to it are dulled, but he is bitterly disappointed that he has lost his capacity to respond to a monument that he recognizes with his intellect to be a great work of art. He is later reassured when he is able to react spontaneously to the simpler beauty of a small church in which he seeks refuge during a storm. In the lightning flashes he glimpses a "fragment of heaven" and sits "among these bursts of glory and passages of darkness as if alternate cantos of the *Paradiso* and the *Inferno* were whirling through him" (*Gods*). Just as the childhood memory of the River Dudden inspired the adult William Wordsworth, so the mere sights and sounds of a river can become for Vance the small, secreted treasures that feed creativity.

Edith Wharton frequently refers, through Vance's voice, to the problems a young writer encounters in trying to maintain his originality and independence. Critics, editors, the influence of other writers, and even the reading of books are all suspect. Vance distrusts critics because, as Halo remarks, they change their standards every day. Halo and, somewhat later, Vance suspect the disinterestedness of editors since they must apply, in the main, commercial criteria to their judgment of art. Editors discourage Vance from being original and prefer him to write in the future what sold well in the past: "the principle of the quick turnover applied to brains as it was to real estate." In her own essays, Edith Wharton found troubling the fact that some of her younger contemporaries refused to read great literature lest they endanger their originality and become derivative in their art. Halo, like Edith Wharton, saw immersion in the tradition as essential to a writer; and she magisterially comments about the New York literary set that "the clever young writers . . . had read only each other and *Ulysses*" (*Gods*).

As a young writer, Vance faces frustration because he can easily copy the facile improvisations and stylistic tricks of his contemporaries but longs to communicate his own vision of the world and his sense of the stark forces that determine man's fate. Edith Wharton herself as a younger writer was undoubtedly annoyed by reviewers who spoke of her cleverness and epigrammatic prose when she was trying to probe deeply into human problems. Vance voices the young author's self-doubt about whether a book composed easily can be good and whether a best-seller can have lasting value. Edith Wharton's own work shows little correlation between the time and effort spent on a novel and its financial success. She herself refused to value as her best works those that sold best. But even in the 1920s she felt the same frustration that Vance voices about the difficulty of his evaluating his own work in the light of hostile criticism.

Again like Edith Wharton in her critical works, Vance distrusts the stream-of-consciousness technique, popular among the other young writers in Paris and in New York. In *The Gods Arrive*, his friends contend that "the art of narrative and the portrayal of social groups had reached its climax" and that now the only hope for attaining new dimensions in fiction is in "the exploration of the subliminal." But Edith Wharton, to the end, saw the use of a structured plot and of dialogue as more effective methods of characterization than the random probing of the inner psyche; and she rebelled against the formlessness, as she saw it, of the stream-of-consciousness technique.

To Vance—as it probably did to Edith Wharton—the stream-of-consciousness technique inevitably associated itself with a deterministic pessimism, derived in large part from the literary Naturalists, though originally these Naturalists had not made much use of the detailed examination of the inner psyche or done much with experimentation in form. While Mrs. Wharton's own work as early as *The House of Mirth* showed the influence of Naturalism, she never fully subscribed to its deterministic tenets; and stream-of-consciousness fiction tends, in Vance's words, to reduce characters "to bundles of loosely tied instincts and habits, borne along blindly on the current of existence" (*Gods*), and inevitably, therefore, to minimize their power of free choice. Like Vance's most sensitive contemporaries, he wants to depict a reality as it is, no matter how somber; but he wants to see a whole man "pitted against a hostile universe and surviving, and binding it to his own uses" (*Gods*).

Edith Wharton also felt that Naturalist novelists tended to use either sensational or grotesque characters to the point of their soon becoming stereotypes. She expressed her dissatisfaction with this tendency in many of her contemporaries through a young Englishman, Chris Churley, and his comments about current American writing. He derides the two extremes in popular fiction, Romantic historical novels and documentary Naturalist novels, since both evince undeveloped characters. He does not understand, furthermore, why modern writers disregard in their work the middle class which comprises so much that is essentially American; instead, these authors choose to write about princesses in Tuscan villas or ignorant peasants, "gaunt young men with a ten-word vocabulary who spend their lives sweating and hauling wood. . . . There's really nothing as limited as the primitive passions—except perhaps those of princesses" (*Gods*).

THE SATIRE OF THE SUPERFICIAL AND THE PROVINCIAL

Beyond her views on literature, Edith Wharton expressed through Vance her scorn for time-serving authors and the venality that motivates them. Her satire may be excessive in depicting the young writers and artists at the Loafers Club and the Coconut Tree Restaurant in New York or at Lorry Spear's apartment in Paris. They are at least dedicated to what they are doing despite their superficiality and false sophistication. But her ridicule of current modes of writing fiction is inescapable and amusing, if sometimes a bit too broad and farcical. The tendencies that she condemned perhaps did not deserve all the attention that she awarded them. But, when her young writers discuss popular novels like *Price of Meat,* now in its seventieth thousand, or *Egg Omelette* (the latter's sales boosted by pulpit denunciations of it), they demonstrate how ridiculous any fad in art can become. Likewise, the quarrel of a prize committee over a book's "exact degree of indecency" and the maneuvering by writers and publishers for the Pulsifer Prize are amusing and contemporaneous aspects of *Hudson River Bracketed* and *The Gods Arrive.* They recall the machinations of George Gissing's characters in the literary world of the 1890s in *New Grub Street.*

The high-powered parties designed to promote the sales of books and to publicize the reputations of writers also come under Mrs. Wharton's steady scrutiny—parties, for example, in which a woman presses an author to identify the originals of his characters and to verify her suspicion that his love scenes reflect his personal life. With the good humor born of long experience with book promotions, she can even laugh indulgently in *Hudson River Bracketed* at the publicity given to books by newspaper interviews with authors: "The heart-to-heart kind ... With a snapshot of yourself looking at the first crocus in your garden; or smoking a pipe, with your arm around a Great Dane."

While Edith Wharton's satire is often biting and precise, at other times it is maladroit, even crude, less controlled than that in *Twilight Sleep* and in *The Children*. In her depiction of the rich, ostentatious tourists in *The Gods Arrive,* she attacked them too directly and harshly; she seemed oblivious to the possibility that her attack might have been outdated because the United States was in the depths of the Depression when this novel appeared and most of the wealthy people of the 1920s had become impoverished. Her satire was, for example, out of place in such comments as "If you're going to buy a Rolls-Royce, buy two—it pays in the end" or "We've run down a little place at last where you can really count on the caviar."

Even more difficult to defend is her snobbish treatment of Vance's Midwestern background and his lack of literary sophistication. For a college graduate interested in the arts, he is impossibly ignorant of literature; American colleges could not have been so provincial as Mrs. Wharton makes them out to be. So his remark to Halo, a stranger, when he skims a book by Coleridge, "Why did no one ever tell me about the Past before?" is totally false (*Hudson*). American education would have done better in those days by Vance than to acquaint him only with James Whitcomb Riley, Ella Wheeler Wilcox, John Greenleaf Whittier, Henry Wadsworth Longfellow, James Russell Lowell, and a little Walt Whitman. Halo Spear is disdainful, as a cultured Easterner, about the Midwest and its purported lack of culture; she imagines that Vance's classmates in the sixth grade were young "savages" about to "maul" the selections in their readers, like *The Ancient Mariner.* Though Mrs. Wharton amused readers with her choice of names—like Prune, Nebraska; and Hallelujah, Missouri—her ridicule of the Midwest through her derision of the forces and the milieu that molded her central character misfired. If Vance is an original genius, as Mrs. Wharton would allege, his region must have contributed more to his development than she is willing to admit.

Yet Mrs. Wharton did have some sympathy for small-town life and regarded some aspects of it with indulgent humor. Vance's father, the real-estate promoter (who names his son "Advance" after his land development in Missouri), and Vance's mother and sisters, with their concern for status, are authentic representatives of the American small town in the 1930s. Their bungalow living room reflects Edith Wharton's interest in interiors and is a typical room for a middle-class house in any town in the United States at this time. The gold-and-grey wallpaper, the phonograph on the library table, the crocheted tablecloth, the religious pictures in Woolworth frames, and the houseplant on a milking stool were ubiquitous "props" in 1930. Realistic, too, and humorous is the general evasiveness characterizing the funeral when quotations from Isaiah and James Whitcomb Riley are "intermingled with a practiced hand" and the word "died" is replaced by "passed over."

Edith Wharton's presentation of provincial life is to be measured largely in terms of the skill with which she envisions her minor characters, Grandpa and Grandma Scrimser, for example. Grandma's ranging and mercurial evangelism is suddenly in demand for lectures in the living rooms of wealthy women in New York. She is an older and more solid version of Pauline Manford in *Twilight Sleep* and of Julia Brant in *A Son at the Front*. An elderly "new woman," Grandma scandalizes her children and grandchildren by her uninhibited behavior. This time the children of a wayward parent are scandalized, not the parents of wayward children. As an evangelist, Grandma is an interesting variation on the religious charlatan in Edith Wharton's other fiction and in a novel like Sinclair Lewis's *Elmer Gantry*. She is more sincere than the evangelists who are typically satirized and feels that she gives something of value to the people whose money she takes. She does, however, confide to Vance that baking gingerbread to sell to the neighbors in Missouri was harder work than "coaxing folks back to Jesus."

Grandpa Scrimser, more unscrupulous, is a variation of the small-town elderly lecher. As a youth, Vance experiences much revulsion when he discovers that Floss Delaney is Scrimser's mistress as well as his own. But Vance comes to pity as well as hate Grandpa when a stroke fells the old man and Vance takes him home from the hotel bar; he is a pitiable figure, "like a marionette with its wires cut, propped on the sofa to which they had hurriedly raised him (*Hudson*). Ironically, when Vance returns to Euphoria as a successful author, he visits with Floss Delaney in the remodelled bar of the hotel (which she now owns) and realizes that Floss seems to have forgotten Grandpa's very existence.

Although Edith Wharton lacked in these two books some of the perceptiveness and practical detachment that had characterized her satire in her earlier works, she revealed, nevertheless, a remarkable capacity to document a social group, to create minor characters in a quick phrase or two, and to evoke a milieu entirely appropriate to the individuals and the events which dominate the novels.

HALO SPEAR: THE DILEMMA OF THE "NEW WOMAN"

In *The Gods Arrive*, Edith Wharton concentrated upon the relationship between Halo Tarrant and Vance Weston which had begun early in *Hudson River Bracketed* before Vance's marriage to Laura Lou. The relationship, as Edith Wharton portrays it, lacks some dimension of veracity, though it is full of interest in many ways. There are some inconsistencies and weaknesses in Vance's characterization. Mrs. Wharton does less well with Halo Spear and seems unable to attain a viable balance between the opposing forces in Halo; and, as a result, Halo emerges as a less sympathetic individual than the author intended her to be. Mrs. Wharton is perhaps not critical enough of Halo's unscrupulousness, her materialism, her egotism, and her selfishness. Halo hardly represents the graciousness of tradition when she argues that her family would have difficulty conversing at dinner if they were to invite their poor relatives, the Tracys, along with Vance: "They talk another language. It can't be helped" (*Hudson*). Condescension and a certain envy mark her attitude toward Vance's creative work from the moment when she interrupts his reading at "The Willows" on his first visit, yet Edith Wharton also inconsistently regarded her as one whose real gift "was for appreciating the gifts of others" (*Hudson*). Other aspects of her actions and motivations seem to be contradictions which Mrs. Wharton does not reconcile, rather than complexities that add richness to Halo's character.

Fortunately, Halo Spear in *The Gods Arrive* is not the same woman in *Hudson River Bracketed*; and this change may be partly, but not entirely, explained by her having attained greater experience and maturity. In the earlier book, she showed a servile willingness to marry Lewis Tarrant for his money and prestige and for the opportunity marriage gave her to leave Paul's Landing for New York City. Edith Wharton tended to equate Halo's limited economic opportunities with those that had been open to Lily Bart in *The House of Mirth* at the turn of the century: "Even had discipline and industry fostered her slender talents, they would hardly have brought her a living . . . what else was there for her but marriage?" (*Hudson*). The total lack of confidence in Halo's ability to earn her own living is inconsistent with the impression that Halo elsewhere conveys of being a character who has enough confidence in herself to bolster Vance's faltering ego in his struggles to realize himself as a writer.

In *The Gods Arrive,* Halo is nothing if not independent; a "new woman," she prefers not to marry Vance, even after Tarrant reluctantly grants her a divorce. Together she and Vance tour Europe for the sake of providing him with inspiration and subject matter for his books. Though society insults and excludes her, Halo refuses to impose sexual and social restrictions upon her lover; and Edith Wharton's own ambivalent feelings about the value of marriage probably appear here. When Halo declares that she wants Vance to feel as free as air, she is reminded paradoxically that a woman who refuses to marry may be chaining her lover all the tighter: "The defenseless woman, and all that. If you were his wife, you and he'd be on a level." The situation in which a woman idealizes her role of mistress when a man advocates marriage had appeared early and frequently in Mrs. Wharton's short stories and had already arisen in the 1920s in both *A Son at the Front* and in *Twilight Sleep.* In *The Gods Arrive,* Mrs. Wharton might have been commenting subtly on the fact that American men were thought to be more chivalrous to the unmarried women they loved than to their wives.

Halo's experiences as Vance's mistress are both inspiriting and distressing. She defends herself vigorously against the criticism of her brother Lorry who hypocritically resents her visiting him, although he lives with a mistress as do his bohemian friends in Paris: "Naturally a man feels differently about his sister." With some conviction, Mrs. Wharton presents marriage, not as a more virtuous alternative to free love, but as a stabilizing institution that prevents a person's life from becoming unduly chaotic. Marriage keeps life in balance as Frenside, the wise philosopher, declares: "We most of us need a frame-work, a support—the maddest lovers do. Marriage may be too tight a fit—may dislocate and deform. But it shapes life too; prevents lopsidedness or drifting." Marriage also becomes a kind of insurance against the inevitable breaking up of strong love—the cynical, but humane, answer to the sometimes ephemeral nature of sexual love. Marriage, by retaining the mere forms of love, prevents the violent tearing up of dying roots, which may still on occasion be reinvigorated. Vance finally sees marriage as providing a way for two people who had once filled each other's universe to hold together as the tide of natural passion and intense involvement recedes.

Actually, Halo's intellectual superiority—sometimes presented as genuine, at other times, as specious—is what Vance comes to resent. The love affair runs aground when Vance resents Halo's dominating influence on his writing and his intellectual growth. The appearance of his old flame, Floss Delaney, for whom surprisingly he feels some of his former passion revive, threatens further complications.

Halo's relationship to Vance provides the major focus of the novel, however, a relationship characterized by much poignancy despite Halo's occasional limitations as a person. For her, sex indissolubly merges with her interest in Vance as an artist; and she can hardly think of love in any terms other than intellectual. She buries her own ambition in order to support her lover's, only to find that she has transferred her own intense ambition to her lover who becomes increasingly restive under the pressure that she exerts. To Halo, the man must succeed in order to satisfy the woman who stands behind him and finds her aspirations satisfied vicariously by his success. The compulsion upon the man in such a case may become unbearable as it does with Vance.

Vance's frustrated love and his desertion of Halo arise from his resentment of the intellectual and artistic pressures that she thrusts upon him, although her interest in his writing had fostered their early love and contributed signally to his own success. He had responded sexually to her in *Hudson River Bracketed* when he first sensed that her imagination was flowing through his and inflaming him as he planned his first novel. In *The Gods Arrive,* she has had to become more passive in her influence: "she listened intelligently, but she no longer collaborated." To this extent, her love as she envisioned it has diminished; she is no longer apparently the chief source of her lover's inspiration; and he may, in fact, have developed beyond her powers to bring him out further. She can never fully accept his view, expressed several months later, of the artist's dependence upon the criticism of others: "My dear child—shall I give you the cold truth . . . the artist asks other people's opinions to please *them* and not to help himself."

Because Halo insists on loving the artist as well as the man, her love becomes finally a repressive influence upon the man she is ironically straining to serve. For him, she becomes "a reproach and a torment," when all he wants is to collect his own thoughts in contemplative peace: "The absorbing interest of seeing his gift unfold under her care had been so interwoven with her love that she could not separate them." A kind of masochism underlies her wish to be subservient to his talent as she asks herself, " 'Shall I have to content myself with being a peg to hang a book on?' and found an anxious joy in the idea." Vance resents her expectant watching for his reactions to new experience, her monitoring of his progress as a potential artist. At Chartres, he grows sulky and baffled and declares he cannot see what she expects him to see. It is as if he has failed her sexual demands and become suddenly impotent before a curious and excessively sympathetic woman: "Halo was elaborately tactful; she waited, she kept silent; she left him to his emotions; but no emotions came. . . . The masculine longing to be left alone was uppermost; he wanted to hate Chartres without having to give any reason."

Halo's emasculating care of Vance extends to his manuscripts themselves. The result is that his frustrations—and her suffering from his rejection—intensify. His books for her become phallic emblems when she judges each new work in terms of its relationship to his masculinity. She resents any lesser book of his as a kind of sexual affront to her, as though it were a symbol of personal weakness and depleted vigor on Vance's part and an insult to her own protective femininity: "What business had a man of Weston's quality to be doing novels like ladies' fancy-work. . . . The next book . . . will show them all what he really is. . . . There were times when she caught herself praying for that next book as lonely wives pray for a child." Later, when she fears that he may be merely following literary fashion in his new novel, instead of expressing his individuality as she knows it, she resents his hiding the manuscript from her; and she equates such furtiveness with a husband's hiding the evidence of sexual infidelity. She refuses to look at the manuscript, just as she would refuse to spy on an affair: "If there had been a letter from a woman in that drawer, she reflected, it would have been almost easier to resist looking at it."

Edith Wharton handled with sympathy and insight Vance's desertion of Halo and her sufferings from this separation in the last chapters of *The Gods Arrive*. Halo simply returns to "The Willows" where her supreme adventure with Vance had begun and mechanically devotes herself to gardening. She refuses to think or feel, and she only responds to the heat of the sun on her neck and the fatigue in her muscles. She tries to kill her suffering by not allowing it to surface to her conscious mind and by resolutely turning her energies to physical pursuits.

Halo's final recognition that Vance had resented her part in his work is more bitter to her than the waning of his passion. Cynically, she had acknowledged that passion cannot last, but she had had faith that a deeper understanding underlay their particular love. "The intellectual divorce" between them became more bitter to her than their physical separation. Conversely, the fact that Halo has allowed this intellectual divorce to occur frees Vance for a renewal of his passion for Halo in the last scene in which he discovers she is pregnant and approaches her simply as a child approaches a protective maternal figure. He wishes her to protect him and to be, in a sense, a mother to him as well as to the child that they have conceived. Vance is not yet ready to accept the intellectual companionship of a woman, though, as a sensitive man, he may eventually be able to do so. In the last scene, he sees her as at one with the soil and the sun in her garden. She is back in "the Past" at "The Willows," and she is at one with nature in her pregnancy. She has, in these respects, fulfilled the romantic dreams that Vance previously associated with her. Perhaps the sincerity that imbues his romanticism will also develop in the future into a full appreciation of Halo's distinction, for Halo has been refined and matured by the suffering which she has in part brought on herself.

CYNTHIA GRIFFIN WOLFF

Ethan Frome:
"This Vision of His Story"

*E*_{*than*} *Frome* was an important book to Edith Wharton. In 1936 when Owen and Donald Davis did a dramatization of the novel, Wharton took the unusual step of writing a short preface. "My poor little group of hungry, lonely New England villagers will live again for a while on their stony hillside before finally joining their forebears under the village headstones," she says. "I should like to think that this good fortune may be theirs, for I lived among them in fact and in imagination, ten years [her ten years of residence at Lenox], and their strained starved faces are still near to me." Wharton was seventy-four when she wrote these words (just a little less than a year before her death), and there is a sense of insistent presence attached to the people of Starkfield that does not emerge when she refers to any other of her fictional creations.

There are other things that signal this novel for special attention. When Scribner's brought out a Modern Student's Library edition of *Ethan Frome* in 1922, Wharton wrote an introduction to it (something she had hitherto refused to do for any of her novels). Some years later Scribner's began to contemplate another edition with a different introduction. Wharton was notified, and she immediately voiced her distress to Mr. Scribner:

> I have a letter from the firm referring to the inclusion of "Ethan Frome" in the Modern Student's Library.

From *A Feast of Words: The Triumph of Edith Wharton.* © 1977 by Oxford University Press. Originally entitled "Landscapes of Desolation: The Fiction, 1889–1911."

> I should be very glad to have it appear in this series, and the royalty suggested is perfectly satisfactory in the circumstances; but I should like, without appearing indiscreet, to ask about the proposed author of the introduction.
>
> I am rather fond of "Ethan Frome," and I should not care to have it spoken of by any one who does not understand what I was trying to do. Would you mind telling me a little about Professor Eskine's capacity for writing of the technique of fiction? How I wish that Mr. Brownell would do this preface for me! Is it quite impossible to persuade him to?

In the end, the novel was issued with her introduction. This is a kind of concern she showed for no other of her works. In *A Backward Glance,* as we have already observed [elsewhere] she points to *Ethan Frome* as the work that marked an end to her long period of apprenticeship. "It was not until I wrote 'Ethan Frome' that I suddenly felt the artisan's full control of his implements. When 'Ethan Frome' first appeared I was severely criticized by the reviewers for what was considered the clumsy structure of the tale. I had pondered long on this structure, had felt its peculiar difficulties, and possible awkwardness, but could think of no alternative which would serve as well in the given case; and though I am far from thinking 'Ethan Frome' my best novel, and am bored and even exasperated when I am told that it is, I am still sure that its structure is not its weak point."

Wharton's sensitive comment on her own novel points directly to the heart of it: the structure of *Ethan Frome*—different from any other of her major fictions—is in an ultimate sense the true subject of the tale.

We must acknowledge the importance of this novel to its author if we are fully to understand it. The perseverance of those images of starvation and loneliness is, perhaps, easiest to understand: Starkfield and its inhabitants must be taken as a map of one portion of her mind, a systematic tracing of the contours of the child's desolation and the young woman's depression. Yet if this fiction *is* an existential statement of the part of Edith Wharton that carried the immutable traces of that early trauma, it is a *controlled* statement, the kind of statement that could be made only by one who was no longer enmeshed in the toils of such a life. The novel was written towards the conclusion of the affair with Fullerton, and as she herself avowed, Wharton had been significantly altered by the experience. "I have drunk of the wine of life at last," she wrote. "I have known the thing best worth knowing, I have been warmed through and through never to grow quite cold again till the end . . ." Never to grow quite cold is not an optimistic prediction; it is not the same thing as remaining forever warmed by the embers of love. But Wharton was in all things a realist, and she was able to accept the limitations even of this liberating experience. A person who will never grow quite cold again is, unavoidably, someone who will always be fearful of the cold, but someone who can discern quite clearly, nevertheless, the differences between her own life and the lives of those who *are* quite cold.

In terms of her personal development, Wharton had begun to explore her passional self, her sexual self. The intimacy of the affair gave her access to these. Eventually her discoveries would be returned to the fictions in novels that dealt primarily with passion—novels like *The Custom of the Country, Summer,* and *The Age of Innocence.* The initial fictional response, however, was not the beginning of a new set of subjects but the conclusion of the ones she had been working with. *Ethan Frome* is the last novel of desolation: it proclaims a triumphant command over both the emotions that shape it and the nature of fiction itself.

The novel has a fascinating provenance. Wharton begins the story for us. "I have a clearer recollection of its beginnings than of those of my other tales, through the singular accident that its first pages were written—in French! I had determined, when we came to live in Paris, to polish and enlarge my French vocabulary. . . . To bring my idioms up to date I asked Charles Du Bos to find, among his friends, a young professor who would come and talk with me two or three times a week. An amiable young man was found; but, being too amiable ever to correct my spoken mistakes, he finally hit on the expedient of asking me to prepare an 'exercise' before each visit. The easiest thing for me was to write a story; and thus the French version of 'Ethan Frome' was begun and carried on for a few weeks. Then the lessons were given up." We cannot date this exercise precisely, but the most likely time is 1906 or 1907; a later date is highly implausible, and an earlier one impossible. This little story in French has survived in its original black notebook and may be found in the Beinecke Library of Yale University.

The French story is short, only eight printed pages, and it is skeletal by contrast with the finished novel. There are but three characters: Hart, his wife Anna, and her cousin Mattie. When the tale opens, Hart and Mattie are conversing intently as they walk through the woods; we soon discover that they are lovers and that Mattie has been asked to leave Hart's home. The story begins with Hart's voice: " 'Tu as raison . . . je ne puis rien pour toi . . . mais ne me quitte pas, chère petite. Je serai raisonnable, tu verras . . .' balbutia-t-il, comprenant que, pour la retenir et pour effacer le souvenir des paroles échangées, le seul moyen était de reprendre courageusement son rôle de frère ainé." The tale is told by an omniscient narrator; there is no frame

story and no first-person narration. The events central to the final novel are
scarcely anticipated, and only one or two short passages (which we shall
remark later) find their way into the longer fiction. Hart and Mattie continue
their walk home, arriving to discover that Anna, who is sickly and com-
plaining, plans a trip to the doctor in a neighboring town. The next day she
makes the trip, and Hart, who is embarrassed and timid, stays at a local
tavern until late in the evening when he returns rather tipsy. The next day
Anna comes home announcing that she has found a job for Mattie in a city
some distance away. Hart protests mildly, but in the end he submits. The
tale concludes as he is putting Mattie on the train. Now the tone of the
French version is flat, the sense of longing and of frustration muted; the
desolation of the sledding accident and of the resultant eternal, infernal triangle is simply not there. What we have in the Black Book *Ethan* is only the
germ of an idea—a lengthy *donnée* that has not yet been explored and shaped
and wrought into a focused fiction. That would come only three or four
years later.

In her introduction to the Modern Student's Library edition of the novel,
Wharton reiterates her interest in the novel's structure. "I make no claim for
originality in following a method of which 'La Grande Breteche' and the
'The Ring and the Book' had set me the magnificent example." (Despite the
pellucidity of its prose and its apparent simplicity, *Ethan Frome* is a tantalizingly literary work; certainly Wharton's careful planning of it followed a
complex tradition, of which the works by Balzac and Browning are only two
examples.) In both "La Grande Breteche" and *The Ring and the Book,* it is
not the "facts" themselves which are of primary importance in the end, but
the collection of facts and—perhaps above all—the impact of these facts upon
the mind of the observer. In *Ethan Frome,* Wharton reminds us, "only the
narrator of the tale has scope enough to see it all, to resolve it back into
simplicity, and to put it in its rightful place among his larger categories." It
is the *relation* of the tale to the narrator's larger categories that must be our
primary interest, the focus of the story as Wharton has defined it. Other
writers, the venerable regionalists of New England, had already given us the
surface view that Wharton scorned: a prettified spectacle of billboard art, a
pastoral land seen through awestruck eyes. Wharton would look through the
surface to discover what was timeless in the human mind, just as Browning
had done before her.

We can follow the subtle associations of her creative intelligence. Browning had had a "source"—a kernel of subject in the Yellow Book which
contained the historical account of Guido's trial; Wharton had an analogue
at hand, the Black Book *Ethan*. But this source alone was now seen to be

an insufficient subject. Browning's narrator impresses the importance of his method upon us in Book I of *The Ring and the Book:* "From the book, yes; / thence bit by bit I dug / The lingot truth, that memorable day / Assayed and knew my piecemeal gain was gold,— / Yes; but from something else surpassing that, / Something of mine which, mixed up with the mass, / Made it bear Hammer and be firm to file." Not situation alone, not narrator alone, but each illuminating the other; the situation filtered *through* the larger categories of a narrator's consciousness (the author outside the work, controlling that delicate relation)—this is to be the subject of the work. In the end, such a method focuses our attention more clearly and precisely on the narrator than on anything else. Refracted thus, a particular event may gain significance beyond the limitations of its time and place, may finally tell us about human consciousness itself. That is the function of Art. ("Why take the artistic way to prove so much? / Because, it is the glory and good of Art, / That Art remains the one way possible / Of speaking truth.")

It helps our understanding of *Ethan Frome* to have this literary kinship dangled before us (perhaps that was Wharton's reason for agreeing to write a preface to the work). But it is not necessary. There are literary affinities inherent in the work itself that force themselves upon us. Outside of *Ethan Frome,* for example, there is no other Zenobia in American literature save Hawthorne's heroine in *The Blithedale Romance;* one of the changes that Wharton made from the Black Book *Ethan* was the change of Anna's name to Zeena (Zenobia), though Mattie's name was left unaltered. Hart's name was changed to Ethan. If we wonder why, we might plausibly connect this change with Hawthorne as well, for the only other notable Ethan in American literature is Ethan Brand of Mount Graylock (a geographical neighbor of Wharton's Lenox and psychological kin of the villagers in Starkfield— amongst whom Wharton lived in imagination for ten years). Ethan Brand had found the Unpardonable Sin in a willed isolation from the brotherhood of humanity. Wharton was not interested in sin, but she was interested in the effect of isolation upon the workings of man's emotional life: thus Ethan Frome is related to Ethan Brand; but his deadening isolation is in the cold world of unloved and unloving inner emptiness—a world of depression, loneliness, and slow starvation. Why, in the end, would Wharton be interested in so deliberately suggesting an affinity between her work and the tales of Hawthorne? Again, we must look to the structure of the novel and the role of the narrator for our answer. In much of Hawthorne (and in that most "Hawthornian" of Edith Wharton's stories—"The Eyes"), we follow the tale principally as a revelation of the teller. *The Blithedale Romance* is, ultimately, about Coverdale. Just so, *Ethan Frome* is about its narrator.

The novel begins with him, begins insistently and obtrusively.

> I had the story, bit by bit, from various people, and, as generally happens in such cases, each time it was a different story.
>
> If you know Starkfield, Massachusetts, you know the post-office. If you know the post-office you must have seen Ethan Frome drive up to it, drop the reins on his hollow-backed bay and drag himself across the brick pavement to the white colonnade; and you must have asked who he was.
>
> It was there that, several years ago, I saw him for the first time; and the sight pulled me up sharp.

We must ask why Wharton would begin thus, assaulting us with the narrator's presence in the very first word. It is a decidedly unusual way to open a fiction. Only two like it come readily to mind: *Wuthering Heights* and "Bartleby the Scrivener." Wharton has informed us that she was consciously indebted to Brontë's work when she wrote *Ethan Frome;* and her preoccupation at the time with the techniques of Hawthorne suggests that she may have had Melville's tale in mind as well. What does all of this suggest? First of all, an extraordinarily literary self-consciousness. Second, a focus on the narrator (for however intricate Brontë's story is, however compelling Melville's vision, it is the *narrator's reaction* that must be deemed the ultimate "subject" in both fictions).

Bearing this fact in mind, let us rush momentarily ahead—to that point in the novel where the "real subject" is generally assumed to begin. An astounding discovery awaits us: the man whom we come to know as the young Ethan Frome is *no more than a figment of the narrator's imagination.* Wharton's method of exposition leaves no doubt. We are not permitted to believe that the narrator is recounting a history of something that actually happened; we are not given leave to speculate that he is passing along a confidence obtained in the dark intimacy of a cold winter's night. No: the "story" of Ethan Frome is introduced in unmistakable terms. "It was that night that I found the clue to Ethan Frome, and began *to put together this vision* of his story . . ." (emphasis mine). Our narrator is a teller of terrible tales, a seer into the realms of dementia. The "story" of Ethan Frome is nothing more than a dream vision, a brief glimpse into the most appalling recesses of the narrator's mind. The overriding question becomes then—not who is Ethan Frome, but who in the world is this ghastly guide to whom we must submit as we read the tale.

The structure demands that we take him into account. Certainly *he* demands it. It is *his* story, ultimately his "vision" of Ethan Frome, that we will get. His vision is as good as any other (so he glibly assures us at the beginning—for "each time it was a different story"), and therefore his story has as much claim to truth as any other. And yet, he is a nervous fellow. The speech pattern is totally unlike Wharton's own narrative style—short sentences, jagged prose rhythms, absolutely no sense of ironic control over the language, no distance from it. Yes, the fellow is nervous. He seems anxious about our reaction and excessively eager to reassure us that had *we* been situated as *he* was, catching a first horrified glimpse of Ethan Frome, we "must have asked who he was." Anyone would. Frome is no mere bit of local color. He is, for reasons that we do not yet understand, a force that compels examination; "the sight pulled me up sharp." (It would pull all of you up sharp, and all of you would have done as I did.)

Certain elements in Wharton's story are to be taken as "real" within the fictional context: Ethan Frome is badly crippled; he sustained his injuries in a sledding accident some twenty-four years ago; he has been in Starkfield for most of his life, excepting a short visit to Florida, living first with his parents and then with his querulous, sickly wife Zeena; there is a third member of the household, his wife's cousin, Miss Mattie Silver; she too was badly crippled in the same sledding accident that felled Ethan. To these facts the various members of the town will all attest—and to *nothing more*. Everything that the reader can accept as reliably true can be found in the narrative frame; everything else bears the imprint of the narrator's own interpretation—as indeed even the selection of events chronicled in the frame does— and while that interpretation *might* be as true as any other, we dare not accept it as having the same validity as the bare outline presented above. Even at the end of the narrator's vision, in the concluding scene with Mrs. Hale, Wharton is scrupulously careful not to credit the vision by giving it independent confirmation.

At this point the narrator himself is still probing. He has now spent a long winter's night in the Frome household, where no one outside the family has set foot for many years, and he is an object of some interest. He responds to that interest by attempting to use it to gain information. "Beneath their wondering exclamations I felt a secret curiosity to know what impressions I had received from my night in the Frome household, and divined that the best way of breaking down their reserve was to let them try to penetrate mine. I therefore confined myself to saying, in a matter-of-fact tone, that I had been received with great kindness, and that Frome had made a bed for me in a room on the ground-floor which seemed in happier days to have been fitted up as a kind of writing-room or study." Despite this tactic, the narrator elicits nothing that he has not already known. Mrs. Hale agrees that "'it was just awful from the beginning. . . . It's a pity . . . that they're all shut up there'n that one kitchen.'" And these fervent platitudes fall so far short of assuring the narrator that he has touched upon the truth that even as they come tumbling inconsequently from her lips, he withdraws into himself. "Mrs. Hale paused a moment, and I remained silent, plunged in the vision of what her words evoked." Her words, vague generalities—driving the narrator back into his own "vision."

If we return now to the opening of the story, we must remind ourselves that the status of the narrator is doubly significant: we are surely meant to credit the information that is given to us in the frame as "true" (and the contrast between the validity of the contents of the frame and the unreliability of the contents of the internal story is clearly signaled by the recurrence of that key word, vision); however, since it, too, is reported by the narrator who has thrust himself before us in the first word of the first sentence, we must recognize that it is biased information and that evaluation and judgments have been built even into the language and choice of incident which make it up. Wharton does not do what Conrad often did, open with a reliable omniscient narrator only to introduce her talkative character when the "facts" have already been established. Instead she forces us to traffic only with the narrator from the beginning; if we are to do that effectively, we must weigh his introduction as carefully as we measure his vision, for only by doing so can we understand, finally, why the vision is so important.

The obsessive anxiety of the narrator's opening statements reveals his need to assure us that we would have reacted just as he did. He wants to elicit our confidence; perhaps he also wants to reassure himself that he is part of our company.

Many of his preliminary remarks about Ethan have a double thrust, carrying the strong implication that he is (or seems) one way, but that he might be (or might at one time have had the option of being) quite dramatically different. It is, indeed, striking how often the narrator's conjuration of Ethan manages to conflate *two* images. "He was the most striking figure in Starkfield, though he was but the ruin of a man. It was not so much his great height that marked him, for the 'natives' were easily singled out by their lank longitude from the stockier foreign breed: it was the careless powerful look he had, in spite of a lameness checking each step like the jerk of a chain." For clarity's sake we must dissect fantasy from fact: Ethan is tall, as are most natives, and he walks with a pronounced limp; yet these simple attributes have been elevated by the narrator's language—"the most striking figure in Starkfield," "but the ruin of a man," "careless powerful look," "each step like the jerk of a chain." Ethan Frome becomes, in the eyes of the teller of his tale, an emblem of vanquished heroism, defeated strength, and foreclosed potentiality—not merely a crippled man, but Manhood brought low. " 'It was a pretty bad smash-up?' I questioned Harmon, looking after Frome's retreating figure, and thinking how gallantly his lean brown head, with its shock of light hair, must have sat on his strong shoulders before they were bent out of shape."

The contrast preys upon the narrator's mind, and he finds himself compelled to pry into the matter. Relentlessly he questions those taciturn New Englanders, and he gets a series of enigmatic and taciturn replies. "Harmon drew a slab of tobacco from his pocket, cut off a wedge and pressed it into the leather pouch of his cheek. 'Guess he's been in Starkfield too many winters. Most of the smart ones get away.' 'Why didn't *he*?' 'Somebody has to stay and care for the folks. There warn't ever anybody but Ethan. Fust his father—then his mother—then his wife.' " Too many winters. The phrase becomes a key to the puzzle. "Though Harmon Gow developed the tale as far as his mental and moral reach permitted there were perceptible gaps between his facts, and I had the sense that the deeper meaning of the story was in the gaps. But one phrase stuck in my memory and served as the nucleus about which I grouped my subsequent inferences: 'Guess he's been in Starkfield too many winters.' "

The narrator offers this phrase to us as a central clue to Ethan's dilemma and to his own investigation; then abruptly, the distance between those two narrows. The narrator becomes implicated in Ethan's fate, and his investigation must be presumed to include himself as well. "Before my own time there was up I had learned to know what that meant. . . . When winter shut down on Starkfield, and the village lay under a sheet of snow perpetually renewed from pale skies, I began to see what life there—or rather its negation—must have been in Ethan Frome's young manhood. . . . I found myself anchored at Starkfield . . . for the best part of the winter." Was the speaker interested in Ethan Frome's history before he (like Ethan) had been constrained to spend a winter at Starkfield? There is no way, really, of knowing, for the entire tale is told retrospectively (and of course, the narrator is insistent—perhaps too insistent—that *anyone* would have felt an interest in the man, the interest that he felt immediately upon seeing him).

Who is the narrator? A busy man—we see the energy that he pours into his quest—a man of affairs: "I had been sent up by my employers on a job connected with the big power-house at Corbury Junction, and a long-drawn carpenters' strike had so delayed the work that I found myself anchored at Starkfield." Nothing else would have brought such a man up here. Even marooned as he is in this desolate spot, he does what he can to keep his

routines regular: he hires Denis Eady's horses to take him daily over to
Corbury Flats where he can pick up a train, and when Eady's horses fall
sick, he hires Ethan Frome. The man has a visionary side; we have already
seen it in the language of his opening remarks. But surely he is at heart an
active man, a man who is part of the larger world, a man who keeps his
options open, a man who bears no essential similarity to these poor folk
among whom he has been thrust. Spending one winter in Starkfield will
surely mean nothing to such a man. "During the early part of my stay I had
been struck by the contrast between the vitality of the climate and the dead-
ness of the community"—the observation of a confident outsider.

And yet, slowly, something within him begins to succumb to this insid-
ious environment. "Day by day, after the December snows were over, a
blazing blue sky poured down torrents of light and air on the white landscape, which gave them back in an intenser glitter. One would have supposed
that such an atmosphere must quicken the emotions as well as the blood;
but it seemed to produce no change except that of retarding still more the
sluggish pulse of Starkfield. When I had been there a little longer, and had
seen this phase of crystal clearness followed by long stretches of sunless cold;
when the storms of February had pitched their tents about the devoted village
and the wild cavalry of March winds had charged down to their support; I
began to understand why Starkfield emerged from its six months' siege like
a starved garrison capitulating without quarter. . . . I felt the sinister force
of Harmon's phrase: 'Most of the smart ones get away.' " And as he begins
to "feel" the force of the phrase—and of the environment which sucks his
confidence and his independence away from him—and as his tale draws
closer and closer to that crucial moment of transition when we move into
the "vision," a peculiar thing begins to happen to his language. The brave
assertion of heroic contingencies falters; what he limns now is capitulation,
and at the heart of the experience is an unavoidable and dreadful image—
"cold" and "starved."

Doggedly, the narrator persists in his quest. He sounds the finer sensibility of Mrs. Ned Hale, who rises only to the platitude that she seems fated
to reiterate without explanation: " 'Yes, I knew them both . . . it was
awful.' "

And yet, it is not entirely clear what *would* satisfy him. He does not
want facts alone; he wants something less tangible, something deeper. "No
one gave me an explanation of the look in his face which, as I persisted in
thinking, neither poverty nor physical suffering could have put there." He
wants an explanation for his own inferences and his own suppositions—we
might call them the projections of his own morbid imagination. Harmon

Gow, who is more loquacious, can be prodded to speak. The "facts" as he sees them look only to those causes which the narrator has already rejected as insufficient, poverty and physical suffering. But the language in which he speaks, language which the narrator records more completely than any other utterance in the frame, addresses itself to the deeper meaning and heightens the horror of the narrator's speculations by reinforcing those images of starvation: "'That Frome farm was always 'bout as bare's a milkpan when the cat's been round; and you know what one of the old water-mills is wuth nowadays. When Ethan could sweat over 'em both from sun-up to dark he kinder choked a living out of 'em; but his folks et up most everything, even then, and I don't see how he makes out now. . . . sickness and trouble: that's what Ethan's had his plate full up with, ever since the very first helping.'"

The narrator's next description of Ethan—drawn during their initial intimate contact as Frome drives him for the first time to the railroad junction—brings all of these themes together. The sight of Frome still calls up visions of ancient heroism and strength; but superimposed upon these images and ultimately blotting them out is a picture of Ethan Frome as the embodiment of some deep mortal misery. Not poverty, merely; not hard work, merely. But something intrinsic to human existence, something imponderable and threatening—something that might swallow up everything else. "Ethan Frome drove in silence, the reins loosely held in his left hand, his brown seamed profile, under the helmet-like peak of the cap, relieved against the banks of snow like the bronze image of a hero. He never turned his face to mine, or answered, except in monosyllables, the questions I put, or such slight pleasantries as I ventured. He seemed a part of the mute melancholy landscape, an incarnation of its frozen woe, with all that was warm and sentient in him fast bound below the surface; but there was nothing unfriendly in his silence. I simply felt that he lived in a depth of moral isolation too remote for casual access, and I had the sense that his loneliness was not merely the result of his personal plight, tragic as I guessed that to be, but had in it, as Harmon Gow had hinted, the profound accumulated cold of many Starkfield winters." And, as we have already observed, this is a winter of the soul that the narrator must now share.

We can see the narrator attempting to assert a distance between himself and this foreboding figure; but in the palpable cold of the region of Starkfield, all things seem to contract. Instead of discovering reassuring distinctions, the narrator finds disconcerting and unexpected similarities. "Once I happened to speak of an engineering job I had been on the previous year in Florida, and of the contrast between the winter landscape about us and that in which I had found myself the year before; and to my surprise Frome said suddenly: 'Yes: I was down there once, and for a good while afterward I could call up the sight of it in winter. But now it's all snowed under.' . . . Another day, on getting into my train at the Flats, I missed a volume of popular science—I think it was on some recent discoveries in bio-chemistry—which I had carried with me to read on the way. I thought no more about it till I got into the sleigh again that evening, and saw the book in Frome's hand. 'I found it after you were gone,' he said. . . . 'Does that sort of thing interest you?' I asked. 'It used to.' . . . 'If you'd like to look the book through I'd be glad to leave it with you.' He hesitated, and I had the impression that he felt himself about to yield to a stealing tide of inertia; then, 'Thank you—I'll take it.'"

The winter landscape reduces the world and obliterates casual surface distinctions. The snow-covered fields lie about the two men, "their boundaries lost under drift; and above the fields, huddled against the white immensities of land and sky, one of those lonely New England farm-houses that make the landscape lonelier." Unknown affinities emerge when everything that fleshes out man's daily existence is taken away—like the ice-age rocks that unpredictably thrust their noses through the frozen ground during winter heaves—shared mortal problems and shared mortal pain. A man must confront himself in such a world, and the narrator is brought to this terrible task in his journey with Ethan Frome. Frome is his Winterman, his shadow self, the man he might become if the reassuring appurtenances of busy, active, professional, adult mobility were taken from him.

The narrator is a man of science; he knows the meaning of cold. Cold is an absence, a diminishment, a dwindling, and finally a death. Everything contracts in the cold. The "place" of the novel is defined by this contraction: from the world to Starkfield; from Starkfield to the thickening darkness of a winter night, "descending on us layer by layer"; from this "smothering medium" to the "forlorn and stunted" farmhouse that is a castrated emblem of its mutilated owner. This relentless constriction of place accompanies a slow shedding of adult personae and leads finally to a confrontation with the core of self that lives beneath these and that would emerge and engulf everything else should the supporting structures of the outside world be lost, somehow. To this point is the narrator reduced—to the edge of nothingness: without identity, without memory, without continuity, without time. All these are outside and beyond. Now there is only the farmhouse. The two men enter it, enter into a small, dark back hallway. The movement is inescapably decreative, and it is captured in a perverse and grotesque inversion of the terms of birth. They move through the hall to the door of a small, warm room. Slowly, the door is opened, and as it opens, the narrator, who is poised on the threshold, starts to "put together this vision" of Frome's story. The fantasy begins.

The fantasy begins with an involuntary echo of the narrator's own world: Ethan Frome, a young man striding through the clear atmosphere of a winter night, "as though nothing less tenuous than ether intervened between the white earth under his feet and the metallic dome overhead, 'It's like being in an exhausted receiver,' he thought"—an association that is plausible in the young Ethan Frome, who had been, so the fantasy postulates, at a technological college at Worcester, but which is much more probably related to the consciousness of the storyteller, who has been sent to Starkfield to work on a power plant. Perhaps the principal thrust of the image is to assert the similarities between the two. They are surely placed similarly. The story brings Ethan to the church where Mattie Silver has gone to dance. He waits for her—poised just outside and looking in—and his position recapitulates the modalities of the narrator's own placement in the framing story, the cold without and the warmth within. However, the implication here is inverted: in young Ethan's life the warmth of the dance represents gaiety, freedom, and love.

The motif of the threshold renders one of the most significant themes of the novel. The narrator's vision begins while he is poised at the edge of the kitchen with the door beginning to swing open. The long fantasy is spun out; it concludes with the terrible, abortive sledding accident, and we return to the framing world of the narrator. "The querulous drone ceased as I entered Frome's kitchen." The entire fantasy has been formulated in the instant that marks the passage from hall to kitchen—that timeless eternity of hesitation upon the threshold. In its essential formulation, the story is about that transition (or the failure to make it). The narrator's fantasy about young Ethan begins by placing him at the juncture of two worlds. Over and over again he is pictured thus. Ethan and Mattie return to the farmhouse, and they are greeted at the threshold by Zeena. "Against the dark background of the kitchen she stood up tall and angular, one hand drawing a quilted counterpane to her flat breast, while the other held a lamp. The light, on a level with her chin, drew out of the darkness her puckered throat and the projecting wrist of the hand that clutched the quilt, and deepened fantastically the hollows and prominences of her high-boned face under its ring of crimping-pins." The next night, after Zeena has gone, the vision is re-enacted with Mattie: "So strange was the precision with which the incidents of the previous evening were repeating themselves that he half expected, when he heard the key turn, to see his wife before him on the threshold; but the door opened, and Mattie faced him. She stood just as Zeena had stood, a lifted lamp in her hand, against the black background of the kitchen. She held the light at the same level, and it drew out with the same distinctness her slim young throat and the brown wrist no bigger than a child's. Then, striking upward, it threw a lustrous fleck on her lips, edged her eyes with velvet shade, and laid a milky whiteness above the black curve of her brows." Since these threshold scenes with Zeena and Mattie are the only two significant passages that have been preserved from the Black Book *Ethan,* we must infer that Wharton chose to use them again because *only these* were appropriate to the story as it is told by the narrator, for only these echo his own spatial position and his own psychological dilemma.

We know what thresholds meant to Edith Wharton long ago, and though we need not have this knowledge to understand the novel, it greatly enriches our reading of it. The threshold of Lucretia's house was a moment of transition for the adolescent girl: at this juncture, the opposing demands of two distinct worlds were visited upon her—the world of adulthood, independence, freedom, and sexual maturity; and the world of childhood, obedience, limitation, and emotional starvation. Every passage of this threshold entailed a momentous and terrible struggle: here Edith Wharton, poised in unbearably protracted psychic conflict, was seized by "a choking agony of terror"—anxiety that took the almost palpable form of a ravening beast at her back. In adolescence, the implications of independence were apparently more frightening than the consequences of submission: the beast who embodied her fears stalked her only when she was outside, and her dreadful anxieties could be relieved by reentering Mother's house. Certainly for many years Edith Wharton did choose to submit herself to the rule of "Mother's house."

And yet, as Wharton eventually discovered, this retrogression had an even more appalling aspect than the dangers that had attended her excursions into the outside world. An adult who has chosen dependency must remain an incomplete and undeveloped human being. Even worse, once systematic diminishment of self has been begun, there is no natural limitation to the process. The only end to diminishment is nullity. The mature Edith Wharton recognized her adolescent mistake. The recovery from the illness of 1898 was a reiteration of this crisis at the threshold, a reenactment in which (given a second chance) the woman chose the outside world and all that went with it: autonomy and initiative. As time passed, her personal struggle opened to her a truth that inheres in the human condition. There is more than a little accuracy in the narrator's obsessive claim—"you must have asked who he was." We all harbor a "Winterman": it is always tempting to cast aside the complexities and demands of adulthood. Within every one of us there lurks a phantom self, not our "real" self, not the self that the world sees, but a seductive shade who calls us to passivity and dependency in a sweet, soft voice. Here is the greatest danger—to relax, to let go, to fall pell-mell, tumbling, backward and down. The horror of the void.

Such is the world we enter as the door to Ethan Frome's kitchen begins to swing slowly open: a world of irrecoverable retreat.

Central to such a world is an inability to communicate: its habitants are inarticulate, mute; and like the patient farm animals they tend to, they are helplessly bound by their own incapacities. The narrator has already experienced Ethan's parsimonious conversation, and his vision repeatedly returns to it. Ethan, walking with Mattie, longing to tell her of his feelings, admiring her laughter and gaiety: "To prolong the effect he groped for a dazzling phrase, and brought out, in a growl of rapture: 'Come along.'" Again and again Ethan "struggled for the all-expressive word" and again and again he fails to find utterance.

Speech is the bridge that might carry Ethan Frome to a world beyond Starkfield, the necessary passport to wider activities and larger horizons. Without it, he is literally unable to formulate plans of any complexity because all such determinations are beyond his limited powers of conceptualization and self-expression. Because he cannot think his problems through in any but the most rudimentary way, he is as helpless as a child to combat the forces that bind him. It is not that he does not feel deeply, for he does. However, one mark of maturity is the ability to translate desire into coherent words, words into action; and Ethan Frome is incapable of all such translations. "Confused motions of rebellion stormed in him. He was too young, too strong, too full of the sap of living to submit so easily to the destruction of his hopes. Must he wear out all his years at the side of a bitter querulous woman? Other possibilities had been in him, possibilities sacrificed, one by one, to Zeena's narrow-mindedness and ignorance. . . . All the healthy instincts of self-defence rose up in him against such waste." Still, he cannot concoct his own plans. All thoughts of another life must come to him ready-made. He gropes among the meager scraps of his experience: there is the "case of a man over the mountain," a man who left his wife and went West. His eye falls on a newspaper advertisement, and he reads "the seductive words: 'Trips to the West: Reduced Rates.'" But these solutions are no better than clothes bought through a mail-order catalogue: they do not fit his situation; they hang loosely on his lank frame, bearing only the general outline of the garment he desires; he must do the finishing work himself, must tailor the garment to fit. And he cannot do such work (how had that other man done it, anyway? how could *he*, Ethan Frome, scrape together enough money to make such a move?). Imprisonment is not inevitably inherent in the external conditions of his world. The example of the other fellow demonstrates as much. But Frome does not have any set of categories available to him that can explain how escape is possible.

It is not too much to say that the entire force of Ethan's life has been exerted merely to hold him at the level of primitive communication he does manage; and the balance of his life, even as he leads it, is precarious and dangerous. A more fully developed capacity to express himself might open avenues of escape. Any further dwindling of his limited abilities would lead in the opposite direction, propelling him down pathways that are both terrifying and fascinating. Further to lose the power of expression would be a diminishment of self; but though loss of self is an appalling specter, there is at the same time a sensuous attraction in the notion of annihilation—of comforting nothingness.

Why had he married Zeena in the first place, for example? Left with his mother after his father's death, Ethan had found that "the silence had deepened about him year by year. . . . His mother had been a talker in her day, but after her 'trouble' the sound of her voice was seldom heard, though she had not lost the power of speech. Sometimes, in the long winter evenings, when in desperation her son asked her why she didn't 'say something,' she would lift a finger and answer: 'Because I'm listening.' . . . It was only when she drew toward her last illness, and his cousin Zenobia Pierce came over from the next valley to help him nurse her, that human speech was heard again in the house. . . . After the funeral, when he saw her preparing to go away, he was seized with an unreasoning dread of being left alone on the farm; and before he knew what he was doing he had asked her to stay there with him." Yet Ethan's own habitual tendency to silence is not relieved by Zeena's presence. The deep muteness of his nature seems to have a life of its own, spinning outside of him and recreating itself in his environment. After a year or so of married life, Zeena "too fell silent. Perhaps it was the inevitable effect of life on the farm, or perhaps, as she sometimes said, it was because Ethan 'never listened.' The charge was not wholly unfounded. When she spoke it was only to complain, and to complain of things not in his power to remedy; and to check a tendency to impatient retort he had first formed the habit of not answering her, and finally of thinking of other things while she talked."

He knows that his silence (so like the silence of his mother who had been "listening" to unearthly voices) is but a short step from pathology. He fears that Zeena, too, might turn "queer"; and he knows "of certain lonely farm-houses in the neighborhood where stricken creatures pined, and of others where sudden tragedy had come of their presence." But his revulsion from silence is ambivalent, for beyond insanity, there is another vision—the close, convivial muteness of death. Ethan feels its attractions each time he passes the graveyard on the hill. At first the huddled company of gravestones sent shivers down his spine, but "now all desire for change had vanished, and the sight of the little enclosure gave him a warm sense of continuance and stability." On the whole, he is more powerfully drawn to silence than to speech. Over and over again, the arrangements of his life reinforce that silence. If his consciousness recoils from it in terror, some deeper inclination perversely yearns toward it.

It is always easier for Ethan to retreat from life into a "vision" (the word is echoed within the fantasy in a way that inescapably reinforces the narrator's deep identification with him). If Ethan is not able to talk to Mattie during that walk home from church, the deprivation is more than compensated for by his imagination. "He let the vision possess him as they climbed the hill to the house. He was never so happy with her as when he abandoned himself to these dreams. Half-way up the slope Mattie stumbled against some unseen obstruction and clutched his sleeve to steady herself. The wave of warmth that went through him was like the prolongation of his vision." The force of such visions is indescribable: it is the appeal of passivity, the numbing inertia that renders Frome impotent in the face of real-world dilemmas. Like a man who has become addicted to some strong narcotic, Frome savors emotional indolence as if it were a sensual experience. In the evening he spends alone with Mattie he is ravished by it. They sit and talk, and "the commonplace nature of what they said produced in Ethan an illusion of long-established intimacy which no outburst of emotion could have given, and he set his imagination adrift on the fiction that they had always spent their evenings thus and would always go on doing so." In truth he is not listening to Miss Mattie Silver with any greater attention than he gives to Zenobia; he is listening to the mermaid voices within himself. Afterwards, the vision lingers. "He did not know why he was so irrationally happy, for nothing was changed in his life or hers. He had not even touched the tip of her fingers or looked her full in the eyes. But their evening together had given him a vision of what life at her side might be, and he was glad now that he had done nothing to trouble the sweetness of the picture." As always, the uncompromised richness of the dream is more alluring than the harsher limitations of actual, realized satisfactions.

In electing passivity and a life of regression, Ethan Frome has chosen to forfeit the perquisites of manhood. The many images of mutilation throughout the story merely reinforce a pattern that has been fully established well before the sledding accident. Ethan flees sexuality just as he has fled self-assertion. When he loses his mother, he replaces her almost without a perceptible break in his routines; and the state of querulous sickliness to which Zeena retreats after a year of marriage might plausibly be seen as a peevish attempt to demand attention of some sort when the attentions more normal to marriage have not been given. It is not Zenobia's womanliness that has attracted Ethan: "The mere fact of obeying her orders . . . restored his shaken balance." Yet the various components of this wife-nurse soon grate upon Ethan Frome's consciousness. "When she came to take care of his mother she had seemed to Ethan like the very genius of health, but he soon saw that her skill as a nurse had been acquired by the absorbed observation of her own symptoms." Ethan and Zeena have been brought together by their mutual commitment to the habits of caretaking; now they have become imprisoned by them.

At first, Ethan's affection for Mattie seems to have a more wholesome basis. However we soon realize that the sensual component in that relationship is of a piece with the sensuality of death. It thrives on exclusions and cannot survive in the rich atmosphere of real-world complexities, Ethan features Mattie as someone who can participate in his visions, and he does not allow the banality of her actual personality to flaw that supposition. One evening they stand watching the blue shadows of the hemlocks play across the sunlit snow. When Mattie exclaims: "'It looks just as if it was painted!' it seemed to Ethan that the art of definition could go no farther, and that words had at last been found to utter his secret soul." His imagination can remedy the deficiencies of genuine conversation; if worse comes to worst, he can ignore genuine conversation altogether (as he has in his relationship with Zeena) and retreat to the more palatable images of his fancy.

By far the deepest irony is that Ethan's dreams of Mattie are not essentially different from the life that he has created with Zeena; they are still variations on the theme of dependency. Mattie "was quick to learn, but forgetful and dreamy. . . . Ethan had an idea that if she were to marry a man she was fond of the dormant instinct would wake, and her pies and biscuits become the pride of the country; but domesticity in the abstract did not interest her." The fantasies here are doubly revealing. As always he substitutes make-believe for reality—loving his vision of Mattie rather than Mattie herself. However, even when Ethan is given full rein, even when he can make any imaginary semblance of Mattie that he wants, he chooses a vision that has no sexual component. He does not see her as a loving wife to warm his bed in the winter. No. She is, instead, a paragon of the kitchen, a perfect caretaker, someone who can fill his stomach—not satisfy his manhood. She is, in short, just what he had imagined Zeena might be. And there is no reason, even at the beginning of the tale, to suppose that Mattie Silver would be any better in the role than Zeena.

Ethan and Mattie are never pictured as man and woman together; at their most intimate moments they cling "to each other's hands like children." At other times, they envision a life in which they exchange the role of care-taker and protector: if Mattie might become the best cook in the county; Ethan longs "'to do for you and care for you. I want to be there when you're sick and when you're lonesome.'" When they finally do come together in their momentous first kiss, even that physical contact is described in terms that remove it from the world of adult passion and reduce it to the modalities of infancy: "He had found her lips at last and was drinking unconsciousness of everything but the joy they gave him."

The sled ride is a natural climax to all of the themes that have been interwoven thoughout the story. It is, or ought to be, a sexual culmination—the long, firm sled; the shining track opening up before them; the swift, uneven descent, now plunging "with the hollow night opening out below them and the air singing by like an organ," now bounding dizzily upward only to plunge again with sudden exultation and rapture past the elm until "they reached the level ground beyond, and the speed of the sled began to slacken." The description of their long, successful first ride gives some inti-mation of the possibilities before them. Nevertheless, the language does not remain fixed; the vision is not steady. By this time the story has achieved such a palpable air of veracity that the reader is apt to accept this language as a more or less adequate description of what "really happened." Of course it is not. Even at this point—especially at this point—we must recollect that Ethan's world and all of the decisions in it (all the language that renders those decisions) is no more than the narrator's vision. We have finally reached the heart of that vision—the ultimate depths of the shadow world in which the narrator has immersed himself—and the inescapable implications of it crowd about us like the shades that gather dusk together and enfold the world in night.

The story becomes a veritable dance around the notion of vision. Ethan's eyesight is keen. "'I can measure distances to a hair's breadth—always could.'" he boasts to Mattie. And she echoes his thought: "'I always say you've got the surest eye.'" Yet tonight "he strained his eyes through the dimness, and they seemed less keen, less capable than usual." Other visions are competing against his clear-eyed view. The couple discovers that each has ached throughout the long six months before, dreaming of the other, dreams defying sleep. This, too, is a climax; for the mingling of their love-fancies becomes the most explicit bond between them. It is a more compelling vision even than the long, smooth, slippery track before them, a vision that is compounded by the potent imagery of Mattie's despair. "'There'll be that strange girl in the house . . . and she'll sleep in my bed, where I used to lay nights and listen to hear you come up the stairs.'" Vision calls to vision, and Ethan, too, succumbs to the stealing softness of his own dreams. "The words were like fragments torn from his heart. With them came the hated vision of the house he was going back to—of the stairs he would have to go up every night, of the woman who would wait for him there. And the sweetness of Mattie's avowal, the wild wonder of knowing at last that all that had happened to him had happened to her too, made the other vision more abhorrent, the other life more intolerable to return to."

It is Mattie who suggests death (though her plea has the urgency of a lingering sexual appeal): "'Ethan! Ethan! I want you to take me down again!'" And he resists her—as he has always resisted any action.

In the end, he is seduced by the vision; her words do not even penetrate. "Her pleadings still came to him between short sobs, but he no longer heard what she was saying. Her hat had slipped back and he was stroking her hair. He wanted to get the feeling of it into his hand, so that it would sleep there like a seed in winter." Not the violence of passion, but the loving, soothing release of sleep. Never has the silence been more profound (her words lost entirely into the cold and empty ether—that exhausted receiver of sky inverted over earth). The close conviviality of the grave has overwhelmed his imagination at last: "The spruces swathed them in blackness and silence. They might have been in their coffins underground. He said to himself: 'Perhaps it'll feel like this . . .' and then again: 'After this I sha'n't feel anything.'" The indivisible comfort of nothingness.

The delicate balance has swung finally to the side of retreat; time and space rush forward, and Ethan Frome lapses back into the simplicities of childhood, infancy. Words will not suffice to reach him now. Nothing does, save one sound—"He heard the old sorrel whinny across the road, and thought: 'He's wondering why he doesn't get his supper.'" Food—and then sleep—the very oldest memories, the persistent, original animal needs, nothing more. Mattie urges him, but he responds only to the "sombre violence" of her gesture as she tugs at his hand. Slowly they take their places. But then, Ethan stops. "'Get up! Get up!'" he urges the girl. "But she kept on repeating: 'Why do you want to sit in front?' 'Because I—because I want to feel you holding me,' he stammered, and dragged her to her feet." This is how he must go, cradled in the embrace of her arms.

The ride begins. Down the hill—no farewell but the gentle neighing of the sorrel. Down and down again, a "long delirious descent [in which] it seemed to him that they were flying indeed, flying far up into the cloudy night, with Starkfield immeasurably below them, falling away like a speck in space." "'We can fetch it'"; he repeats the refrain as the sled wavers and then rights itself toward the looming elm. "The air shot past him like millions of fiery wires, and then the elm. . . ."

Afterwards, there seems nothing left but silence; silence at first, and then "he heard a little animal twittering somewhere near by under the snow. It made a small frightened *cheep* like a field mouse. . . . He understood that it must be in pain. . . . The thought of the animal's suffering was intolerable to him and . . . he continued to finger about cautiously with his left hand, thinking he might get hold of the little creature and help it; and all at once he knew that the soft thing he had touched was Mattie's hair and that his hand was on her face." He has come to the very verge, but he has not managed to go over. His own final threshold remains uncrossed. He has not quite died. He has only been reduced, irretrievably reduced, to the sparse simplicities of animal existence.

Having plunged thus far from the world of adult possibilities, having brought Mattie and Zeena with him, he is doomed, after all, to wait for the end—possibly to wait for a long time. The last words of the vision measure the level of reality to which he has consigned himself. "Far off, up the hill, he heard the sorrel whinny, and thought: 'I ought to be getting him his feed.'" Thus the vision concludes, and the narrator steps finally through the kitchen door into the unchanging world of Ethan Frome, his wife, and Miss Mattie Silver. The condition of static misery that he infers, the life that has been Frome's scant portion, is an inevitable consequence of those dark impulses that lead past madness to the edge of oblivion.

We leave the narrator reflecting upon the tale he has told. It is not "true" except as an involuntary expression of his own hidden self; nevertheless, this purgatory of the imagination becomes ominously insistent, and the "self," having had life breathed into it, grows stronger even as the narrator assembles his story. Mrs. Hale's banal chatter falls upon deaf ears: he heeds her no more than Ethan has heeded Zeena or Mattie; and like Ethan, he has a parsimonious way with conversation. "Mrs. Hale paused a moment, and I remained silent, plunged in the vision of what her words evoked." Insidiously, the vision possesses him.

Wharton issues a grisly invitation to compare this frozen horror with the works of the New England regionalists. It is grotesque—this tale of appalling bleakness, this novel of the apocalypse measured against those wistful, nostalgic, sentimental evocations of "rural simplicities." The contrast is so bizarre that we might be tempted to rest with the obvious differences, and that would be a mistake.

Ethan Frome introduces us to terrible contingencies of the human condition; it also compels us to examine a nightmare that inheres in the deluding allurements of all literary embodiments of the Romantic vision. If we remove the accidents from the work of a writer like Sarah Orne Jewett (even one with such mastery), what will we find? What is the subject of her loving attention? In social terms, we must speak of a diminished world where all pleasure, all hope, all energy have been focused into the simplest acts of subsistence. We read of early-morning blueberries and succulent fresh fish, of hot tea and cold milk, and of long, chilly, dreamless summer nights. The disruptions in such a world are few (and they often come as unwelcome invasions from the world outside), but peace has been purchased at the price of passion. There is no rage, and the climax of sexual fulfillment has been indefinitely suspended. It is a twilight world; perhaps a world of senescence, but more probably an evocation of childhood. It recalls to the reader that time in his own life when days were longer and pleasures simpler. But—such an evocation is at base a sham. What we are invited to savor is a memory of childhood as it never was, as it never could be. Childhood is but one stage, a *real stage,* in a process of development. It is passionate, and it is constantly changing—its essence is change, its sanity resides in its capacity for change. Only adult memories of childhood are static. Only adult dreams and fantasies of childhood can invest that time with such a pleasing illusion of permanent happiness. And if by some terrible chance we should achieve the world of that dream—a world where our entire energies are focused into the acts of eating and sleeping and being taken care of, a world devoid of emotions powerful enough to change it or disrupt it, a world where man's deep harmony with nature makes his life virtually indistinguishable from the lives of simple animals (like Ethan's sorrel, whose hungry whinny is the only sound to penetrate the final moments of the vision, or like the small, cheeping field mouse into which Miss Mattie Silver has been transformed)—if we should sink into the oblivion of such a world, we would go mad. Taken seriously, the beckoning vision of the New England regionalists becomes a nightmare.

Ethan Frome is, of course, the explication of a private nightmare as well. Wharton never lost her fear of animals; but by the time she wrote *Ethan Frome,* she had a detailed understanding of the many meanings of that fear. It was among other things, the fear of muteness, of helplessness, of confinement to those elemental activities of eating and sleeping. Above all—and Wharton understood that it was above all—her nightmare was a fear of that part of herself that forevermore longed to retreat from adult complexities into the terrible diminishments of such a world. It was a terror of the desire to regress. Wharton had controlled that fear by repressing any feelings that might produce it—ultimately, by suppressing virtually all feeling. When she first began writing, she had postulated her private bondage as the necessary condition for *any* kind of coherent existence. Repression seemed an existential necessity of life; thus, when she made fictions, the worlds in them were landscapes of unrelieved desolation.

Now, at last, Wharton is able to recognize the horror *as* horror—and to reject it. The literary device of the "frame" in this story makes an important assertion: the narrator's "vision" is just that, a vision. The life of the young Ethan Frome that he has conjured is *not* a description of necessary human hopelessness; it is no more than a private nightmare (like Wharton's nightmare of twelve years past, perhaps). Beyond it and outside is a whole world—made "real" by multitudinous possibilities.

Finally, *Ethan Frome* is a statement of Edith Wharton's coming of age as a novelist. What had she meant when she said that "it was not until I wrote 'Ethan Frome' that I suddenly felt the artisan's full control of his implements"? One thing she might have meant was that she had finally learned to distinguish between a "vision" and a "fiction." By her own admission: "No picture of myself would be more than a profile if it failed to give some account of the teeming visions which, ever since my small-childhood, and even at the busiest and most agitated periods of my outward life, have incessantly peopled my inner world." A vision must be hammered into shape. It is, perhaps, the germ of a fiction; but it is not yet a fiction. A vision is a primitive expression of self; a fiction is the creation of an independent world that stands apart from self. Within *Ethan Frome* the narrator lapses into a vision (the tale of Ethan which is, as we have seen, a terrified expression of the narrator's latent self—his *alter ego*, his "Winterman"). The *novel*, *Ethan Frome*, focuses on the narrator's problem: the tension between his public self and his shadow self, his terror of a seductive and enveloping void.

We might almost fancy Edith Wharton going back to her own first efforts—"Mrs. Manstey's View" or "The Fullness of Life"—and regarding them with a mature and critical eye. But these are only partial fictions, she might say; my own dilemmas intrude into them, my own need to find expression of self prevents them from standing independently of me. These are visions more than fictions—visions of reduction and isolation. I have grown beyond that now. Let me complete the cycle before I go on. Let me write a novel that captures the compulsive qualify of vision-making. And so she did. And then, she went on.

ALLAN GARDNER SMITH

Edith Wharton and the Ghost Story

Edith Wharton's feminist contributions to the novel have been extensively admired, to the point of inspiring an enthusiastic analysis by Josephine Jessup in *The Faith of Our Feminists*. In the genre of the realist novel, however, Wharton obeyed the constraints of the visible; she adhered, perforce, to what could be seen by her society, to the areas of consensus—however critical— about the "real" state of that society and its interpersonal relations. In the genre of the ghost story, on the other hand, she was able to penetrate into the realm of the *un*seen, that is, into the area that her society preferred to be unable to see, or to construe defensively as super (i.e. not) natural. Schelling's definition of the *unheimlich* or uncanny held it to be the "name for everything that ought to have remained . . . hidden and secret and has become visible," a formulation which drew Freud toward a sexual implication, but which seems to me to retain a reservoir of unexplored content in the possibility of socially legitimated reticence or ideological denial, beyond the repressions of an individual ego or characteristic neurosis.

The most distinctive suppressed material (I use the term in distinction to "repressed," which is by definition unconscious) is sexual: the description of conduct which could not be acknowledged even in fiction. After the researches of R. W. B. Lewis, who has published the pornographic fragment "Beatrice Palmato" (which Wharton intended as background for a less explicit and therefore publishable version of the story, to appear in a volume

From *Gender and Literary Voice* (Women and Literature, n.s. vol. 1). © 1980 by Holmes and Meier Publishers, Inc.

significantly titled *The Powers of Darkness*), we know that Wharton explored this field, with a remarkable intensity. But I am concerned with material that is sexual not in unsanctioned eroticism and explicitness so much as in the sense of a "sexual pathology of everyday life," surfacing in stories of the invisible.

To disentangle this "sexual pathology of the everyday" from the erotic it is useful to examine "All Souls'" (1937, the last story that Edith Wharton sent to her publisher) which isn't, the narrator remarks, "exactly a ghost story" because it contains a mystery but no apparitions. An elderly woman, left alone in her house with an injured ankle, experiences a day that others claim did not exist, finding that the electricity and telephone have been cut off, and the servants [are] mysteriously absent. The evening before, October 31st, she had met an unknown woman on her way to the house to "visit one of the girls," but thought little about it after fracturing her ankle. The injury which makes her a prisoner, a sudden snowfall, and the size of her house intensify Mrs. Claymore's helplessness and fear as she stumbles from room to room, oppressed by silence that is "folded down on her like a pall" and that the presence of any other human, however secret, would have flawed "as a sheet of glass is flawed by a pebble thrown against it." The controlling, rational presence of the mistress of the house has to be inscribed on this flawless silence in the absence of her servants, who have apparently gone to join in an orgiastic coven (which, an epilogue suggests, will draw inexorably any who have entertained the remotest wish to assist at it and will thereafter make them move heaven and earth to take part again). The crippled intellect stumbling in its empty house carries sexual implications which are confirmed by the location of Mrs. Claymore's profoundest source of fear, a man's voice, speaking in low, emphatic tones in the "back premises," specifically, the kitchen, which normally belongs to the servants. The peripeteia which occurs at this point replaces sexual threat with the bathos of absence; the voice, in a foreign language unknown to her, proceeds from a portable radio, and she faints in shock.

Several lines of thought are suggested by this story. The first is that "All Souls'" can be read as a parable of frustration: Mrs. Claymore, delirious after the fall that damaged her ankle, fantasizes a situation which expresses her sexual desires in suitably censored and transformed version. This is the sort of reading suggested by the perceptive remark of R. M. Lovett, who noted as early as 1925 (before "All Souls'" was written) that "the wellings-up from the turbid depths of the subconscious she prefers to treat by the symbolism of the supernatural, and to draw the obscure creatures of the depths into the light of day as apparitions." Passing over the emotive color-ation of Lovett's dictum, this seems to me an accurate proposition which, applied to "All Souls,'" shows how Mrs. Claymore's "illicit" desires are projected onto the servants but kept offstage and by this absence are intensified in suggestiveness, becoming an unspeakable witches' coven.

The next line of thought qualifies this reading without denying it, in suggesting that "All Souls'" dramatizes the psychic deformations entailed by Mrs. Claymore's inheritance of an authoritarian male position in relation to the house and servants. Since the death of her husband she has maintained an almost compulsive control over the household, dressing for dinner, and ruling her five retainers with an "authoritative character" so that the house is always immaculate, even down to the empty servants' rooms. Her terror of something going wrong in this regime acknowledges the irrationality and instability of her financial and class-determined position beneath the rationality or common sense of her acceptance of it. The servants are as much a threat as a comfort, especially the faithful Agnes, who has been with her mistress for so long without revealing her affinity with the inconceivable "fetch" who calls for her. Mrs. Claymore, masquerading as male, inherits with her costume the terror of the female that suggests, as in earlier periods, the accusation of witchcraft.

The aggressive modernity of the portable radio in "All Souls'" enshrines Edith Wharton's contention in the Preface to *Ghosts,* her 1937 collection of stories, that, contra Osbert Sitwell, ghosts did not go out when electricity came in, because she could imagine them "more wistfully haunting a mean house in a dull street than the battlemented castle with its boring stage properties," and it documents her interest in the haunting *by absence* in everyday life rather than by presence in an extraordinary one. Mrs. Claymore's unacknowledged terrors and longings take on pathos in a confrontation with the absent male, foreign (revolutionary?) voice, which expresses a hollowness even at the center of threat, paralleling the emptiness of the snow outside, the silence within the house, or the emptiness and silence within herself.

In these respects "All Souls'" can be paired with "The Looking Glass," published two years before, in 1935, which explores the pitiable emptiness of a woman clinging to her beauty after it has gone, and to the memory of a distant encounter, in which no words were spoken. Duped by a version of what those words might have been, she leaves a considerable inheritance to the woman who misled her, a masseuse. Yet here Edith Wharton raises the possibility that the Word *has* been spoken: the young man employed by the masseuse for verisimilitude in her communications from "beyond" dies, leaving a last letter, which is the only communication to convince, but remains unseen both by the reader and the charlatan. Thus the absence within the text becomes a possible reproach to the materialism of the masseuse's heavily processed first-person account. An irony of the story is, however, that the most significantly unspoken (i.e. unseen, unacknowledged) element within the story is precisely the full extent of that *materialism*: the masseuse believes that she saved her patient from the "foul people" who might have exploited her belief in spirits, whereas she has done exactly that herself.

Taken together, these two stories illustrate Edith Wharton's complexity of approach to such issues as the unease of women in male roles, mistrust between women and the distortions of the master/servant, employer/employee situations, in which the unspoken, suppressed issue of status and suborned affection return in terror or the attribution of occult powers, and the servant/ employee is perceived as a witch or spiritualist with access to psychic forces denied to the ostensibly superior woman. Two further instances of a similar exploration may be cited, the tales "Bewitched" and "Miss Mary Pask," both of 1925 and both, again, concerned with the problems of women's aging.

In "Bewitched," set like *Ethan Frome* in rural New England, a barren and archaic environment, an elderly woman accuses her husband of meeting with a young girl who "walks," and he agrees that the girl has "drawn" him to her for over a year, turning him into a haggard wretch. In a compli- cated misconception, the dead girl's father shoots what he takes to be her spirit, and the narrative covers over a probable, ugly sequence of events under the screen of a limited point of view, showing only the outline of a corpse: the dead girl's sister has suddenly been carried off by "pneumonia." This leaves the attribution of witchcraft to fall on its inceptor, Mrs. Rutledge, whose Saul, it seems, had married the witch, not met her. Mrs. Rutledge now reminds the narrator of a stone figure, with marble eyeballs and bony hands, a reference that picks up his earlier reminiscence of "soft bony hands" belonging to mad aunt Cressida, who strangled the canary he brought her as a boy. "Witchcraft" here is shown as a two-edged weapon, used for manipulations between women and exploiting residual superstition for per- sonal ends which may or may not be unconscious, thus filling an empty concept with new significance.

"Miss Mary Pask," again a tale of an old woman, brings to light an aspect of male attitudes which is not "secret" (like Mrs. Rutledge's manip- ulations) within the terms of the story, but is unexpressed by the narrator because it is invisible to him. The combined effects of foreign travel, incipient fever, a dark and misty night, and a missing fragment of information result in his belief that he has been conversing with a ghost, the wraith of a woman for whom he never had much time when she was alive. The encounter dramatizes a sentimental and clinging quality in Mary Pask, and also dramatizes the narrator's frantic recoil. Her insistent loneliness, her evidently rambling mind, her appeals to him to stay send him bolting outside, tearing loose with a jerk from the trailing scarf or sleeve he cannot see in the dark, and slamming the door on her "pitiful low whimper." The episode employs traditional motifs of the spine-chilling convention: a stress on clamminess, darkness, flesh that is too soft, like a toadstool that the least touch resolves to dust, and familiar devices of claustrophobia, confusion, entrapment; but it employs them to investigate male responses to *un*desirable females in a very conscious way, and doubles back on itself to make a deeper point about self-defensive and romanticized sympathy. In absence, and believing her to be dead, the narrator's horror of the "childish wiles of a clumsy capering coquetry," the signals of an inappropriate, threatening sexual content in her gestures, recedes into an appreciation of the possibility that something of the woman had survived, enough, as he puts it: "to cry out to me the unuttered loneliness of a lifetime, to express at last what the living woman had always had to keep dumb and hidden." The thought moves him "curiously," he weeps over it, and supposes that "no end of women were like that . . . and perhaps, after death, if they got their chance they tried to use it . . ." This is what the narrator can see; what he cannot see is that such comfortable sympathy depends first on the idea that she is dead, and secondly on the belief that her spirit cried out to him. When he learns that the woman he met was actually alive, his sympathy vanishes and he concludes: "I felt I should never again be interested in Mary Pask, or in anything concerning her." The apparent indifference of this thrown-off conclusion elides its larger significance in a way characteristic of Edith Wharton; it is [what she calls in *The Writing of Fiction*] "that careful artifice which is the real carelessness of art."

The stories I have discussed so far would all fit comfortably within Tzvetan Todorov's definition of the genre of the uncanny, which lies (in the same way as William James's realm of the subconscious) touching the fantastic on one side, merging into the realistic on the other. The fantastic is, for Todorov, a hesitation, albeit momentary and shaded by its bulking neighbors, between the uncanny and the marvelous. The out-and-out marvelous contains improbable, unbelievable affairs which violate the laws of nature; the uncanny, however, is the genre of those works which relate events we can account for by the laws of nature, but find incredible, shocking, disturbing, or unexpected. The definition is broad, as he admits, but nevertheless it rapidly proves incompetent in practice, and Edith Wharton's stories show this up. There is no significant difference between those of her ghost stories which depend upon a rational explanation, as do the above; those which are predicated on the marvelous, such as "The Triumph of Night," or "Pomegranate Seed"; and those which reside in the evanescent realm of the fantastic as Todorov defines it, of which I think "The Eyes" is Wharton's only example. Rational explanation of some sort is usually possible in any story—always if we read the story as a creation of a writer and a reader—but to stress the ultimate explicability is to pass over the places in the text where the uncanny effect arises in favor of a comprehensive "reading" of the whole.

Actually the issue of whether Faxon, say, in "The Triumph of Night" encounters a phantom version of Mr. Lavington or merely hallucinates one, like the debate over the governess in *The Turn of the Screw,* means almost nothing. If he sees the phantom, it appears to *him,* as a person susceptible to its meaning; if he hallucinates it, that does not mean he was incorrect. In either case the issue is *why* rather than *whether.* Locally, that is, within the terms of the story, the phantom is clearly an illustration of the actual malignity of Lavington, beneath his mask of ingratiation and benevolence, as he cheats his nephew out of an inheritance. Structurally, the apparition provides a turning point, since Faxon's response to it (fleeing in horror) occasions young Rainer's death (seeking Faxon in the blizzard); hermeneutically, it suggests the vicious requirements of business practice beneath a bland mask, and it also belongs to a larger pattern in Edith Wharton's writing in which mature men are seen as tyrannical in respect of women and younger men. In none of these areas is the question of the apparition's reality of any weight—what matters is what it points to, material not repressed but suppressed in the overt recognitions of the group.

"Afterward" offers another indictment of this kind, when a woman comes to realize, through her husband's disappearance, that he had cheated a partner out of his rights and thus caused his death. The ghostly ectoplasm is a coalescence of her husband's guilt, a veridical haunting to dramatize the suppressions of business mores, kept from the wife but surfacing in conditions of "continuity and silence." The ghost itself dramatizes, in its indeterminateness, the difficulty she experiences in bringing this material to consciousness and recognition or becoming aware of the foundations of her domestic milieu. As in many of her stories, Edith Wharton here utilizes the estrangement of silence and stillness (often realized through sudden snowfall) to provoke the irruption of the strange within the familiar, with the consequent possibility of defamiliarized perception.

The *unheimlich,* in Freud's speculations, is the divergence between the familiar and the strange, in which infantile fears that we have repressed, or primitive fears that have been surmounted, return to haunt us. Such fears, and the fear of death, are necessarily indefinite, strange, and secret. In Helen Cixous's reading of Freud's essay, because the unconscious makes no place for the representation of mortality, the representation of death is itself "that which signifies without that which is signified," and the ghost is the fiction of our relationship to this unthinkable. However, to leap to infantile or primitive generators of the uncanny is to pass over a range of estrangements which are less closely related to the infancy of the individual or the species than to linguistic and social experience. Linguistically, any indefiniteness or reference may open the door to the uncanny, which is, as Cixous notes, "a concept whose entire denotation is a connotation," and the effect is enhanced by poetic defamiliarization and the imperialisms of metaphor. Here is occasion for close attention to the uncanny text rather than the assumption of its transparency in tracing the redoublings of a writer's own phantoms. And socially the case is particularly challenging, for we can see the intersection and divergence of the familiar and the strange as a procedure for the interrogation of convention and ideology (especially where the "natural" is so much at issue) and therefore a vehicle for the articulation of what, ideologically, "ought to have remained . . . hidden and secret."

Perhaps these claims are too bold. The extraordinary delicacy by which a "realistic" text may quietly twist into the uncanny is more the province of Henry James in, for example, "The Jolly Corner," than his pupil's, especially in view of her statements about the genre.

In the Preface to *Ghosts* she called her stories "ghostly strap-hangers," alluded to the "thermometrical quality" of ghost stories, and concluded that the only suggestion she could make was that the teller of supernatural tales should be well frightened in the telling. It may be argued that the suppressed conflicts and indecencies of relationship that surface in her tales are commonplaces of social and sexual experience. With regard to both reservations I argue that Edith Wharton's work is subtler than immediately appears and deserves close attention.

For example, in reading "Mr. Jones," it is easy to miss, as Margaret B. McDowell did, the significance of this servant in the story (which might have been better titled "Also His Wife," after the headstone of its heroine). Ms. McDowell says that Mr. Jones's motives for suppressing the family history are trivial, and "his implication in the destinies of the family does not run deep." But Juliana, it appears from the family documents, had been kept in close confinement by Mr. Jones, who was given absolute authority by the Viscount over his dumb wife, and she must have been especially exposed to Jones after the Viscount's death in 1828, before her own in 1835. The

investigation of an authoritarian male tradition gains greatly from the fact
that a servant maintains that authority over a wife, though he is much lower
in the social scale, and the personification of this tradition in Mr. Jones's
ghostly immortality dramatizes its persistence. A similarly "silent" note is
struck in "Kerfol," when a woman supposed to have murdered her husband,
and not convicted on the grounds of insufficient evidence (she said that the
ghosts of her dogs, which he strangled, had killed him), is handed over to
her husband's family. Naturally they shut her up in the keep at Kerfol, where
she died many years later, "a harmless madwoman."

The suggestiveness of Mrs. Wharton's language in its shifts into uncan-
niness can also be missed, as in this example, when the metaphor striving
to be born is thrust back again:

> The life [of Lyng] had probably not been of the most vivid order:
> for long periods no doubt, it had fallen as noiselessly into the
> past as the quiet drizzle of autumn fell, hour after hour, into the
> fishpond between the yews; but these backwaters of existence
> sometimes breed, in their sluggish depths, strange acuities of
> emotion.
>
> ("Afterward")

Here the past is likened to the fishpond, between the yews, which suggest
death, in the depths of which monstrous creatures breed: a premonition of
Boyle's disappearance and the ghost of Elwell, but this metaphor is resisted
by Mary, who turns it into a positive possibility, "strange acuities of emotion." Ironically that *is* what the place breeds, since after her husband's
disappearance she sees him properly.

It may be belaboring the obvious to point out that the values Edith
Wharton associated with the ghost story and the capacity to "feel" ghosts,
"continuity," and "silence," have been historically ascribed to females, or to
show that the victims in Edith Wharton's stories generally display such features themselves, while on occasion being victimized precisely by these qualities. Her stories depend heavily on the expression of the inarticulate. So, a
man's obsession with his dead wife comes to the surface in a series of letters
he receives, which appear to be blank paper with an indecipherable imprint,
but are interpreted by his second wife Charlotte as being from the woman
whose place she has taken:

> What difference does it make if her letters are illegible to you and
> me? If even you can see her face on that blank wall, why shouldn't
> he read her writing on this blank paper? Don't you see that she's

everywhere in this house, and the closer to him because to everyone else she's become invisible?

("Pomegranate Seed")

The fact that is absent from the wall, but leaves its afterimage, footprints of
bare feet in the snow, indecipherable letters, records which suppress—like
the inscription: "Also his wife"—a day that does not exist, the words spoken
in a silent encounter, disappearance that makes evident an unpleasant truth;
all these marks of elision are the negative inscriptions that register deformations in experience. Most of them are records of male sadism, though
there are exceptions to this, as in "Pomegranate Seed" or "All Souls'" and
"Bewitched," but even in these stories, if the sadism is absent or female, the
suffering is female too. Occasionally, as in "The Triumph of Night," it is a
sensitive young man who is victimized.

The most powerful of Edith Wharton's ghost stories, "The Eyes," unites
horror of male oppression and sadism with distaste for homosexuality. The
descriptions of the eyes which haunt Culwin whenever he has done (as he
thinks) a virtuous action, like proposing to a cousin he doesn't love, or telling
a handsome young man that he can write well when he produces rubbish,
are virtuoso, and would almost lead one to suppose that Wharton had taken
Freud's meaning in his account of Hoffman's Sandman:

> There they hung in the darkness, their swollen lids dropped
> across the little watery bulbs rolling loose in the orbits, and the
> puff of flesh making a muddy shadow underneath—and as their
> stare moved with my movements, there came over me a sense of
> their tacit complicity, of a deep hidden understanding between
> us that was worse than the first shock of their strangeness.
>
> ("The Eyes")

Culwin's failure to recognize himself in the image he describes is not shared
by his auditors, a circle of young men ("He liked 'em juicy," as one puts it),
and the reaction of one of them, his current protegé, is enough to let him
see himself for the first time. He and his image in the glass confront each
other "with a glare of slowly gathering hate," apt summary of the indictment
contained in his "dry tale." With Culwin's furiously suppressed recognition
of the other that is his own self, Edith Wharton moves decisively into the
grotesque, impressing upon the reader this final discrimination: in her ghost
stories the horror of what is, of the suppressed "natural," is greater than the
horror of what is not, of the conventionally "supernatural." Perhaps it has
been in an unspoken deference to this disquieting perception that her con-
tribution to the genre has on the whole been neglected.

JUDITH FRYER

Purity and Power
in The Age of Innocence

Society does not exist in a neutral, uncharged vacuum. It is subject to
external pressures; that which is not with it, part of it and subject to
its laws, is potentially against it. . . . ideas about separating, purifying,
demarcating and punishing transgressions have as their main function
to impose system on an inherently untidy experience. It is only by ex-
aggerating the difference between within and without, above and be-
low, male and female, with and against, that a semblance of order is
created.

—MARY DOUGLAS, *Purity and Danger*

The classical house is a prefiguration of a society which affirms a hier-
archy of values. These are the ground rules. All this is, of course, op-
posed to the contemporary odyssey of the self-centered self.

—EDITH WHARTON, *The Decoration of Houses* (Introduction)

"Once upon a time," begins one of Edith Wharton's earliest tales, a
series of parables entitled "The Valley of Childish Things, and Other Emblems,"

> a number of children lived together in the Valley of Childish
> Things, playing all manner of delightful games, and studying the
> same lesson books. But one day a little girl, one of their number,
> decided that it was time to see something of the world about
> which the lesson books had taught her; and as none of the other
> children cared to leave their games, she set out alone to climb the
> pass which led out of the valley.

From *American Literary Realism 1870–1910* 17, no. 2 (Autumn 1984). © 1985 by
The Department of English, The University of Texas at Arlington.

> It was a hard climb, but at length she reached a cold, bleak
> tableland beyond the mountains. Here she saw cities and men,
> and learned many useful arts, and in so doing grew to be a
> woman. But the tableland was bleak and cold, and when she had
> served her apprenticeship she decided to return to her old com-
> panions in the Valley of Childish Things, and work with them
> instead of with strangers.

On the way back she meets one of her old playmates, who has also been out
in the world. They talk of building bridges and draining swamps and cutting
roads, and she thinks to herself, "Since he has grown into such a fine fellow,
what splendid men and women my other playmates must have become!" But
she is disappointed. Instead of growing into men and women, her playmates
have remained little children, playing the same old games. When she tries to
tell them about the great things being done beyond the mountains, they pick
up their toys and go further down the valley to play. Turning to her fellow
traveler, who is making a garden out of cockleshells and bits of glass and
broken flowers for a dear little girl, she asks him if he wants to set to work
building bridges, draining swamps, and cutting roads. He replies that at the
moment he is too busy; and as she turns to go, he adds, "Really, my dear,
you ought to have taken better care of your complexion."

This is a story that Wharton would retell the rest of her life. She herself
would leave the Valley, a confining space where women were expected to
remain as children, withdrawn from the grown-up activities of the outer
world. She would map out her own spaces, both figuratively— in her first
book, *The Decoration of Houses*—and literally, in her own houses in Massachusetts and in France. She would assert herself by plotting carefully the
boundaries of her own retreat—the place where she wrote every morning—
and separating it from the as-carefully zoned social spaces of the house for
her afternoon entertaining. But in her novels the women were usually confined to and trapped in the (with)drawing-room, the room she had called in
The Decoration of Houses a place of "exquisite discomfort." Posed there
like the subject of a Sargent painting, the picturesque woman became herself
the chief decoration of houses.

The protagonist of *The Age of Innocence* is male. His name seems to
promise the reader a hero something like Henry James's Christopher New-
man and a novel something like *The Portrait of a Lady* (which James intended, at least, to center in the young woman's own consciousness).
Wharton's celebrated Pulitzer Prize-winning novel is not about her hero,
however, but about the "little hieroglyphic world" in which Newland Archer
lives. In fact, despite its deceptively innocent tone, *The Age of Innocence* is

much more like James's "The Jolly Corner" and Wharton's autobiography, *A Backward Glance,* and for good reason. Each of these is a tale written at the end of its author's life, "a backward glance o'er travel'd roads" in order, as James says in his story, to wake "all the old baffled forsworn possibilities . . . into such measure of ghostly life as they might still enjoy." James's protagonist is a returned American who wanders by night through the house of his youth in search of his lost self: "with habit and repetition he gained to an extraordinary degree the power to penetrate the dusk of distances, . . . to resolve back into their innocence the treacheries of uncertain light, the evil-looking forms taken in the gloom by mere shadows," until he meets his *doppelgänger,* a man with a mutilated hand, becoming "in the apparitional world, an incalculable terror." Wharton's search for her lost self is likewise a ghostly venture, as the reader is warned by the dedication to her friends who come each year on All Souls' Night—the night when the dead can walk. This is a literal invitation, for all of the characters in *A Backward Glance* whom Wharton calls back for a visit are dead people; bringing them back in her own declining years helps her to fix her image. *The Age of Innocence* is played upon the stage of everyday life, but like its ghostly counterpart it represents—and for similar reasons—Wharton's search in her own past for a hidden treasure.

Like the hero of "The Jolly Corner" and like Ellen Olenska in *The Age of Innocence,* Wharton lived most of her life abroad: she stayed in France all through the First World War, an experience which fueled *The Marne, A Son at the Front, Fighting France,* and *French Ways and Their Meanings.* At the same time, she had to distance herself from the deathly horrors of the war and the rape of her beloved country. She had seen, for example, the ruined town of Gerbéviller, "simultaneously vomited up from the depths and hurled down from the skies, as though she had perished in some monstrous clash of earthquake and tornado"; it filled her with cold despair to know that this was no accident of nature "but a piously planned and methodically executed human deed":

> From the opposite heights the poor little garden-girt town was shelled like a steel fortress; then, when the Germans entered, a fire was built in every house, and at the nicely-timed right moment one of the explosive tabloids which the fearless Teuton carries about for his land—*Lusitanias* was tossed on each hearth. . . . One old woman, hearing her son's death-cry, rashly looked out of her door. A bullet instantly laid her low among her phloxes and lilies; and there, in her little garden, her dead body was dishonoured.
> [*Fighting France, from Dunkerque to Belfort*]

In these same years, sorrows came for Wharton "not single spies but in battalions," bringing the deaths of her friends Henry James, Howard Sturgis, Egerton Winthrop, among others. She wrote in *A Backward Glance*:

> My spirit was heavy with these losses, but I could not sit still and brood over them. I wanted to put them into words, and in doing so I saw the years of the war, as I had lived them in Paris, with a new intensity of vision. . . . But before I could begin to deal objectively with the stored-up emotions of those years, I had to get away from the present altogether. . . . Meanwhile I found a momentary escape in going back to my childish memories of a long-vanished America, and wrote "The Age of Innocence."

These two works, *A Backward Glance* and *The Age of Innocence*, spring from the same impulse; and both begin with the purpose of fixing an image of security, the one with the child dressed for and engaged in the ritual of taking a walk with her father (the little girl, ruffled, muffled, veiled, and encased "like a Valentine") and the other with the childlike world of Old New York dressed for and engaged in the ritual of attending the Opera, standing for a good world in which, according to the epigraph from Goethe in *A Backward Glance*, it is impossible to write poetry.

Wharton's *intention*, then, is similar in the two works (though I by no means wish to argue that a novel is the same as an autobiography): she journeys into her own past, a past which she had rejected, in order to recapture a time of lost stability and to achieve a reconciliation with that past. We know from both *A Backward Glance* and *The Age of Innocence* that Edith Wharton and Newland Archer live divided lives. The novelist described both in *A Backward Glance* as "real" and "tangible," as "totally unrelated," but coexisting "side by side, equally absorbing but wholly isolated from each other." Similarly, Newland Archer lives one life committed to his responsibilities to his family, profession, and community, but at the same time he has another life which seems equally real, a "kind of sanctuary" for "his secret thoughts and longings," which becomes for him "the scene of his real life, of his only rational activities." It is not at all clear, however, that a reconciliation is achieved, either in *A Backward Glance* or in *The Age of Innocence*. Both Edith Wharton and Newland Archer are fifty-seven years old at the end of *The Age of Innocence*, and Archer, a free man at last, having traveled to Paris to stand beneath the windows of the woman he has loved in tormented secrecy for twenty-nine years, says to himself, "it's more real to me here than if I went up"; and "the fear lest that last shadow of reality should lose its edge" sends him slowly back to his hotel alone. If Archer has accepted his own past, we do not know what he has received from family and community which compensate him for the possibility of a companionate and passionate relationship with Ellen Olenska; we see only that he chooses to live in the world of his imagination rather than to risk the jeopardy of a relationship now, after so many years of denial. But this is not, finally, Newland Archer's story.

The two problems which Wharton investigated in this novel are related: one is the moral issue of the needs of the individual versus the claims of family, tradition, and community; and the other is the nature of that community. Or, to put it another way, Wharton confronted with the engines of technology that had wreaked havoc on France in World War I was much like her contemporary Henry Adams, who, standing in front of the Corliss Engine at the Paris exhibition of 1900, saw two kingdoms of force which he called "Virgin" and "Dynamo," the one having inspired all the great works of art and the other responsible for the new era of technology—and between them an "abysmal fracture" [*The Education of Henry Adams*]. Wharton's perception, however, was different from Adams's. While he unequivocally mourned the past, she was ambivalent about its comfort, particularly for women. The past stood for a kind of order that was a necessary counterbalance to war and death, but there was something to be said for disorder, too. Moreover, it was not all that clear that the family *was* nurturing, at least in America. If *The Age of Innocence* were a novel of reconciliation, one would expect to find serenity in the later novels and the kind of conservatism that pervades *The Education of Henry Adams*. For one who felt stifled by family and defensive always in her family circle about her writing, the presentation of the family as destructive and oppressive in the early fiction is understandable: driving Lily Bart to suicide, for example, in *The House of Mirth* (1905), when she chooses not to marry for convenience and thus becomes "unsphered"; trapping a man and two women in a living tomb of coldness and silence in *Ethan Frome* (1911); full of incestuous attraction and distrust in *The Reef* (1912) and in *Summer* (1917); or ineffectual in *The Custom of the Country* (1913), a novel whose subject is the divorce between the sexes in American life. However, the novels which follow *The Age of Innocence* present even more devastating depictions of the family as perverted and destructive: a "hideous and degrading" competition between two women for one daughter in *The Old Maid* (1924), the competition between a mother and daughter for the same man in *The Mother's Recompense* (1925), the meaninglessness and outrage of all family intercourse in *Twilight Sleep* (1927), incestuous attraction again and the destruction of children by irresponsible parents in *The Children* (1928). And while she was writing *The Age of Innocence* (in 1919), Wharton began an "unpublishable fragment" for a ghost story, "Beatrice Palmato." The story was never completed, but in the written fragment and plan for the tale, she described an incestuous relationship between a father and daughter and wrote an erotically-detailed scene of oral sexual intercourse between the two which takes place in the mother's drawing-room.

Given all of this, it is difficult to see *The Age of Innocence* as a novel of reconciliation—or as a successful novel of reconciliation. Rather, it is the pivotal novel in the Wharton canon, the imaginative work in which the moral claims of family and of the individual are held in perfect tension. Anthropologist Edward Hall is helpful here: in *The Silent Language* he describes times of transition as a time of breaking with prevailing group patterns and warns that new patterns must be generated, or else the parts of one's environment do not relate to each other in a meaningful way. It is because *The Age of Innocence* was written at a time of the breakdown of old patterns that Wharton turned to the past to consider a time of stability. Newland Archer might see "good in the old ways" and "good in the new order too." Wharton, however, saw the repression of the self in the old ways and fragmentation of the self in the new ways; the best she could do to achieve a reconciliation, or a resolution, was to tack back and forth between her own two created lives.

In this she was like her contemporary Virginia Woolf, who, likewise responding to the cataclysmic events of the early twentieth century, saw two structures in *Mrs. Dalloway*—one of war and the other of roses. In this novel, Lee Edwards has written, Virginia Woolf was examining modes of social organization: "solitude, fragmentation, rigidity, and death on the one side, or communion, harmony, spontaneity, and life on the other. Wars and parties, shell shock and roses, authority and individuality, death and life, 'manly' and 'feminine' are counters. . . . The politics of *Mrs. Dalloway* are such that life is only possible when roses, parties, and joy triumph over war, authority, and death. Clarissa's celebrations—ephemeral and compromised though they may be—are a paradigm of sanity, a medium through which energy can flow in a world otherwise cruel, judgmental, and frozen."

The masculine structure of war and the feminine structure of roses were horribly clear to Edith Wharton, but not in *The Age of Innocence*. In *Fighting France* she wrote of the war as a deliberate destruction of all that gave life meaning: "The photographs on the walls, the twigs of withered box above the crucifixes, the old wedding-dresses in brass-clamped trunks, the bundles of letters laboriously written and as painfully deciphered, all the thousand and one bits of the past that give meaning and continuity to the present—of all that accumulated warmth nothing was left but a brick-heap and some twisted stove-pipes!" And even worse was the violation of Ypres, bombarded to death, but with the outer walls of the houses still standing so that it presented the distant semblance of a living city, while nearby it seemed a disembowelled corpse:

> Every window-pane is smashed, nearly every building unroofed, and some house-fronts are sliced clean off, with the different stories exposed, as if for the stage-setting of a farce. In these exposed interiors the poor little household gods shiver and blink like owls surprised in a hollow tree. A hundred signs of intimate and humble tastes, of humdrum pursuits, of family association, cling to the unmasked walls. . . . It was all so still and familiar that it seemed as if the people for whom these things had a meaning might at any moment come back and take up their daily business.

Wharton found that in hundreds of such houses in hundreds of open towns the hand of time had been stopped; she found a convent where the orderly arrest of life symbolized the senseless paralysis of a whole nation's activities: "Here were a houseful of women and children engaged in useful tasks and now aimlessly astray over the earth." But she found, too, women beginning to build again the structures that support life—nuns, for example, at work in the fields, one of whom, turning up a hob-nailed sole, told her: "All the women are working the fields—we must take the place of the men," and, Wharton wrote, "I seemed to see my pink peonies flowering in the very prints of her sturdy boots!"

Wharton carried these flowers back half a century to *The Age of Innocence,* which was for her an oasis, a compromised oasis, a frozen world of ritual that offered sanity in its very repetition: she held before her scenes in "suitable" rooms in Old New York houses and pictures from summers at Newport where athletic rituals were carried out on the hemmed turf of the small bright lawns.

The repetition of rituals is characteristic of female structures, anthropologists tell us: woman's body, for one thing, assigns her to a repetitive role in the reproduction of the life cycle, while the male transcends the life cycle "artificially," through the medium of technology and symbols, asserting and declaring this transcendence ("culture") superior to "nature." Lacking in value or status to the extent that they are confined to domestic activities, cut off from the social world of men and from each other, women gain power and a sense of value in one of two ways: they can transcend domestic limits either by entering the men's world or by creating their own society. In a separate society, purity rituals become particularly important—elaborate norms for "strict dress and demeanor, modesty, cleanliness, prudishness"— because these are devices for contrasting their world with the men's world and of establishing grounds for order and status. The convent is the most extreme example of such a world: it is a pure and moral society of women, a world wholly their own in which "the very symbolic and social conceptions that appear to set women apart and to circumscribe their activities may be used by women as a basis for female solidarity and worth" [Michelle Zimbalist Rosaldo, "Women, Culture, and Society: A Theoretical Overview," in *Women, Culture, and Society,* Michelle Zimbalist Rosaldo and Louise Lamphere, eds. (Palo Alto: Stanford University Press, 1974)].

We know that Wharton knew a great deal about cultural anthropology; one learns from *A Backward Glance* that she had been reading Darwin, Huxley, Spencer, "and various popular exponents of the great evolutionary movement." She made skillful use particularly of *The Golden Bough* in analyzing her own former world in tribal terms and in dramatizing its rituals, from the performance of the Old New York audience attending the Opera, with which the novel opens, to the final scene where Newland Archer waits beneath Ellen Olenska's windows until the lights go on, and "as if it had been the signal he waited for"—as if the play were over—he "got up slowly and walked back alone to his hotel." The repetitive rituals of *The Age of Innocence* are the signs of a female society—but a female society in decline, with frozen rituals. Old New York may once have been ruled by the matriarchal Grandmother Mingott, with her "strength of will and hardness of heart, and a kind of haughty effrontery"; but by 1870 "Catherine the Great," as she is called, is fat and immobile: an "immense accretion of flesh" has changed her from an active woman into "something as vast and august as a natural phenomenon." Because of the burden of her flesh, she can no longer go up and down stairs, and all the family come to her, where with "moral courage" she still suggests the disorder of the "inaccessible wilderness near the Central Park," startling and fascinating her visitors with her ground-floor arrangement of sitting-room giving onto an unexpected vista of bedroom, recalling "scenes in French fiction, and architectural incentives to immorality such as the simple American had never dreamed of." It is, however, only "a stage-setting of adultery," as Newland Archer reflects when he goes with May, a Mingott granddaughter, to receive their betrothal blessings—like the stage-settings for the other scenes in the novel; in it old Catherine leads a blameless life. Her empty place in the family opera box signifies her diminishing importance; it is filled with the younger representatives of the female order, among them her daughter Augusta Welland and Augusta's daughter May, a young girl in white with fair braids who lowers her eyes now and then to her bouquet of lilies-of-the-valley (which Newland has sent her and will send every day until their wedding), touching the flowers softly with her white-gloved fingertips. There is one exception to the "abysmal purity" of this box, and that is another Mingott granddaughter, the Countess Ellen Olenska, who shocks the Old New York audience by her offense against "Taste" in wearing a simple dress which has no tucker and slopes away from her shoulders; her grandmother will later say that Ellen is the only one of the family like her.

Wharton gives here two simultaneous performances. Onstage, the performers follow the "unalterable and unquestioned law of the musical world [which] required that the German text of French operas sung by Swedish artists should be translated into Italian for the clearer understanding of English-speaking audiences." It is significant that the opera is *Faust* and that the first person we meet in *The Age of Innocence* is Christine Nilsson, the opera singer of whom Henry James had written, "What a pity she is not the heroine of a tale, and that I didn't make her!" James probably meant by this that Madame Nilsson seemed to him even more vital, more energetic, larger, and bolder than someone like his own actress Miriam Rooth of *The Tragic Muse*. Christine Nilsson was no innocent Marguerite or Gretchen, but a woman of charm and experience who has *chosen* to play this part, and plays it with deliberation and genius. The contrast between Madame Nilsson's power and the repeated ritual of performance—at the end of the novel the same people will gather again to see "the same large blonde victim ... succumbing to the same small brown seducer"—must have been striking to Wharton; knowing her Goethe, she was certainly aware that Part II begins with Faust's invocation to "The Mothers," dangerous powers of darkness. But for the audience the Opera is an occasion for another sort of performance, an ongoing ceremony which is taken for reality itself, with laws unalterable and unquestioned: the pre-Opera dinner; the arrival in Brown coupes—late because "in metropolises it was 'not the thing' to arrive early ... and what was or was not 'the thing' played a part as important in Newland Archer's New York as the inscrutable totem terrors that had ruled the destinies of his forefathers thousands of years ago"; the costumes of the audience, as prescribed and as elegant as those of the actors; and the visiting back and forth from one box to another. All of this seems as natural to Newland "as all the other conventions on which his life was moulded: such

as the duty of using two silver-backed brushes with his monogram in blue
enamel to part his hair, and of never appearing in society without a flower
(preferably a gardenia) in his buttonhole."

All of these details of the social ritual of Old New York have little to
do with Newland Archer's profession as a lawyer, or with his thinking self—
for despite his dilettantish qualities he reads a great deal in his own library
(in fact he reads the same books as Wharton, in *A Backward Glance*, admits
to reading), but they have a great deal to do with his day-to-day behavior,
for after his brandy, cigars, and conversation with the men, he must always
return to the drawing-room world of the women. He values that world, and
he even wishes to protect and preserve it, just because of the sense of continuity and stability it offers. When he turns his eyes to the Mingott box,
therefore, his first response to the observation of something that offends
against "Taste" is to rush to the box to persuade May to announce their
engagement early, adding the strength of his family to that of hers to affirm
their respectability—or reinforce their boundaries—in face of what he perceives as disorder.

One way to read this novel is to see May Welland and Ellen Olenska as
the traditional light and dark ladies of this script, as two ways of dealing
with "reality"—the ways of the two girls in "The Valley of Childish
Things"—two choices for Newland Archer in this novel. He perceives May
as "a light under ice"; she embodies "the steadying sense of an inescapable
duty." Where Newland has originally imagined her as a comrade, once freed
from her "abysmal purity" by his "enlightening companionship," he will
come to see that "such a picture presupposed, on her part, the experience,
the versatility, the freedom of judgment, which she had been carefully trained
not to possess"; he will come to fear that her "niceness" carried to the
supreme degree is only "a dull association of material and social interests
held together by ignorance on the one side and hypocrisy on the other." May
is the "terrifying product of the social system he belonged to and believed
in, the young girl who knew nothing and expected everything." Repeatedly
described as Diana, as May Archer she will still have that kind of innocence
"that seals the mind against imagination and the heart against experience."

In contrast to the safe and ordinary way of May, Ellen suggests "tragic
and moving possibilities outside the daily run of experience." Her eclectic
education has been "expensive but incoherent," including such unimagined
things as "drawing from the model" and playing in quintets with professional
musicians. Unlike May, who is stiffly bedecked and elaborately bejewelled
for each social occasion, Ellen chooses unadorned dark velvet for the Opera,
a fur-trimmed lounging robe at home—clothes which seem exotic in their

simplicity, and suited to no other occasion than Ellen's mood, her body. Unlike the varnished, tufted, and gilded extension of her mother's house that May will furnish, Ellen's house—in which time literally has stopped—is "intimate, 'foreign,' subtly suggestive of old romantic scenes and sentiments," pervaded by "the scent of some far-off bazaar, a smell made up of Turkish coffee and ambergris and dried roses." Ellen Olenska offers the possibilities of individual freedom and experience, instinct and variety, cultural and sexual richness, and recognizing this, Newland sends her not lilies-of-the-valley, but yellow roses which are "too rich, too strong, in their fiery beauty."

The "too rich" tells us already which way Newland will choose, but to read the novel in this way is to fail to see that he is not really part of either world; it is to fail to take account of his limitations and of the limits of his perception. Wharton took repeated care to point up the differences between Newland and Ellen—they admit to each other, for example, that they don't speak the same language—but the most significant difference is that he is "at heart a dilettante, and thinking over a pleasure . . . often gave him a subtler satisfaction than its realization," while she is characterized most of all by *passion*. (Wharton in fact tried other versions of *The Age of Innocence* in which Newland and Ellen marry, only to separate because of their difference from each other.) Likewise, however, Newland is excluded from the world of May. His sense of the power of her female world, which he does not understand and in which he has no part, makes him suspect that May's innocence is an artificial product—"Untrained human nature was not frank and innocent, it was full of the twists and defenses of an instinctive guile"— and feel "oppressed by this creation of factitious purity, so cunningly manufactured by a conspiracy of mothers and aunts and grandmothers and long-dead ancestresses."

Newland Archer is trapped in this world—both by his own limitations and by forces he does not understand. A journalist-friend, Ned Winsett, sees these limitations clearly: "You're like the pictures on the walls of a deserted house: 'The Portrait of a Gentleman,'" he tells Archer. ". . . you've got no center, no competition, no audience." The accuracy of Winsett's perception is borne out by Archer's confession of his own passivity: he mentally responds, "A gentleman simply stayed at home and abstained." Similarly, his seemingly radical words about human freedom on another occasion— "Women ought to be free—as free as we are"—have been meaningless; he understands that "'nice' women, however wronged, would never claim the kind of freedom he meant, and that generous minded men like himself were therefore—in the heat of argument—the more chivalrously ready to concede it to them. Such verbal generosities were in fact only a humbugging disguise of the inexorable conventions that tied things together and bound people down to the old pattern." What Newland does not realize at this point, of course, is that the "freedom" of the chivalrous men is just as much of a humbugging disguise as their verbal generosity.

To read *The Age of Innocence* as a failed love story, then, is to believe that "the play's the thing"—that the script offers Newland Archer a choice between May Welland and Ellen Olenska, a Faust-like opportunity to transform his reality. But in fact he is fated to remain in the old pattern precisely because there is in May's "innocent" world a shrewdness, even a worldliness which, without asking questions, instinctively protects that world, relentlessly patrolling its boundaries against the forces of disorder. The power of this world is such that the men can be called home from work to give their attention to domestic problems, and even the nature of their work—when it touches on family matters—can be dictated, as when the family makes clear to Newland what sort of legal decision he is expected to make about Ellen Olenska's divorce.

Because Newland's social conditioning makes him more comfortable in May's world than in Ellen's, he flees with "instinctive recoil" from Ellen, the very vocabulary of the freedom she suggests seeming "to belong to fiction and the stage," and from "an atmosphere . . . thick with drama." He flees to May, for her script is safer; it calls for a woman to be static, fixed against a scenic backdrop with a "faculty of unawareness" that makes her blood seem a preserving fluid, and gives her a transparency, a "look of representing a type rather than a person; as if she might have been chosen to pose for a Civic Virtue or a Greek Goddess"—as indeed she does throughout the novel. Newland has one of two predictable responses to May's "Diana-like aloofness": either he feels a "glow of proprietorship," as at that first Opera scene, when he walks with her in the park, or at the Newport archery match; or he communicates with her in "the code in which they had both been trained," "an atmosphere of faint implications and pale delicacies . . . [where] he and she understood each other without a word"—what their son will later call "a deaf-and-dumb asylum." His May stands for "a kind of hieroglyphic world, where the real thing was never said or done or even thought, but only represented by a set of arbitrary signs." In choosing her, "the world lay like a sunlit valley at their feet."

This hieroglyphic world of Old New York is a kind of "heaven"—a place for the "blessed," where other women do not feel the needs that Ellen Olenska expresses, a place where no one cries, where the people seem like "children playing in a graveyard," or like children "lighting a bunch of straw in a wayside cavern, and revealing old silent images in their painted tomb." It is the world of the luxurious Welland house and of "the density of the Welland atmosphere, so charged with minute observations and emotions" that it becomes for Newland a narcotic: "the heavy carpets, the watchful servants, the perpetually reminding tick of disciplined clocks, the perpetually renewed stack of cards and invitations on the hall table, the whole chain of tyrannical trifles binding one hour to the next, and each member of the household to all the others" makes any other less-systematized and less-affluent existence seem unreal and precarious.

On the other hand, the life Newland is expected to lead as May's husband seems equally unreal and irrelevant. When he flees from Ellen to May, his "here was truth, here was reality," upon seeing her standing Diana-like in the garden of St. Augustine carries the doubled-edged irony of Lawrence Selden's "This was the real Lily Bart" when she stands posed in the *tableaux vivants* of *The House of Mirth*. In fact, it seems that it is impossible for Newland to tell what the "real thing" is at all. May's is the world where "the real thing was never said or done," but Ellen's is the world "of fiction and the stage." The only place where "real" things happen to him is in his library, with its "sincere" Eastlake furniture, or in the theater of his imagination where he plays opposite Ellen Olenska. This is no random metaphor, for he identifies himself and Ellen with the hero and heroine of a play, *The Shaughraun,* which he sees repeatedly for the sake of one scene. In it, after a sad parting from the woman he loves, the hero steals back into the room where she stands with her back to him, her face in her hands. He lifts one of the velvet ribbons of her dress to his lips, and then leaves the room without her having noticed him or changed her attitude.

Ellen has this exact quality of unreality for Newland—but so has he for her, and he and she will reenact this very scene twice. The first time is when he stands by the shore of Granny Mingott's Newport house, watching Ellen, who faces away from him. She seems transfixed, and he says to himself, "If she doesn't turn before that sail crosses the Lime Rock light I'll go back." She does not turn; he walks back up the hill. The second time is at the end of the novel, when an older Newland turns away from Ellen's lit windows in Paris and walks back alone to his hotel. As in the play, Ellen knows Newland is there; in the case of the first scene, she later tells him so. And if one has been reading *The Age of Innocence* as a failed love story, then these scenes prefigure and explain their failed assignation.

That scene points up the difference between Newland and Ellen: it also points out the degrees of their belongingness to the "little hieroglyphic world." Ellen has returned from Washington to be with her stricken Granny

Mingott, whose stroke literally threatens the demise of the old order. Though he feels "burnt up in a great flame" every time he sees her after an absence, Newland tells her when they meet that he understands her reasons "for not wanting to let this feeling between us dwindle into an ordinary hole-and-corner love affair." He has a vision, he tells her, of "much more than an hour or two every now and then, with wastes of thirsty waiting between." Ellen gives a hard little laugh at this and warns him to look not at visions, but at realities. What do you want, exactly, she asks him: "Is it your idea . . . that I should live with you as your mistress—since I can't be your wife?" Her question pulls him up with a jerk, and he flounders, "I want—I want somehow to get away with you into a world where words like that—categories like that—won't exist. Where we shall be simply two human beings who love each other, who are the whole of life to each other; and nothing else on earth will matter." Ellen laughs again, asking, "Oh, my dear,—where is that country? Have you ever been there?" But she offers to come to him once, and then to return to Europe alone. At first Newland thinks to himself, "If I were to let her come, . . . I should have to let her go again." Then, he agrees. He sees her face "flooded with a deep inner radiance," and his heart "beat[s] with awe"—but they look at each other "amost like enemies."

Ellen does not come to Newland; she sends his key back and does not see him again until she departs for good. The reason is that she has had a meeting with May instead. She and May have had "a really good talk," according to May; they have understood each other. May has in fact lied to Ellen about her pregnancy, but she has acted with the knowledge and approval of the family and Granny Mingott has promised to guarantee Ellen's financial independence. The bargain to which Ellen has agreed is sealed in the ritual dinner, a ceremony of inclusion and exclusion, May's triumph.

While the love story of Newland and Ellen has been going forward, another counterplot has been running, but so caught up does one get in the romantic world of Newland and Ellen (perhaps because one is used to reading novels as fables of courtship) that the irony of its language is not at first noticed, and the inexorableness of the offensive which has been launched by the women in *The Age of Innocence* is obscured. Ellen Olenska suggests disorder, but this is not all. Her aunt, Medora Manson, "a gaunt and mincing lady . . . in a wild dishevelment of stripes and fringes and floating scarves," suggests disorder, too, especially in her association with Algernon Carver, itinerant leader of a free-love community. Both Ellen Olenska and Medora Manson are marginal people—that is, they exist on the margins of the community and as such are necessary in defining its boundaries; but where Medora's kind of disorder is frivolous and ineffectual (like Algernon Carver's

"Valley of Love"), Ellen Olenska's spoils pattern and suggests both danger and power in some potential pattern of its own. She is what anthropologist Mary Douglas would call a "polluting person," who as such is always in the wrong. She has "simply crossed some line which should not have been crossed and this displacement unleashes danger for someone" [Mary Douglas, *Purity and Danger: An Analysis of Concepts of Pollution and Taboo* (New York: Praeger, 1966)]. It is not just that Ellen has been married (to a notorious European count), for Medora Manson has been married several times; it is not just that Ellen is rumored to have had affairs (though this is never proved); she represents the European kind of threat to the "official innocence" of May's world that Madame de Vionnet, for example, represents to the world of Woollet, Massachusetts, in Henry James's *The Ambassadors*. She threatens to engulf the little world of order and purity in a world of sexual and cultural richness that would destroy it.

We know from Wharton's earlier *The Custom of the Country* that "the money and the motors and the clothes" tossed to the American woman by her preoccupied husband do not constitute life; in such a world the woman is a mere parenthesis. This is not to suggest that Wharton would have opted for a separate world of women: we know from *French Ways and Their Meanings,* for example, or from *A Backward Glance,* that she valued a world in which men and women intermingled, a world of conversation and stimulation, of continuity and tradition embodied, for example, in Laura Fairford's dinner party in *The Custom of the Country,* where conversation is a "concert," with Laura "drawing in the others, giving each a turn, beating time for them with her smile, and somehow harmonizing and linking together what they said." Nor is this to suggest that Wharton believed that a society of women was a way to real power—power in the world of men, political power. Surely she understood that the elevation of woman to deity on the one hand, the downgrading of her to child on the other, produced the same result—permanent residence in "The Valley of Childish Things." And yet the community of women in *The Age of Innocence* has greater importance than, say, Henry James gives a similar community in *The Bostonians*. This is a useful comparison, for while both writers present a female society in decline, Wharton's is the decline of the matriarchal vigor and daring of Grandmother Mingott into a Bachofean kind of matriarchal deity—the Victorian "perfect woman" of "unblemished beauty . . . chastity and high-mindedness." As woman's real power declines, I think she would argue, so her need to protect her separate world—a world characterized by purity and order—increases. The world of cultural and sexual richness for which Ellen Olenska stands is impossible in America precisely *because* Ellen's is a heterosexual world, a shared world, a world "rich and deep" because it is "based on the recognised interaction of influences between men and women" [*French Ways and Their Meanings*]. But the world to which she comes for relief, for escape from the "horrors" of the European world (in the person of her unscrupulous husband) offers some other qualities which even she—the intruder who cannot be tolerated in that world—sees as worth preserving. For May's world is not all bad: May herself is brave and strong and generous, as when she offers, during their engagement, to set Newland free to love another woman, or when she tells their son that she has understood Newland's sacrifice of what he wanted most in life.

And so May's triumphant dinner, the "tribal rally around a kinswoman about to be eliminated from the tribe" is an expressive reaffirmation of female loyalty; it is a statement of where the boundaries of the community are and of an intention to protect and delineate those boundaries as a means of protecting the community. We have seen this motive in action throughout the novel—when the women decide at first that Ellen should be offered protection, that she must live in an appropriate neighborhood, that she should not seek a divorce, and finally that she should return to her husband, whatever his qualities, because in attracting Newland, who belongs to May, she threatens the community itself. And in all of these family judgments, once May has held up the straw to the wind to see which way his loyalties lie, Newland has been excluded—just as at the final dinner he is not even there: he floats "somewhere between chandelier and ceiling," the music he hears in the two syllables of Ellen's name flickering against the social reality of May, "a band of dumb conspirators" eating canvasbacks, taking life in the Old New York way "without effusion of blood." He does not understand how all of this has come about: the menu and the guest list and the flowers have been chosen by May, her mother, and her mother-in-law in the same way as Ellen has gone in her grandmother's carriage to visit the shunned and humiliated cousin Regina Beaufort—while the men ignore her husband; and in the same way May and Ellen have had their talk which has led to the agreement that Ellen return to Europe. When he looks at Ellen's long pale fingers, Newland says to himself that he must follow her; but just as one has known that she would send back his key, one knows that he will not follow her, remembering his "A gentleman simply stayed at home and abstained." They have been able to remain near to each other only so long as they have not come too near; since she has told him, "I can't love you unless I give you up," it has depended on him to keep her "just there, safe but secluded." And that is the way she becomes for him—so dreamlike that he will not even be able to imagine what her life is like; he will come to think of her "abstractly, serenely, as one might think of some imaginary beloved in a book or picture: . . . the composite vision of all he had missed."

Whatever kind of escape Ellen finds must remain for Newland conjectural, for choosing to live in the world of May, his vision is limited to the orderliness her boundaries impose. By the end of the novel, although May is dead, their daughter makes no attempt to maintain the twenty-inch waist, and their son marries a Beaufort bastard, it is too late for Newland Archer to redefine himself. If he has missed something, Ellen Olenska, apparently, has not: at least her life on the same street in Paris as Edith Wharton's suggests that she has created her own sources of tradition and continuity, of richness and of power. Newland Archer does well not to enter this world. Had he done so, no doubt Ellen Olenska would have received him graciously, but he would not have felt at home: he would have found the atmosphere "too dense and yet too stimulating for his lungs," an "incessant stir of ideas, curiosities, images and associations."

CAROL WERSHOVEN

The Divided Conflict
of Edith Wharton's Summer

When Bernard Berenson complimented Edith Wharton on her latest novel,
Summer, and expressed admiration for its predominant male character, Lawyer Royall, Wharton replied, "of course *he*'s the book."

Wharton's statement has been largely ignored by critics who view the
book as Charity Royall's story, and who classify Lawyer Royall as an old
windbag, a pompous drunkard, or worse. The popular interpretation ignores
not only Royall's central position in the plot, but Royall's central role in the
novel's subtle and unfolding themes. For *Summer* is not just Wharton's variation on the old seduced-and-abandoned theme; it is a story of *two* protagonists, both of whom must come to terms with their destructive illusions in
order to lead adult lives.

The ability to "look life in the face," to confront reality without flinch-
ing or evasion, was, for Wharton, an essential quality in mature conduct.
She repeatedly traced the conflicts of characters faced with the choice of
escape through evasion or a more painful but adult recognition of things as
they are. In the majority of her novels, Wharton chronicles this conflict
through the use of an outsider heroine, one who exposes the reality of situation and self in confrontation with a weak male. This male figure, unable
to face the truths the heroine reveals, rejects her. Such is the pattern of Ellen
Olenska and Newland Archer in *The Age of Innocence,* of Lily Bart and
Selden in *The House of Mirth,* as well as of Wharton's lesser-known novels.
(Among them: *The Reef, The Custom of the Country* [where several heroes

From *Colby Library Quarterly* 21, no. 1 (March 1985). © 1985 by Carol Wershoven.

are drawn to an intruder heroine but reject what she reveals], *The Valley of Decision, New Year's Day.*) What is unusual about *Summer* is, as Wharton herself noted, that a man, Royall, is at the center of the book, that the conflict between suffocating illusions and painful but liberating reality is not expressed through Wharton's customary plot structure.

Granted, the traditional elements of a Wharton novel—ineffective and evasive male and outsider female—are here, Lucius Harney qualifying as the first and Charity Royall as the second. But in *Summer,* Wharton departs from her usual pattern by splitting the character and conflict of the intruder into male and female, and by resolving the conflict through a union of the two. It is a union which not only satisfies the requirements of plot, but which delineates what, Wharton felt, an adult marriage must be. *Summer,* Wharton's most uncharacteristic book, is both Charity and Lawyer Royall's story, a dual conflict and, more importantly, a dual growth achieved through "looking life in the face."

As Blake Nevius has noted, Charity Royall and her guardian Lawyer Royall are twins. They share certain characteristics which set them apart from, and above, the stifling environment of North Dormer. Both are rebels, rejecting the restraints of village life: Royall, by his drunkenness and dissipation, Charity, in her affair with a city gentleman. Both are village outsiders: Charity, because of her ties to the Mountain; Royall, because he is too large a figure for small town life. They share a desire for more of an existence than North Dormer provides, and, in seeking that life, both resort to fantasies which are destructive and essentially paralyzing.

Trapped in a society they scorn and in lives they despise, Royall and his ward resort to a common consolation: the fantasy of escape. In a new place, they feel, they will become new persons. Royall laments his diminishing law practice and his own degeneration, but blames them both on his environment; had he stayed in Nettleton, he reasons, he would be a bigger man. He camouflages his own self-hatred by surrounding himself with younger men, men like Harney, in whom he sees his own wasted potential, and young drunkards, who will flatter him through their inferiority.

Charity has her own fantasies of escape—to Nettleton, to a larger world with Harney as guide, even to the Mountain. Anywhere is better than North Dormer, for Charity has "a childish belief in the miraculous power of strange scenes and new faces to transform her life and wipe out bitter memories." Royall and Charity both evade change from within, believing that a new place will make them new persons.

Charity's fantasy of escape from self by a change of place is paired with an even more destructive fantasy—the dream of deliverance through romantic love. Her affair with Harney is grounded on the classic feminine fantasy of romantic submission, on an abdication of will (and self) through absorption into the loved one. From their initial meeting, Charity feels inferior to Harney, and senses "the sweetness of dependence" on him. After her sexual initiation, Charity chooses a masochistic, servile role in Harney's life: "she could imagine no reason for doing or not doing anything except for the fact that Harney wished or did not wish it. All her tossing contradictory impulses were merged in a fatalistic acceptance of his will." Rather than resolve her conflicts and develop an adult identity through painful yet free choices, Charity hides in her dream of a self defined by her lover: "her own life was suspended in his absence." Their relationship becomes the stereotypical romance of patriarchy; Harney, the superior guide, educating, dominating, forming his inferior mistress, who has sold all sense of self in exchange for his protection. It is no wonder that Wharton associates Harney with a musty "vault" of a library, with decayed and empty houses, with man-made enclosure in the midst of natural, open beauty. For Harney, not Royall, represents the dangerous paternal power opposed to Charity; he fathers her child, thus making her a prisoner of her body. More importantly, he reduces her to the status of a dependent, both a child, relying on him for her very identity, and a prostitute, selling her emerging self for the security of his indulgent and patronizing care.

This destructive fantasy of love is shared by Royall. He, like his ward, seeks a way out of the prison of isolation through the avenue of romantic love. The love he envisions is, essentially, the same kind of love chosen by Charity, a relationship of master/slave, of woman submitting to man's superior will. His fantasy is expressed, grotesquely, in his drunken assault upon Charity one lonely night, yet the model of love it expresses is, at bottom, the model of Charity and Harney's romance. The paternal lust of the father for the child only parodies the dynamics of Harney, representative of money, old New York and its suffocating superiority, seducing the poor and adoring country girl.

The subtle and hidden plot of *Summer,* then, is the revelation of these fantasies to the two main characters. It is a gradual exposure of destructive illusions accomplished, by Wharton, through the use of mirror images. Charity and Royall, twins in their weaknesses, must come to terms with themselves by repeatedly confronting one another. When Royall makes his sexual advance upon Charity, for example, she forces him to face himself, in shame. "How long is it since you've looked at yourself in the glass?" she asks, and she mocks his appearance, his age, his lecherousness. Similarly, Royall repeatedly shatters Charity's dream of Harney. When Royall refuses to board

Harney any longer, suspecting Harney's motives regarding Charity, Charity surreptitiously observes her lover, and sees "a look of weariness and self-disgust on his face: it was almost as if he had been gazing at a distorted reflection of his own features. For a moment Charity looked at him with a kind of terror, as if he had been a stranger under familiar lineaments." Royall's action exposes Harney to himself and to his lover.

Two major episodes highlight the use of mirror images. The first is the Fourth of July celebration, where Harney and Charity, who is intoxicated by the fireworks, the crowds, and her first lingering kiss, meet Royall, drunk, on the arm of the local prostitute, Julia Hawes. When Royall calls Charity a whore, she has "a vision of herself, hatless, dishevelled, with a man's arm about her," a whore confronted, ironically, by a whoremonger. The further irony is, of course, that while Royall calls her a whore, Harney will make her one.

And still the illusions persist, for Charity continues to believe in her deliverance through an all-consuming love, and Royall, though repeatedly shamed by Charity, undergoes no radical change of character. It is not until near the end of summer (the season and the book) that Royall, facing himself, reaches out to Charity, to force her to face herself.

The scene is the Old Home Week festivity, a time when North Dormer gathers to celebrate its sense of place and to welcome those who have left the village back "home." The keynote speaker for the occasion is Lawyer Royall, and his speech, delivered to the entire town, is symbolically directed at only two people—himself and Charity. It is an oral resolution of his own conflicts, an acceptance of his own shortcomings, and a plea to Charity to "come home" to reality, to abandon her fantasies and accept herself.

In a masterful speech of reconciliation, expressing his own dignity and courage, Royall confronts himself, exhorting his listeners with Wharton's favorite theme: "let us look at things as they are."

> Some of us have come back to our native town because we've failed to get on elsewhere. One way or other, things have gone wrong with us . . . what we'd dreamed of hadn't come true. But the fact that we had failed elsewhere is no reason why we should fail here . . . even if you come back against your will—and think-ing it's all a bitter mistake of Fate or Providence—you must try to make the best of it, and to make the best of your old town; and after a while . . . I believe you'll be able to say, as I can say today: "I'm glad I'm here."

For both Charity and Royall, who so closely associate self with place, the return "home," for "good," as Royall specifies, represents the return to one's self, an acceptance of one's self and of one's limitations. Royall, having faced himself, can only appeal to Charity to do likewise, to seek growth and identity in the real world of "home," rather than to escape into dangerous illusions.

Eventually, Charity does come home, to North Dormer and to herself. She begins to face the suffocating and deathlike nature of her romance: "she felt as if they were being sucked down together into some bottomless abyss"; "she had lost all spontaneity of feeling, and seemed to herself to be passively awaiting a fate she could not avert." Finally, pregnant, alone, deprived of the fantasy of a world of love apart from the real world, Charity seeks one last escape, one last place—the Mountain. It is Royall who must bring her down from the horror of the primitive place, and bring her home. And he brings her love, not particularly romantic love, not particularly passionate love, but a love that will allow her to be free of illusions and free to redefine herself.

Much has been said about the vile nature of Charity and Royall's marriage. It has been called sick, incestuous, and, superficially, it does signal Charity's return to the prison of North Dormer, where things never change, where people just get used to them. What such interpretations dismiss, however, are the changes which have taken place within the protagonists, and the subtle yet positive signs Wharton distributes through her final scenes. For what Wharton describes is not the incestuous marriage of father and child, the paradigmatic marriage of old New York, but a union of equals, of adults who have grown through confrontation and acceptance of themselves and of each other.

The marriage is, first of all, the marriage of two people who will never become model citizens of North Dormer. The pregnant girl has already scandalized the village, and the man who weds her knows full well that he is violating village norms. Both Charity and Royall will always be "too big" to fit comfortably into North Dormer, which Royall calls "a poor little place," but, as he said in his homecoming speech, a place which can become bigger "if those who had to come back . . . wanted to come back for *good.*" Rather than get used to North Dormer, Charity and Royall can work to change it.

Unlike the union of Harney and his society fiancée, Annabel Balch, the marriage of Charity and Royall is not incestuous. Charity is no innocent child-bride, no ornament to be displayed and broken by New York aristocrats. When Royall offers Charity his name and his life, he does so with sensitivity and compassion, so that Charity may salvage her dignity and pride from the shambles of her pain.

The man who had attempted to rape his ward sleeps in a rocking chair on their wedding night, and exhibits delicacy and tact by asking no questions about her pregnancy. He gives Charity money to spend as she wishes, and in Wharton's world, where money represents male power and female submission to that power, the incident is noteworthy. When Charity chooses to spend that money to preserve the memory of her summer with Harney, Royall makes no comment. At home, Charity has always ruled in Royall's house and she will continue to do so. Spared the sexual violation of the traditional wedding night, spared the enslavement of economic control, Charity is given the liberty of a different kind of marriage. The young girl who "had never known how to adapt herself," and "could only break and tear and destroy," has broken herself and her romantic dreams. Now, like Royall, she must rebuild herself and must learn when to adapt, never forgetting when to rebel.

The young girl trapped in loneliness can change, and fight for good, with a new partner. Even Charity, in her misery, can see a new Royall, one from whom "all the dark spirits had gone out," and for whom she now feels "a stir of something deeper than she had ever felt." In the marriage of Charity and Lawyer Royall, Wharton proposes a new and radical union: not of father and child, but of adults, coming together without illusions but with tolerance and compassion, with appreciation of the others' strengths and acceptance of weaknesses. The marriage is nothing like a surrender to the status quo of Harney and old New York, but a coming home to a union built together out of loneliness and pain and shame, and dedicated to working together, as equals, for *good*.

WAI-CHEE DIMOCK

Debasing Exchange:
Edith Wharton's The House of Mirth

"... you got reckless—thought you could turn me inside out and chuck me in the gutter like an empty purse. But, by gad, that ain't playing fair: that's dodging the rules of the game. Of course I know now what you wanted—it wasn't my beautiful eyes you were after—but I tell you what, Miss Lily, you've got to pay up for making me think so."

"Pay up?" she faltered. "Do you mean that I owe you money?"

He laughed again. "Oh, I'm not asking for payment in kind. But there's such a thing as fair play—and interest on one's money—and hang me if I've had as much as a look from you—"

(The House of Mirth)

The most brutal moment in *The House of Mirth* dramatizes not so much the centrality of sex as the centrality of exchange. Sexual favors are what Gus Trenor wants, but his demands are steeped in—and legitimated by— the language of the marketplace, the language of traded benefits and reciprocal obligations. Odious as it may seem, Trenor's speech merely asserts what everyone assumes. "Investments" and "returns," "interests" and "payments": these words animate and possess Wharton's characters, even in their world of conspicuous leisure. The power of the marketplace, then, resides not in its presence, which is only marginal in *The House of Mirth,* but in its ability to reproduce itself, in its ability to assimilate everything else into its domain. As a controlling logic, a mode of human conduct and human association, the marketplace is everywhere and nowhere, ubiquitous and invisible. Under its shadow even the most private affairs take on the essence

From *PMLA* 100, no. 5 (October 1985). © 1985 by The Modern Language Association of America.

of business transactions, for the realm of human relations is fully contained within an all-encompassing business ethic. Some characters—Trenor and Rosedale, for instance—obviously speak the voice of the marketplace, but even those who hold themselves aloof (as Lawrence Selden does) turn out to be more susceptible than they think.

Of all the characters, Lily Bart has the most puzzling and contradictory relation to the marketplace. A self-acknowledged "human merchandise," she is busy marketing herself throughout most of the book, worried only about the price she would fetch. She tries to induce Percy Gryce to purchase her, and if she had succeeded she would have been "to him what his Americana had hitherto been, the one possession in which he took sufficient pride to spend money on it." Much later, as she forces herself to accept Rosedale's attentions, she consoles herself by calculating "the price he would have to pay." Lily is clearly caught up in the ethos of exchange. And yet her repeated and sometimes intentional failure to find a buyer, her ultimate refusal to realize her "asset"—as her mother designates her beauty—makes her something of a rebel. She is not much of a rebel, of course, and that is precisely the point. For Lily's "rebellion," in its very feebleness and limitation, attests to the frightening power of the marketplace. It attests as well to Wharton's own politics, to her bleakness of vision in the face of a totalizing system she finds at once detestable and inevitable.

The persistent talk of "cost" and "payment" in *The House of Mirth* raises the question of *currency*. How does one compute the "cost" of an action, what constitutes a "debt," and in what form must "payments" be made? Money, the standard medium of exchange, is not the only currency in circulation. Trenor clearly does not wish to be paid back with a check. In fact, "payment in kind" is never expected in transactions in the social marketplace, and this unspoken rule makes for a plethora of business opportunities. A "society" dinner, for instance, is worth its weight in gold. Since the likes of Rosedale habitually "giv[e] away a half-a-million tip for a dinner," Jack Stepney regularly "pay[s] his debts in dinner invitations." Others—even those who protest—eventually follow Stepney's example, for the simple reason that Rosedale is "placing Wall Street under obligations which only Fifth Avenue could repay." There are other expenses, other debts, and other means of payment as well. Lily's visit to Selden's bachelor apartment is a "luxury" that is "going to cost her rather more than she could afford." Still she might have "purchased [Rosedale's] silence" if she had only allowed him to take her to the train station, since "to be seen walking down the platform at the crowded afternoon hour in the company of Miss Lily Bart would have been money in his pocket." Business, in the social world, operates by what we might call the commodification of social intercourse. Everything has a price, must be paid for, just as—on the opposite end—everything can be made to "count as" money, to be dealt out and accepted in lieu of cash. Dispensed in this manner, social gestures lose their initial character and figure only as exchange values: the dinner invitations, for Stepney and Rosedale, presumably have no meaning except as surrogate cash payments. (A social world predicated on business ethics is an essentially reductive world, and the power of money lies not so much in its pristine form as in its claim as a model, in its ability to define other things in its own image.) The fluidity of currencies in *The House of Mirth*, the apparently endless business possibilities, attests to the reduction of human experiences to abstract equivalents for exchange.

The principle of exchange, the idea that one has to "pay" for what one gets, lays claim to a kind of quid pro quo justice, and it is this justice, this "fair play," that Trenor demands from Lily. What he does not (or chooses not to) recognize is that what he calls "fair" is by no means self-evident and certainly not computable on an absolute scale. The problem stems, of course, from the rate of exchange, from the way prices are fixed. After all, why should a single dinner cost Rosedale a tip worth half a million (why not a quarter of a million, or a million)? And, for that matter, why should a ride in the park *not* be sufficient "payment" for the money Lily owes Trenor? In both instances, the "price" for the received benefit could easily have been otherwise, since the rate of exchange is altogether variable, altogether an artificial stipulation. In other words, two items might be yoked in one equation, pronounced of equal worth, but their "equality" will always remain imputed rather than inherent. Prices will remain arbitrary as long as the exchange rests on a negotiated parity between the exchange items—negotiated according to the bargaining powers of the contracting parties. Not everyone pays a half million dollars for a dinner invitation. Some pay nothing at all. The manipulatable rate of exchange makes it a treacherous model for "fair play." Lily "owes" Trenor the payment that he now demands only according to his rate of exchange—not hers—and his ability to set the rate and impose it on Lily says nothing about fairness, only something about power.

Power in *The House of Mirth*, many critics have suggested, is patriarchical. They are right, no doubt, about the basis for power, insofar as power is economic and insofar as money making is a male prerogative, but the actual wielders of power in the book are often not men but women. On the whole, Wharton is interested less in the etiology of power than in the way power comports itself, in the mode and manner of its workings. She is most interested, that is to say, in the mediated and socialized forms of power,

power that women do enjoy and that they use skillfully and sometimes bru-
tally. Within the orbits of exchange, power resides in the ability to define
the terms of exchange, to make one thing "equal" to another. That privilege
belongs, obviously, to only one of the partners, and this intrinsic inequity
gives the lie to Trenor's notion of fairness. A presumed model of justice and
mutuality, exchange really grows out of an imbalance of power, which it in
turn reconstitutes. Its "fair play" is in fact a fiction masking a deeper reality
of unfairness, for the rate of exchange is no more than a tautological reflection of the inequity that is the condition as well as the result of its operations.

Nowhere is the injustice of exchange more clearly demonstrated than
on board the *Sabrina*. Lily's presence on the yacht is, as everyone recognizes,
simply a business arrangement. "We all know that's what Bertha brought
her abroad for," Carry Fisher observes. "When Bertha wants to have a good
time, she has to provide occupation for George . . . and of course Lily's
present business is to keep him blind." Afterward Lily seems to realize this
fact equally well: "That was what she was 'there for': it was the price she
had chosen to pay for three months of luxury and freedom from care." But
the "price" turns out to be steeper than Lily thinks, for she pays eventually
with her good name and, indirectly, with her aunt's inheritance. The luxurious yacht cruise is a rotten deal for Lily, but it remains a "deal." And
without deviating from the model of exchange, Bertha has managed to get
her money's worth from Lily; she has simply managed to get away with a
good bargain. Like Trenor, Bertha has come up with a rate of exchange to
suit herself; unlike Trenor, she is eminently successful in exacting payments
from Lily. Thanks to her adroit management, the reconciliation with her
husband is "effected at [Lily's] expense." Bertha has got everything she wants
without any significant expenditure. This feat is all the more remarkable
because—if the logic of exchange were to be faithfully followed—she ought
to have paid a heavy price for her affair with Ned Silverton. But Bertha, in
her "cold determination to escape [the] consequences" of her actions, has
raised nonpayment to an art.

Bertha's success summarizes the contradiction that energizes and sus-
tains the system of exchange. The art of nonpayment requires, after all, the
most brazen sort of doublethink. The principle that enables Bertha to collect
payments from Lily is the same principle that enables her to shrug off her
own debts, and Bertha's ability to master that contradiction entitles her to
her considerable rewards. For doublethink is the very essence of the exchange
system, a system in which use and abuse are the same thing, in which leg-
islations violate and violations legislate, in which, to play by the rules, one

must break the rules. Doublethink explains why a system based on exchange should have nonpayment as its secret motto.

"The hatred of expenditure," Georges Bataille has written, "is the raison d'être of and the justification for the bourgeoisie." Bertha Dorset's bold miserliness—her absolute refusal to "pay"—is therefore only the extreme and ruthless version of a prevailing stinginess, observable in duller and stodgier persons. A case in point is Mrs. Peniston, Lily's aunt. She is quite willing to give her niece room and board and occasional checks for clothes in return for "the reward to which disinterestedness is entitled." But she is loath to give anything else. "When I offered you a home, I didn't undertake to pay your gambling debts," she informs Lily. Apparently she is not ready for other kinds of expenditure either. When Lily intimates that she has "had worries," Mrs. Peniston "shut[s] her lips with the snap of a purse closing against a beggar." Obviously no spendthrift, emotional or otherwise, Mrs. Peniston manages her affections economically and keeps her obligations minimal. Both her generosity and her forbearance have limits, which Lily in time exceeds. Mrs. Peniston has not bargained for the troubles Lily gets into, and she "recognize[s] no obligation" to help. But she is quick to detect any breach of contract on Lily's side and to retaliate accordingly. Nothing can be more logical than her eventual decision to disinherit her niece. Since Lily has failed to meet her obligations, Mrs. Peniston sees no reason to meet *hers*. If there is something hard and mechanical in the aunt's moral accounting, it is no more than what is considered "just" among those who stick to business principles. Mrs. Peniston is not alone in turning away from Lily. Her conditional affection parodies that of another character. In the same chapter in which Lily looks in vain to her aunt for help, she also waits in vain for Lawrence Selden to come to her (chapter 15).

Selden has other things in common with Lily's aunt aside from their shared abandonment of Lily. Like Mrs. Peniston, who chooses to be a "looker-on" in life, Selden relishes his "spectatorship" and "indolent amusement." In the opening scene we find him amused in just this way: he is "divert[ed]" by Lily, "enjoy[ing]" her "as a spectator" "with a purely impersonal enjoyment." Unlike Mrs. Peniston, however, Selden does not always remain a spectator. He has had his share of action (an affair with Bertha Dorset, for instance), and even in his indolent enjoyment of Lily he is not without other intentions. For Selden also happens to be a connoisseur, an investor in aesthetic objects, a man equipped with the "lingering, appraising, inventorial mind of the experienced collector" [Cynthia Griffin Wolff, *A Feast of Words*]. Selden collects, Wharton explains, "as much as a man may who has no money to spend"; now and then he "pick[s] up something in the rubbish heap, and [he goes] and look[s] on at the big sales." Selden remains a spectator when he cannot afford to buy, but he is not averse to pocketing little tidbits when they can be had for a small price. The investor picks up where the spectator leaves off, and in making the most of his resources, in getting the most from exchange, Selden shows more speculative instinct than he would like to admit.

"Speculation" is precisely what draws Selden to Lily. "[H]e could never see her without a faint movement of interest," we learn as soon as the novel opens; "it was characteristic of her that she always roused speculation." Selden is "interest[ed]" in Lily—curious about what she will do—but he is "interested" also in another sense, as every investor would be in an eminently collectible item. To be sure, Selden is not half as crude as the others: while they notice Lily's "outline," he admires the "modelling of her little ear, the crisp upward wave of her hair," "the thick planting of her straight black lashes," and "her hand, polished as a bit of old ivory, with its slender pink nails." Lily would have been a valuable acquisition, and Selden knows it. "Ah, well, there must be plenty of capital on the lookout for such an investment," he muses as they discuss her marriage prospects. Selden himself, apparently, has no such "capital" to "invest" and chooses simply to look on. His "admiring spectatorship" costs him nothing, involves "no risks," and allows him to enjoy the goods without the responsibility of paying for them.

Why does Selden not invest in Lily? On the face of it, he cannot afford to: he has "nothing to give" her. That is true as far as money goes, but money is not the only asset in Selden's portfolio, nor does he always count himself indigent. What holds him back, indeed, is not so much the thought of having "nothing to give" as the thought of what he might have to lose. And Selden stands to lose a great deal. His currency is not money, of course, but spiritual stocks, and in this currency he has been saving and hoarding for so long that he is afraid there might be "a chance of his having to pay up." If he has so far kept his riches to himself, he has done so "not from any poverty of feeling" but from a conscious sense of his accumulated wealth and from a determination to safeguard that wealth. Lily now presents him with an opportunity to "invest," and the question for Selden is whether she can be trusted with his emotional capital, whether he can "stake his faith" on her. The quandary he faces is not unlike that of his friends on the stock exchange, and the way he settles the question puts him in good company, which is to say, the company of the nonpayers, the company of Mrs. Peniston and Bertha Dorset.

Selden is loath to part with his assets in the hazardous business of exchange. This self-serving conservatism comes through most vividly in a seemingly jesting moment between him and Lily:

"Do you want to marry me?" she asked.

He broke into a laugh. "No, I don't want to—but perhaps I should if you did!"

Never is romance so unpassionate, so bluntly contractual. "Perhaps I should if you did"—the niggardly proposition epitomizes Selden's love for Lily. He will not propose to her until he knows that she will accept him; indeed, he will not love her until he knows that she will love him in return, until he can be "as sure of her surrender as of his own." Short of this assurance—and all through the book Selden is never completely sure—he will not part with his spiritual capital; he will not take "risks" with it. For Selden love is a form of exchange, and he will hear of nothing but profits.

The discipline of business determines which of the two roles, spectator or investor, Selden chooses to play. The spectator turns into the investor at the point where returns are guaranteed. These, then, are the two faces of the speculator—for Selden is no less business-minded when he "looks on" than when he "picks up" a find—and their equal congeniality enables him to perform some heady emotional flip-flops. As a spectator Selden remains cynically amused by Lily; as an investor he seeks to acquire her hand. Disparate as these sentiments may seem, for Selden they are both "options," to be taken up or put aside at will, and he trades options with daunting facility. Meeting him for the first time after Bellomont, Lily is struck by his having "gone back without an effort to the footing on which they had stood before their last talk together." But such adaptability is to be expected from someone who computes his love as if it were on a balance sheet, "proportion[ing]" his expenditure to anticipated returns. Selden's "speculation" is the sort that will brook no risks (and certainly no losses), and Lily is simply not a sound enough investment for him. The sight of her emerging late at night from the Trenor house shatters his slim confidence, and Selden is quick to pull out. When they meet again he has once more become a spectator. In Monte Carlo he can "give his admiration the freer play because so little personal feeling remained in it," and he sticks to this convenient role all through Lily's subsequent troubles.

Still, the investor in Selden is not quite willing to give up. As the book closes he is ready to make another move, to trust once again to his "sense of adventure." Of course, he arrives just a few hours too late for the adventure to take off, but even that unfortunate fact has no meaning for him except as a "loss" to himself. Faced with Lily's death, he will only "accuse himself for having failed to reach the height of his opportunity." Selden does not seem aware of his responsibility—of his complicity—in her death. Like Mrs. Peniston, he "recognize[s] no obligation" toward Lily's welfare and accords himself no blame for her demise. Indeed, the worst thing that Selden can say about himself is that he has not been enterprising enough, that he has missed his "opportunity." And so he remains, to the end, a closet speculator. Selden's lament is one that Rosedale would have understood and might even have made himself. The "republic of the spirit" turns out to be less a republic than a refined replica of the social marketplace, of which Selden is a full participating member.

Selden is a "negative hero," then, as Wharton herself admits, not a high-minded dissident but very much "one of them." Like the others, he too exudes a cold stinginess, a desire for acquisition without risk and without expenditure. It is not Selden but Lily, the woman he tutors and scolds, who comes closest to breaking away from the rules and premises of the marketplace. Lily is also, of course, the only one who pays routinely and scrupulously, and often with currency she can little afford. "You think we live *on* the rich, rather than with them," Lily observes to Gerty, "and so we do, in a sense—but it's a privilege we have to pay for!" She is right. It is no accident that the one who pays most regularly is also the one with the scantest means, for nonpayment, as we have seen, is a privilege of the powerful, those who fix the rate of exchange. Lily is therefore the obverse of, and the needed complement to, three characters: Bertha Dorset, who avoids paying by making others foot the bill; Mrs. Peniston, who scrimps on her obligations; and Lawrence Selden, who pulls out when the deal seems overly risky. "Paying" is Lily's habitual way of being, and she is at it almost as soon as the book opens. It is she, not Selden, who has to "pay so dearly for" her visit to his apartment. Lily goes on to pay for her stay at Bellomont by performing "social drudgery" for Mrs. Trenor as well as by incurring gambling debts. She pays for her momentary truancy from Percy Gryce. She pays Trenor, though not to his satisfaction. She pays Bertha for the cruise on the *Sabrina,* just as she pays Norma Hatch for her brief stay at the Emporium Hotel. And she pays, finally, for those extravagant sentiments she permits herself to feel toward Selden.

Lily's dutiful payments are altogether in keeping with the principle of exchange. She is merely doing what the system requires of her, what she is supposed to. And yet—such is the irony of exchange—it is precisely this strict compliance that marks her as a deviant. Lily is working, after all, within a system in which nonpayment is the norm, in which violation is the only mode of conformity. She is penalized, then, not for breaking the rules but for observing them. This sort of absurdity is the logic of nightmare, but it is just this absurd logic that makes the exchange system work. In its disfiguring light Lily's "rebellion" takes on the correspondingly absurd form of playing by the rules, of rebellion by submission.

Lily's paradoxical conformity and deviance come across most clearly in her dealings with Trenor. Having taken almost nine thousand dollars from him and finding her obligation "not the sort . . . one could remain under," she proceeds to settle her debt as soon as she receives her aunt's legacy—a decision that "cleans [her] out altogether," as Rosedale rather indelicately puts it. In repaying Trenor, Lily is indeed complying with the rules of exchange, but she is also challenging the very basis of exchange. Trenor never expects to be paid back in quite this way. "Payment in kind," the most primitive form of barter economy, has no place in a highly developed social marketplace, which trades on the putative equivalence between disparate entities. By paying back the exact monetary amount, by equating nine thousand dollars with nine thousand dollars, Lily at once obeys the principle of exchange and reduces it to tautology. Her nine-thousand-dollar debt is now just that; a nine-thousand-dollar debt, not some ill-defined and possibly limitless obligation. In other words, by making money its own equivalent, Lily reduces it to its own terms and defies its purchasing power. She has understood what it means to live under the "intolerable obligation" of an all-consuming system of exchange, and she now tries to exorcise its influence by facing up to what she owes—in all the crudeness and brutality of its cash amount—just to rescue from its dominion the other strands of her life. What appears as a gesture of submission turns out to be a gesture of defiance, for by adhering literally to the terms of exchange Lily turns the system on its head. And yet, as every reader must recognize, defiance of this sort is ultimately unavailing. The exchange system can easily accommodate rebellion like Lily's: Trenor, no doubt, will take the money and even circulate it anew. Lily's action hurts no one but herself. It remains a challenge to the exchange system in spirit but not in fact.

When Lily returns the money, her rebellion by submission assumes its final and characteristically self-defeating form, the only form it is permitted to take within the exchange system. We see the beginning of that pattern in her earlier and grateful refusal of the "plain business arrangement" Rosedale offers her. What Rosedale proposes is this:

> "Well, I'll lend you the money to pay Trenor; and I won't—I— see here, don't take me up till I've finished. What I mean is, it'll

be a plain business arrangement, such as one man would make with another. Now, what have you got to say against that?"

Lily's blush deepened to a glow in which humiliation and gratitude were mingled, and both sentiments revealed themselves in the unexpected gentleness of her reply.

"Only this: that it is exactly what Gus Trenor proposed; and that I can never again be sure of understanding the plainest business arrangement." Then, realizing that this answer contained a germ of injustice, she added, even more kindly: "Not that I don't appreciate your kindness—that I'm not grateful for it. But a business arrangement between us would in any case be impossible, because I shall have no security to give when my debt to Gus Trenor has been paid."

This reply is surely an impressive statement from someone who, not so long ago, believed that "her modest investments were to be mysteriously multiplied" with Trenor's help. Lily has since found out what even "the simplest business arrangement" entails, and on this occasion she is careful to keep "business" to its strictest possible definition. She is in fact blunter, more matter-of-fact than Rosedale himself, but by being so implacably businesslike, Lily paradoxically obstructs, rather than facilitates, business opportunities. By insisting on money as the only legitimate currency, she limits the field of action as well as the available material for exchange. There is something heroic in her refusal to accept money when she knows she has no money to give in return, and yet such principles are surely suicidal, when the point of exchange is to get and not to give. What is honorable from a moral point of view is plain foolishness within the context of the marketplace. Like her decision to return Trenor's money, Lily's rejection of Rosedale's loan leaves the exchange system intact and hurts only herself. Where the marketplace is everywhere, in refusing to do business Lily is perhaps also refusing to live—an implication Wharton takes up at the end.

Meanwhile Lily is left to commit two more business errors. The more serious one (from a practical point of view) concerns the disposition of Bertha's letters. These are valuable assets, and Rosedale, the consummate businessman, has no doubt about how Lily should use them. "The wonder to me is that you've waited so long to get square with that woman, when you've had the power in your hands," he declares. After all, Bertha had saved her own skin "at Lily's expense," she "owes" Lily, and nothing would be more natural than an attempt to right the balance. Of course, there are different ways of "getting even." Going to Bertha's husband with proof of her infidelity could be one way, but from a "purely business view of the question" Rosedale does not recommend this method, since "in a deal like that, nobody comes out with perfectly clean hands." He has a much better "deal" in mind. Lily is to use the letters not to destroy Bertha but to cow her, to "get [her] into line." Unlike the other deal, a risky business, this one is guaranteed to work:

> [Rosedale's plan] reduced the transaction to a private understand-ing, of which no third person need have the remotest hint. Put by Rosedale in terms of business-like give-and-take, this under-standing took on the harmless air of a mutual accommodation, like a transfer of property or a revision of boundary lines. It certainly simplified life to view it as a perpetual adjustment, a play of party politics, in which every concession had the recog-nized equivalent; Lily's tired mind was fascinated by this escape from fluctuating ethical estimates into a region of concrete weights and measures.

Properly managed, even revenge can become a form of exchange. And in the hands of Rosedale, exchange will be very good business indeed—completely without risk, with profits guaranteed. Lily's grievances are to be paid back with "recognized equivalent[s]"; they are to count as credits with which to exact payment (and indeed interest) from the offending party. The past wrongs are to be set right by a little "adjustment" between the two women in the form of a "private transaction," a "transfer of property," from which Lily is to be—for once—the receiving rather than the paying party.

Lily has not always been averse to righting her balance. Much earlier, when she was contemplating marriage to Percy Gryce, she had looked for-ward to the "old scores she would pay off as well as old benefits she could return." Still, she cannot bring herself to use Bertha's letters. Even though Rosedale will not carry her unless she is "reconciled" with Bertha and "re-habilitated" in society and even though marriage is her only remaining hope, Lily cannot carry out the "private transaction" he has so plainly laid out. To strike a deal with Bertha, Lily is required not only to "trade on [Selden's] name and profit by a secret from his past" but to "trade on" and "profit by" her past wrongs. Rosedale's method represents the ultimate commodi-fication of experience, the reduction and quantification of moral outrage into "concrete weights and measures" for exchange. Lily cannot do it. This, too, is a business opportunity she must reject. If she refuses to pay her debts with surrogate money, she also refuses to "cash in" on her injuries. Since she will not make Bertha "pay back" what Bertha "owes" her, she must leave the imbalance between herself and Bertha unredressed. What Lily is rejecting is not so much the idea of revenge as the degradation of revenge in the arena of exchange.

As Lily leaves Selden's apartment, she quietly slides the packet of letters into the fire. Rosedale would have been horrified. Her last "asset" is now destroyed and with it any hope of rehabilitation. But Lily has not planned to burn the letters—she does so on the spur of the moment—and her sudden decision probably has something to do with another mistake she makes during the same visit, the mistake of indulging in "the passion of her soul." Hardly anyone else in the book has been guilty of this mistake, and it becomes all the more startling against the background of Selden's tepid civilities. He offers her tea—"that amount of hospitality at my command," he tells her. Lily sees that "her presence [is] becoming an embarrassment to him," she notices his "light tone" and his all-too-evident "linger[ing] in the conventional outskirts of word-play and evasion." But his demeanor no longer holds her back; for once she can accept the disparity between her sentiments and his. In Wharton's wonderful phrase, Lily has "passed beyond the phase of well-bred reciprocity, in which every demonstration must be scrupulously proportioned to the emotion it elicits." In destroying Bertha's letters, she is offering Selden a great deal more than he has offered her or will ever offer her. But Lily no longer weighs and "proportion[s]" her feelings; she is no longer deterred by thoughts of "profits" and "returns." As she throws away her love in an act of wanton expenditure, she is making what is perhaps her most eloquent protest against the ethics of exchange.

And yet this protest, like her other ones, is ultimately futile, ultimately contained, absorbed, and exploited by the very system against which it is directed. The exchange system has room for money foolishly returned and loans foolishly refused, just as it has room for sentiments foolishly indulged in. Far from being a threat to the system, Lily's gesture of defiance merely recapitulates its assignation—merely reaffirms its sovereignty—for in giving Selden more than she gets from him, Lily is simply reverting to her customary role within the exchange system: her role as the one who "pays."

Even more ironically, Lily's extraordinary expenditure, like her previous ones, is not valued by those who benefit from it; it literally goes unnoticed. For a man who prides himself on his spectatorship, Selden is surprisingly blind to the moral drama unfolding before his very eyes. "When she rose, he fancied that he saw her draw something from her dress and drop it into the fire; but he hardly noticed the gesture at the time." The gesture will never be noticed; it is not meant to be. Lily's delicacy of feeling, her rectitude and generosity—all these are lost on Selden. They will always be unrecognized, unrewarded even by his gratitude. But that, too, is only to be expected. For the nobility of her action surely lies in its fruitlessness, in its utter lack of material consequence, in its erasure from history.

With her death Lily's moral triumph evaporates as if it had never taken place. In the last chapter of *The House of Mirth,* Wharton presents us with the spectacle of Selden rummaging through Lily's papers, fretting over the check made out to Trenor, feeling sorry for himself—and remaining, all the while, abysmally ignorant of what she has done for his sake. Wharton could not have written a stronger or more bitter commentary on the loneliness and futility of Lily's "rebellion." But even if her secret had somehow been revealed, it would have made no sense to her friends. They would have dismissed it as a species of folly. Private morality is finally defenseless against an exchange system that dissolves the language of morality into its own harsh, brassy parlance. Within this totalizing system moral rectitude simply counts as another exchange value, another commodity—and an insanely expensive one, as it turns out. For this ultimate luxury Lily pays with her life. Her few moments of moral triumph, translated into the idiom of the marketplace, merely figure as moments of ill-advised improvidence, altogether in keeping with her lifelong habit of spending "more than she could afford." Morality, in *The House of Mirth,* provides no transcendent language, no alternative way of being, but feeds directly into the mechanisms of the marketplace. Lily's rebellion, which appeals to and presupposes a transcendent moral order, is doomed for that very reason.

"A frivolous society can acquire dramatic significance only through what its frivolity destroys. Its tragic implication lies in its power of debasing people and ideas," Wharton once said about *The House of Mirth.* Such debasement and destructiveness she conveys with devastating clarity. Her difficulty arises only when she is confronted with the need to imagine an alternative to the exchange system, a positive ideal to complement her ringing critique. To do so Wharton can only invoke an absent ideal—something that it has never been Lily's privilege to experience:

> And as [Lily] looked back she saw that there had never been a time when she had had any relation to life. Her parents too had been rootless, blown hither and thither on every wind of fashion, without any personal existence to shelter them from its shifting gusts. She herself had grown up without any spot of earth being dearer to her than another: there was no centre of early pieties, of grave endearing traditions, to which her heart could revert and from which it could draw strength for itself and tenderness for

others. In whatever form a slowly-accumulated past lives in the blood—whether in the concrete image of the old house stored with visual memories, or in the conception of the house not built with hands, but made up of inherited passions and loyalties—it had the same power of broadening and deepening the individual existence, of attaching it by mysterious links of kinship to all the mighty sum of human striving.

Wharton's image of the sanctified ancestral home, like the house of custom and ceremony Yeats prays for, is a quintessentially aristocratic ideal. As metaphor and as fact, the ancestral house stands aloof, in all its feudal strength, from the contemporary world of commodities, the world of "the wares / Peddled in the thoroughfares" [W. B. Yeats, "A Prayer for My Daughter"]. It is Wharton's fantasy of a transcendent order, for an organic life based on "blood" and "root[s]" is indeed antithetical to the mechanical exchange of capitalism. Wharton's critique of the marketplace is essentially an aristocratic critique, a critique from the standpoint of "early pieties," "grave endearing traditions," and "inherited passions and loyalties." And yet, even as she articulates her ideal, she sees that it does not exist, will not exist, and indeed has never existed, either in her own experience or in Lily's. The ideal is declared impossible even as it is invoked. The ancestral home is no alternative to the commodified "house of mirth," irrevocably present and here to stay.

Still, Wharton is not quite willing to give up the idea of transcendence. She finally compromises, ingeniously if not altogether convincingly, by grafting her ideal on a lower social order, the working class. The fantasized ancestral house does appear in the book after all, if only in the modernized and modified form of a working-class tenement. And to the occupant of this humble habitation, Nettie Struther, Wharton entrusts her vision of a life antithetical to the one she condemns. It is in Nettie's kitchen that Lily catches her "first glimpse of the continuity of life." She sees in Nettie someone who seems "to have reached the central truth of existence." It is not clear how Nettie accomplishes that feat (aside from her good fortune in having found a trusting husband); nor is it clear how her haphazard life as a wage laborer can withstand the ravages of the marketplace. As an ideal, Nettie remains curiously unsubstantiated, curiously unexamined: Wharton seems to have suspended her ironic incisiveness, her withering sense of all that entraps and compromises the human spirit. She does not look more closely at Nettie, one suspects, because she cannot afford to. Wharton is not completely persuaded by the virtues of the working class, nor is she altogether sympathetic to their causes. Even though she looks instinctively to the "poor little working girl" in her search for a redemptive figure, she sees Nettie less as the representative of the working class than as the embodiment of a private ideal—Wharton's ideal. Nettie, then, is to be *from* the working class but not too militantly, not too clamorously *of* it. To be all that Wharton wants her to be, Nettie must be abstracted from the all-contaminating exchange system. She must be romanticized and, to some extent, insulated—transported, in short, from the social realm into another realm, what we might call the realm of nature, a realm Wharton metaphorically invokes. Nettie's makeshift tenement, Wharton would have us believe, has "the frail, audacious permanence of a bird's nest built on the edge of a cliff." As an organic force, a principle of tenacity and continuity, Nettie takes her place within the "permanence" of natural history, at once more primitive and (Wharton hopes) more enduring than the exchange system.

A "naturalized" working class represents Wharton's best hope for an organic life beyond the marketplace. It is the only romanticism she permits herself in the book, but even this ideal is not always easy to sustain. On a number of occasions—most particularly when Nettie expresses her innocent hope that her daughter ("Marry Anto'nette") will grow up to be just like Lily—we see the corrosive vision of the ironist subverting the "alternative" she has so painstakingly set up. The book is fueled, then, by an almost exclusively critical energy directed at the marketplace Wharton disdains. She can only confusedly gesture toward a redeeming alternative: for her, the house of mirth has no exit.

ELAINE SHOWALTER

The Death of the Lady (Novelist):
Wharton's House of Mirth

*The lady is almost the only picturesque survival in a social order
which tends less and less to tolerate the exceptional. Her history is distinct from that of woman though sometimes advancing by means of it,
as a railway may help itself from one point to another by leasing an
independent line. At all striking periods of social development her status has its significance. In the age-long war between men and women,
she is a hostage in the enemy's camp. Her fortunes do not rise and fall
with those of women but with those of men.*
       —EMILY JAMES PUTNAM, *The Lady* (1910)

Perfection is terrible, it cannot have children.
       —SYLVIA PLATH, "The Munich Mannequins"

At the beginning of Edith Wharton's first great novel, *The House of Mirth*
(1905), the heroine, Lily Bart, is twenty-nine, the dazzlingly well-preserved
veteran of eleven years in the New York marriage market. By the end of the
novel, she is past thirty and dead of an overdose of chloral. Like Edna Pontellier, Kate Chopin's heroine in *The Awakening* (1899), who celebrates her
twenty-ninth birthday by taking a lover, Lily Bart belongs to a genre we
might call "the novel of the woman of thirty," a genre that emerged appro-
priately enough in American women's literature at the turn of the century.
These novels pose the problem of female maturation in narrative terms: What
can happen to the heroine as she grows up? What plots, transformations,
and endings are imaginable for her? Is she capable of change at all? As the

From *Representations* 9 (Winter 1985). © 1985 by The Regents of the University of
California.

nineteenth-century feminist activist and novelist Elizabeth Oakes Smith
noted in her diary, "How few women have any history after the age of
thirty!"

Telling the history of women past thirty was part of the challenge Wharton faced as a writer looking to the twentieth century. The threshold of thirty
established for women by nineteenth-century conventions of "girlhood" and
marriageability continued in the twentieth century as a psychological observation about the formation of feminine identity. While Wharton's ideas about
personality were shaped by Darwinian rather than by Freudian determinants,
she shared Freud's pessimism about the difficulties of change for women. In
his essay "Femininity," for example, Freud lamented the way that women's
psyches and personalities became fixed by the time they were thirty. While
a thirty-year-old man "strikes us as a youthful, somewhat unformed individual, whom we expect to make powerful use of the possibilities for development opened up to him by analysis," Freud wrote, a woman of thirty
"often frightens us by her psychical rigidity and unchangeability. Her libido
has taken up fixed positions and seems incapable of exchanging them for
others." From Wharton's perspective Lily Bart is locked into fixed positions
that are social and economic as well as products of the libido. Her inability
to exchange these positions for others constitutes an impasse in the age as
well as the individual.

Wharton situates Lily Bart's crisis of adulthood in the contexts of a
larger historical shift. We meet her first in Grand Central Station, "in the
act of transition between one and another of the country houses that disputed
her presence at the close of the Newport season," and indeed *The House of
Mirth* is a pivotal text in the historical transition from one house of American
women's fiction to another, from the homosocial women's culture and literature of the nineteenth century to the heterosexual fiction of modernism.
Like Edna Pontellier, Lily is stranded between two worlds of female experience: the intense female friendships and mother-daughter bonds characteristic
of nineteenth-century American women's culture, which Carroll Smith-
Rosenberg has called "the female world of love and ritual," and the disso-
lution of these single-sex relationships in the interests of more intimate
friendships between women and men that was part of the gender crisis of
the turn of the century. Between 1880 and 1910, patterns of gender behavior
and relationship were being redefined. As early as the 1880s, relationships
between mothers and daughters became strained as daughters pressed for
education, work, mobility, sexual autonomy, and power outside the female
sphere. Heroines sought friendship from male classmates and companions as
well as within their single-sex communities.

These historical and social changes in women's roles had effects on women's writing as well. Pre–Civil War American women's fiction, variously described as "woman's fiction," "literary domesticity," or "the sentimental novel," celebrated female solidarity and revised patriarchal institutions, especially Christianity, in feminist and matriarchal terms. Its plots were characterized by warmth, intense sisterly feeling, and a sacramental view of motherhood. As these "bonds of womanhood," in Nancy Cott's term, were being dissolved by cultural pressures toward heterosexual relationships, women's plots changed as well. In 1851, for example, Susan Warner's best-selling novel *The Wide, Wide World* tearfully recounted the history of a girl painfully separated from her mother. But in 1882, in Warner's artistically superior but less-celebrated *Diana,* we are given an astringent and startling modern analysis of the psychological warfare between mother and daughter and the mother's fierce efforts to thwart her daughter's romance. As women's culture came under attack, so too its survivors clung desperately to the past, seeing men as the interlopers in their idyllic community. While some women writers of this generation championed the New Woman, others of the older generation grieved for the passing of the "lost Paradise" of women's culture. In their fiction, male invaders are met with hostility, and the struggle between female generations is sometimes murderous. By the century's end, as Josephine Donovan explains, "the woman-centered, matriarchal world of the Victorians is in its last throes. The preindustrial values of that world, female identified and ecologically holistic, are going down to defeat before the imperialism of masculine technology and patriarchal institutions."

The writers and feminist thinkers of Wharton's transitional generation, Elizabeth Ammons has noted, wrote "about troubled and troubling young women who were not always loved by their American readers." This literature, Ammons points out, "consistently focused on two issues: marriage and work." Seeing marriage as a form of work, a woman's job, it also raises the question of work and especially of creativity. The fiction of this transitional phase in women's history and women's writing is characterized by unhappy endings, as novelists struggled with the problem of going beyond the allowable limits and breaking through the available histories and stories for women.

Unlike some other heroines of the fiction of this transitional phase, Lily Bart is neither the educated, socially conscious, rebellious New Woman, nor the androgynous artist who finds meaning for her life in solitude and creativity, nor the old woman fiercely clinging to the past whom we so often see as the heroine of the post–Civil War local colorists. Her skills and morality are those of the Perfect Lady. In every crisis she rises magnificently to the occasion, as we see when Bertha insults her, her aunt disinherits her, Rose-dale rejects her. Lawrence Selden, the would-be New Man to whom she turns for friendship and faith, criticizes Lily for being "'perfect' to everyone"; but he demands an even further moral perfection that she can finally only satisfy by dying. Lily's uniqueness, the emphasis Wharton gives to her lonely pursuit of ladylike manners in the midst of vulgarity, boorishness, and malice, makes us feel that she is somehow the *last* lady in New York, what Louis Auchin-closs calls the "lone and solitary" survivor of a bygone age.

I would argue, however, that Wharton refuses to sentimentalize Lily's position but rather, through associating it with her own limitations as the Perfect Lady Novelist, makes us aware of the cramped possibilities of the lady whose creative roles are defined and controlled by men. Lily's plight has a parallel in Wharton's career as the elegant scribe of upper-class New York society, the novelist of manners and decor. Cynthia Griffin Wolff calls *The House of Mirth* Wharton's "first Kunstlerroman," and in important ways, I would agree, Wharton's *House of Mirth* is also a fictional house of birth for the woman artist. Wolff points out that *The House of Mirth* is both a critique of the artistic representation of women—the transformation of women into beautiful objects of male aesthetic appreciation—and a satiric analysis of the artistic traditions that "had evolved no conventions designed to render a woman as the maker of beauty, no language of feminine growth and mastery." In her powerful analysis of Lily Bart's disintegration, Wharton "could turn her fury upon a world which had enjoined women to spend their artistic inclinations entirely upon a display of self. Not the woman as productive artist, but the woman as self-creating artistic object—that is the significance of the brilliant and complex characterization of Lily Bart." In deciding that a Lily cannot survive, that the lady must die to make way for the modern woman who will work, love, and give birth, Wharton was also signaling her own rebirth as the artist who would describe the sensual worlds of *The Reef, Summer,* and *The Age of Innocence* and who would create the language of feminine growth and mastery in her own work.

We are repeatedly reminded of the absence of this language in the world of *The House of Mirth* by Lily's ladylike self-silencing, her inability to rise above the "word-play and evasion" that restrict her conversations with Sel-den and to tell her own story. Lily's inability to speak for herself is a muteness that Wharton associated with her own social background, a decorum of self-restraint she had to overcome in order to become a novelist. In one sense, Lily's search for a suitable husband is an effort to be "spoken for," to be suitably articulated and defined in the social arena. Instead, she has the opposite fate: she is "spoken of" by men, and as Lily herself observes, "The truth about any girl is that once she's talked about, she's done for, and the more she explains her case the worse it looks." To become the object of male discourse is almost as bad as to become the victim of male lust; "It was horrible of a young girl to let herself be talked about," Mrs. Peniston reflects in agitation. "However unfounded the charges against her, she must be to blame for their having been made."

Whenever Lily defies routine, the male scandalmongers are there to re- cycle her for their own profit. After the *tableaux vivants,* her performance and her relationship with Gus Trenor are so racily described in *Town Talk* that Jack Stepney is perturbed, although the elderly rake Ned Van Alstyne, "stroking his mustache to hide the smile behind it," comments that he had "heard the stories before." When Bertha Dorset announces that Lily is not returning to the yacht, the scene is witnessed by Dabham, the society col- umnist of "Riviera Notes," whose "little eyes," Selden fears, "were like tentacles thrown out to catch the floating intimations with which . . . the air at moments seemed thick." These men can rewrite the story of Lily's life, as they can also enjoy the spectacle of her beauty and suffering.

Although Lily has a "passionate desire" to tell the truth about herself to Selden, she can only hint, can only speak in parables he is totally unable to comprehend. Even the body language of her tears, her emaciation, and her renunciatory gestures are lost on him. On her deathbed, as she is drifting into unconsciousness, Lily is still struggling with the effort to speak: "She said to herself that there was something she must tell Selden, some word she had found that should make life clear between them. She tried to repeat the word, which lingered vague and luminous on the far edge of thought. . . . If she could only remember it and say it to him, she felt that everything would be well." Yet she dies with this word of self-definition on her lips, not the bride of a loving communication, but rather the still unravished bride of quietness. After her death, Selden kneels and bends over her dead body on the bed, like Dracula or little Dabham, "draining their last moment to its lees" (as he has earlier led Gerty on, "draining her inmost thoughts"), "and in the silence there passed between them the word which made all clear." This word, Susan Gubar argues, "is Lily's dead body; for she is now con- verted completely into a script for his edification, a text not unlike the letters and checks she has left behind to vindicate her life. . . . Lily's history, then, illustrates the terrors not of the word made flesh, but of the flesh made word. In this respect, she illuminates the problems Wharton must have faced in her own efforts to create rather than be created."

Among the issues the novel raises is the question of writing itself, both in terms of female creativity and in terms of a relationship to literary traditions. Whereas mid-nineteenth-century American women writers, unlike their English and European counterparts, had explicitly and in their writing styles rejected a male literary tradition that seemed totally alien to their culture, Wharton's generation of women writers, who defined themselves as artists, were working out their relationship to both the male and female literary heritage.)*The House of Mirth* revises both male and female precursors, as Wharton explores not only the changing worlds of women, but also the transformed and equally limiting worlds of men. In a number of striking respects, *The House of Mirth* goes back to adapt the characteristic plot of mid-nineteenth-century "woman's fiction" and to render it ironic by situating it in the post-matriarchal city of sexual commerce. This plot, as Nina Baym has established, concerned "a young girl who is deprived of the supports she had rightly or wrongly depended on to sustain her throughout life and is faced with the necessity of winning her own way in the world." Despite hardships and trials, the heroine overcomes all obstacles through her "intelligence, will, resourcefulness, and courage." Although she marries, as an indication that her progress toward female maturity has been completed, marriage is not really the goal of this heroine's ordeal, and men are less important to her emotional life than women.

Lily Bart's story alludes to but subverts these sentimental conventions of nineteenth-century women's literature, conventions that dozens of female bestsellers had made familiar. Lily has certainly been deprived of the financial and emotional supports she has been raised to expect and has been even more seriously deprived of the environment for the skills in which she has been trained. First of all, Wharton puts the question of youth itself into question. At twenty-nine, Lily sees eligible "girlhood" slipping into spinsterhood and faces the impending destruction of her beauty by the physical encroachments of adulthood—not simply the aging process, but also anxiety, sexuality, and serious work. Secondly, in contrast to the emotionally intense relationships between mothers, daughters, sisters, and friends in most nineteenth-century women's writing, women's relationships in *The House of Mirth* are distant, formal, competitive, even hostile. Selden deplores "the cruelty of women to their kind." Lily feels no loving ties to the women around her; in her moment of crisis "she had no heart to lean on." Her mother is dead and unmourned; "Her relation with her aunt was as superficial as that of chance lodgers who pass on the stairs." Her treatment of her cousin Grace Stepney is insensitive and distant, and Grace is bitterly jealous of her success. Lily sees and treats other women as her allies, rivals, or inferiors in the social competition; she is no different from the "best friends" she describes to Selden as those women who "use me or abuse me; but . . . don't care a straw what happens to me."

Whereas childbirth and maternity are the emotional and spiritual centers of the nineteenth-century female world, in *The House of Mirth* they have been banished to the margins. Childbirth seems to be one of the dingier attributes of the working class; the Perfect Lady cannot mar her body or betray her sexuality in giving birth. There are scarcely any children occupying the Fifth Avenue mansions and country cottages of Lily's friends. (Judy and Gus Trenor have two teenaged daughters, briefly glimpsed, but not in their mother's company. Judy refers to them only once as having to be sent out of the room because of a guest's spicy stories.)

And whereas the heroine of women's fiction triumphs in every crisis, confounds her enemies and wins over curmudgeons and reforms rakes, Lily is continually defeated. The aunt who should come to her rescue disinherits her; Bertha Dorset, the woman friend who should shelter her, throws her out in order to protect her own reputation; the man who should have faith in her cannot trust her long enough to overcome his own emotional fastidiousness. With stark fatalism rather than with the optimism of woman's fiction Wharton takes Lily from the heights to her death. As Edmund Wilson first noted in his 1937 essay "Justice to Edith Wharton," Wharton "was much haunted by the myth of the Eumenides; and she had developed her own deadly version of the working of the Aeschylean necessity. . . . She was as pessimistic as Hardy or Maupassant." Indeed, Lily's relentless fall suggests the motto of Hardy's *Tess of the D'Urbervilles*: "The Woman Pays." Despite being poor, in debt, disinherited, an outsider in a world of financiers and market manipulators, speculators and collectors, Lily is the one who must pay again and again for each moment of inattention, self-indulgence, or rebellion. "Why must a girl pay so dearly for her least escape from routine?" she thinks after her ill-timed meeting with Rosedale outside Selden's apartment. But while Tess pays with her life for a real fall, Lily pays only for the appearance of one, for her inability to explain or defend herself.

In other respects, many details of the novel allude to an American female literary tradition. As Cynthia Griffin Wolff has shown, the name "Lily" referred to a central motif of art nouveau: the representation of female purity as lilies adapted from Japanese art themes, "Easter lilies, tiger lilies, water lilies, liquescent calla lilies, fluttering clusters of lily-of-the-valley." It was also a name with a special history in nineteenth-century women's writing. Amelia Bloomer's temperance and women's rights journal of the 1850s was called *The Lily,* to represent, as the first issue announced, "sweetness and purity."

In women's local-color fiction, "Lily" was a recurring name for sexually attractive and adventurous younger women, as opposed to women of the older generation more bound to sisterly and communal relationships. In Mary Wilkins Freeman's most famous story, "A New England Nun," Lily Dyer is the blooming girl to whom the cloistered Louisa Ellis thankfully yields her red-faced suitor. In Freeman's later "Old Woman Magoun," "Lily" represents the feminine spirit of the new century, a sexuality terrifying to the old women who guard the female sanctuaries of the past. In this stark and terrifying story, Old Woman Magoun has managed to keep her pretty fourteen-year-old granddaughter, Lily, a child within a strictly female community; but when it becomes clear that she will lose the orphaned girl both to adolescence and to the predatory sexuality of the male world, the grandmother poisons her.

Furthermore, Wharton's pairing of Lily Bart with her nemesis, Bertha Dorset, echoes the pairing of Berthas and Lilys in an earlier feminist text: Elizabeth Oakes Smith's *Bertha and Lily* (1854). Oakes Smith's novel describes the relationship of a mother (Bertha) and her illegitimate daughter (Lily). While the erring Bertha's life has been painful and limited, Lily's future is presented as radiantly hopeful: "She will be an artist, an orator, a ruler . . . just as her faculties impel." Lily seems to represent the possibilities of the creative buried self Oakes Smith felt in her own stifled career.

Constance Cary Harrison's *The Anglomaniacs* (1890), a successful novel of the *fin de siècle* set in the same upper-class New York milieu as *The House of Mirth,* also has a heroine named Lily, a young heiress who is presumed to marry a titled Englishman she does not love in order to satisfy her mother's social ambitions. Like Lily Bart, Lily Floyd-Curtis has the graceful figure of a "wood-nymph," socializes with a sensitive bachelor friend who lives "in the Benedick with his violincello," and attends a charity ball where the dinner table is set to represent a Veronese painting and she herself is dressed as a Venetian princess.

Wharton is ironically aware of the way that Lily Bart becomes the object of male myths and fantasies, like that of the wood nymph, that must be revised from the woman's perspective. Selden insists on seeing her as a "captured dryad subdued to the conventions of the drawing-room," yet the image of the dryad is as much one of these drawing-room conventions as that of the woman of fashion. Indeed, Lily, as Wharton tells us, "had no real intimacy with nature, but she had a passion for the appropriate." For her role in the *tableaux vivants,* Lily chooses to represent the figure of Sir Joshua Reynolds's *Mrs. Lloyd,* in a draped gown that revealed "long dryad-like curves that swept upwards from her poised foot to her lifted arm." Selden is enraptured by her performance, finding the authentic Lily in the scene; but it is rather the carefully constructed Lily of his desire that he sees. The "streak of sylvan freedom" he perceives in her is rather what he would make of her, and we are reminded that Ezra Pound at this same period was imposing the title "Dryad" on the equally plastic H. D.

The myth of Tarpeia was another case of differing male and female interpretations. Simon Rosedale tells it in garbled form to Lily when he comes to propose to her: "There was a girl in some history book who wanted gold shields or something, and the fellows threw 'em at her, and she was crushed under 'em; they killed her." Tarpeia, the Roman who betrayed her city to the Sabines by opening the Capitoline citadel in exchange for gold bracelets and was crushed by the shields of the invading Sabine army, was also the subject of Louise Guiney's well-known poem of the 1890s that dramatized the paradox of a woman's being condemned by her society for the mercenary and narcissistic values it has encouraged.

Wharton's major revision of a male text, as those critics not obsessed with her alleged apprenticeship to Henry James have noted, was with relation to Oscar Wilde's *Picture of Dorian Gray* (1890). Lily's picture is in one sense her mirror, but it is more fully her realization of the ways in which her society has deformed her. In contrast to Dorian Gray's portrait, Lily's monster in the mirror is not one whose perfect complexion has been marred by lines of worry, shame, or guilt, but rather a woman with a "hard, brilliant" surface. In the aftershock of her encounter with Gus Trenor in his empty house, Lily recognizes "two selves in her, the one she had always known, and a new abhorrent being to which it found itself chained." As she tells Gerty, this self seems like a "disfigurement," a "hideous change" that has come to her while she slept; a moral ugliness that she cannot bear to contemplate.

Some feminist critics have argued that this "stranger" in Lily, this second and abhorrent self, is the female personality produced by a patriarchal society and a capitalist economy. As Elizabeth Ammons notes, "the system is designed to keep women in divisive and relentless competition" for the money and favor controlled by men. "Forbidden to aggress on each other directly, or aggress on men at all, women prey on each other—stealing reputations, opportunities, male admirers—all to parlay or retain status and financial security in a world arranged by men to keep women suppliant and therefore subordinate." Women employ, exploit, and cheat each other as cold-bloodedly as their Wall Street husbands carry out deals, but "by nature" women "feel no necessity to harm each other."

Yet the nature of both men and women is in question in the novel rather than given. It is often overlooked that Wharton develops a full cast of male characters in *The House of Mirth,* whose dilemmas parallel those of the women. As historians now recognize, the period 1880–1920 redefined gender identity for American men as well as for American women. Among the characteristics of progressivism and of the masculinity crisis was the increased specialization of men as workers marginal to the family and culture: "According to the capitalistic ethos, men were expected to promote industry and commerce, which they did in abundance, often spending long hours at the office, the plant, or in the fields and forests. With their energies spent, they came home too weary and worn to devote much time and interest to family or friends."

Wharton's critique of the marriage system is not limited to the economic dependency of women but also extends to consider the loneliness, dehumanization, and anxiety of men. Lily's father, a shadowy figure in the prehistory of the novel, establishes the theme of the marginal man. This "neutral-tinted father, who filled an intermediate space between the butler and the man who came to wind the clocks," is a dim and pathetic fixture of Lily's scant childhood memories. "Effaced and silent," patient and stooping, he is an exhausted witness to the stresses his society places on men. Even on vacation at Newport or Southampton, "it seemed to tire him to rest, and he would sit for hours staring at the sea-line from a quiet corner of the verandah, while the clatter of his wife's existence went on unheeded a few feet off." Mr. Bart does not so much die as get discarded; to his wife, once he had lost his fortune "he had become extinct," and she sits at his deathbed "with the provisional air of a traveller who waits for a belated train to start." Unable to love her father, to feel more for him than a frightened pity, or to mourn him, Lily nonetheless comes to identify with him in her own trial, recalling his sleepless nights in the midst of her own and feeling suddenly "how he must have suffered, lying alone with his thoughts."

The story of Mr. Bart, who in his enigmatic solitude and marginality here strongly resembles Mr. Bartleby, lingers in our consciousness as we read *The House of Mirth,* coloring our impression of even the crudest male characters. If Gus Trenor is beefy and stupid, he is nonetheless repeatedly used by the women in the book, and there is some justice in the words, if not the tone, of his complaint to Lily: "I didn't begin this business—kept out of the way, and left the track clear for the other chaps, till you rummaged me out and set to work to make an ass of me—and an easy job you had of it, too." To Lily, we have seen earlier, Trenor is merely "a coarse dull man . . . a mere supernumerary in the costly show for which his money paid; surely, to a clever girl, it would be easy to hold him by his vanity, and so keep the obligation on his side." Lily repays her financial debt to Trenor, but never her human one.

If women in this system harm each other, they also do an extraordinary amount of harm to men. It's hard not to feel a sympathy for shy Percy Gryce when Lily sets out to appeal to his vanity and thus to make an ass of *him*: "She resolved so to identify herself with her husband's vanity that to gratify her wishes would be to him the most exquisite form of self-indulgence." Despite the loss to Lily, we must feel that Gryce is better off with even the "youngest, dumpiest, dullest" of the Van Osburgh daughters.

Edmund Wilson described the typical masculine figure in Edith Wharton's fiction between 1905 and 1920 as "a man set apart from his neighbours by education, intellect, and feeling, but lacking the force or the courage either to impose himself or to get away." Selden is obviously such a figure, a man who seems initially to be much freer than Lily but who is revealed to be even more inflexible. His failed effort to define himself as the New Man parallels Lily's futile effort to become a New Woman; "In a different way," as Wharton points out, "he was, as much as Lily, the victim of his environment." Selden's limitations are perhaps those of the New Man in every period of gender crisis. Cautious about making a commitment, successful and energetic in his law practice, fond of travel, taking enormous pleasure in his Manhattan apartment with its "pleasantly faded Turkey rug," its carefully chosen collectibles, and its opportunities for intimate entertaining, Selden lacks only jogging shoes and a copy of *The Color Purple* on his coffee table to fit into the culture of the 1980s.

Real change, Wharton shows us in the novel, must come from outside the dominant class-structures. Thus the figure of Simon Rosedale, the Jewish financier making it big on Wall Street, takes on increasing importance as the novel develops. He plays one of the main roles in the triangle with Lily and Selden, and while Selden asserts too late that he has faith in Lily, Rosedale demonstrates his faith by coming to see her in her dingy exile and by offering her money to start again. Rosedale's style is certainly not that of the Perfect Gentleman, and even to the last Lily's ladyhood cannot quite accept him: "Little by little, circumstances were breaking down her dislike for Rosedale. The dislike, indeed, still subsisted; but it was penetrated here and there by the perception of mitigating qualities in him: of a certain gross kindliness, a rather helpless fidelity of sentiment, which seemed to be struggling through the surface of his material ambitions." In order to break out of the social cage, Lily must make compromises with elegance, compromises that ultimately are beyond her scope. But Rosedale, the only man in the novel who likes children (we see him through Lily's eyes "kneeling domestically on the drawing room hearth" with Carry Fisher's little girl, offers the hope of continuity, rootedness, and relatedness that Lily finally comes to see as the central meaning of life.

Lily's changing perceptions of Rosedale are a parallel to the most radical theme in the novel: her growing awareness and finally her merger with a community of working women. With each step downward, each removal to a smaller room, Lily's life becomes more enmeshed with this community, and she sees it in more positive terms. We see her first as an exceptional figure, silhouetted against a backdrop of anonymous female drones in Grand Central Station, "sallow-faced girls in preposterous hats and flat-chested women struggling with paper bundles and palm-leaf fans." For the observant Selden, the contrast to "the herd" only brings out Lily's high gloss: "The dinginess, the crudity of this average section of womanhood made him feel how specialized she was."

The crudest of these women is the charwoman, Mrs. Haffen, whose appearance frames the first part of the novel as that of the typist Nettie Struther frames the end. Leaving Selden's apartment, Lily encounters this woman scrubbing the stairs, stout, with "clenched red fists . . . a broad, sallow face, slightly pitted with smallpox, and the straw-coloured hair through which her scalp shone unpleasantly." In her hardness, ugliness, poverty, and age, Mrs. Haffen is the monstrous specter of everything Lily most dreads, the very heart of dinginess. Trying to make money out of Bertha Dorset's love letters, she also embodies the moral corruption Lily has come to fear in herself, the willingness to sacrifice all sense of value to the need to survive.

Lily's gradual and painful realization that her status as a lady does not exempt her from the sufferings of womanhood is conveyed through her perceptions of her own body as its exquisite ornamentality begins to decline. Her luxuriant hair begins to thin, as Carry Fisher notices; her radiant complexion too will become "dull and colourless" in the millinery workshop. In the beginning, she is one of the lilies of the field, who neither toils nor spins, nor, certainly, scrubs; her hands are not the "clenched red fists" of anger, labor, rebellion, but art objects "polished as a bit of old ivory." Yet in her confrontation with Gus Trenor, Lily is suddenly aware that these lovely hands are also "helpless" and "useless." Lily has had fantasies of her hands as creative and artistic, dreaming of a fashionable shop in which "subordinate fingers, blunt, grey, needle-pricked fingers" would do all the hard work, while her delicate fingers added the distinctive finishing touch. In reality, she learns, her "untutored fingers" are blundering and clumsy; like the hands of the working women, her hands too have "been formed from childhood for their special work," the work of decoration and display, and they can never compete in the workaday world. When Selden sees her for the last time in his apartment, noting "how thin her hands looked" against the fire, it is as if they are fading and disappearing, vestigial appendages useless to her solitary existence.

At the center of Lily's awakening to her kinship with other women is Gerty Farish's Working Girls' Club. Gerty works with a charitable association trying "to provide comfortable lodgings, with a reading-room and other modest distractions, where young women of the class employed in downtown offices might find a home when out of work, or in need of a rest." Visiting this club as Lady Bountiful, Lily nonetheless makes the first imaginative identification between herself and the working girls, "young girls, like herself, some perhaps pretty, some not without a trace of her finer sensibilities. She pictured herself leading such a life as theirs—a life in which achievement seemed as squalid as failure—and the vision made her shudder sympathetically."

Yet when she "joins the working classes," Lily also sees "the fragmentary and distorted image of the world she had lived in, reflected in the mirror of the working-girls' minds." They idealize the society women whose hats they trim. Lily Bart herself has become a kind of romantic heroine for Nettie Struther, the working girl she meets in Bryant Park on her return from Selden's apartment. Nettie has followed Lily's social career in the newspapers, reading about her dresses, thinking of her as "being so high up, where everything was just grand." She has named her baby daughter "Marry Ant'nette" because an actress playing the queen reminded her of Lily. Their encounter is the strongest moment of female kinship in the novel, as Lily also sees herself mirrored in Nettie and her baby, and recognizes that Nettie's achievement is far beyond any she has previously conceived for herself.

Nettie is a typist who has had an unhappy affair with a man from a higher social class, a man who promised to marry her but deserted her. (Margaret B. McDowell, one of Wharton's critics, leaps to the false conclusion that Nettie has been a prostitute.) Although Nettie felt that her life was over, she was given the chance to begin again by a man who had known her from childhood, knew that she had been seduced, and loved her enough to marry her anyway. There is even an ambiguity about the paternity of the child; Nettie may have been pregnant when George married her. This testament of male faith and female courage stands in sharp contrast to Selden's caution and Lily's despair.

The scene between the two women is unique in *The House of Mirth* for its intimacy and openness (Lily too tells Nettie that she is unhappy and in

trouble), for its setting in the warm kitchen (the ritual center of much nineteenth-century woman's fiction), for the presence of the baby, and for its
acknowledgment of physical needs. In holding Nettie's baby, the untouchable
Lily gives in at last to her longing for touch. Holding the baby, she is also
being held, expressing her own hunger for physical bonding: "As she continued to hold it the weight increased, sinking deeper, and penetrating her
with a strange sense of weakness, as though the child entered into her and
became a part of herself."

Some feminist critics, however, have tended to see the images of the
mother and child in this scene, and in Lily's deathbed hallucination of holding
the infant, as sentimental and regressive. Patricia Meyer Spacks, for example,
criticizes Lily's "escapist fantasy of motherhood." Cynthia Griffin Wolff
maintains that the scene with Nettie "gives poignant evidence of Lily's inability to conceive of herself in any other way than as the object of aesthetic
attention," that she is once again self-consciously arranging herself in a
tableau vivant for Nettie's admiration. Wolff also argues that in her death
Lily is relinquishing her "difficult pretenses to adulthood." Thus in Wolff's
view the extraordinary passage in which Lily, as she is succumbing to the
drug, feels "Nettie Struther's child . . . lying on her arm . . . felt the pressure
of its little head against her shoulder" is a sign of Lily's own retreat into the
safety of infantilization.

It seems to me, however, that this hallucination speaks rather for Lily's
awakened sense of loving solidarity and community, for the vision she has
had of Nettie's life as representing "the central truth of existence." That
Nettie should be the last person to see Lily alive and that Gerty should be
the first to discover her death suggests that Lily's death is an acknowledgment
of their greater strength. Doing justice to Lily Bart requires that we see how
far she has come even in her death. Unlike the infantilized Edna Pontellier,
who never awakens to the dimensions of her social world, who never sees
how the labor of the mulatto and black women around her makes her narcissistic existence possible, Lily is a genuinely awakened woman, who fully
recognizes her own position in the community of women workers. Whereas
Edna's awakening is early, easy, incomplete, and brings a warm liquid sense
of satisfaction, Lily's enlightenment is gradual and agonizing: "It was as
though a great blaze of electric light had been turned on in her head. . . .
She had not imagined that such a multiplication of wakefulness was possible;
her whole past was re-enacting itself at a hundred different points of consciousness." Although her awakening proves unendurable, she really tries to
overcome rejection, failure, and the knowledge of her own shortcomings.
The House of Mirth ends not only with a death, but with the vision of a

new world of female solidarity, a world in which women like Gerty Farish and Nettie Struther will struggle hopefully and courageously. Lily dies—the lady dies—so that these women may live and grow. As Elizabeth Ammons observes, "In the arms of the ornamental, leisure-class Lily lies the working-class infant female, whose vitality succors the dying woman. In that union of the leisure and working classes lies a new hope—the New Woman that Wharton would bring to mature life in her next novel."

For Edith Wharton as novelist, then, *The House of Mirth* also marked a transition to a new kind of fiction. Like Lily Bart, Wharton had retreated from touch, from community, from awakenings to her own sexuality and anger. While the standard pattern for nineteenth-century American women writers was a strong allegiance to the maternal line and the female community, Wharton belonged to the more troubled and more gifted countertradition of women writers who were torn between the literary world of their fathers and the wordless sensual world of their mothers. These two lines of inheritance are generally represented in the literary history of American women writers by the spatial images of the father's library and the mother's garden. Like Margaret Fuller, Edith Wharton felt that "the kingdom of her father's library" was the intellectual center of her development. But unlike Fuller, she did not have the childhood alternative of her mother's garden— a space of sensuality, warmth, and openness. Instead Lucretia Wharton was a chilly woman who censored her daughter's reading, denied her writing paper (as a child Wharton was "driven to begging for the wrappings of the parcels delivered to the house"), withheld physical affection, and met her literary efforts with "icy disapproval."

Nonetheless in her literary memoir, *A Backward Glance,* Wharton called her writing a "secret garden," echoing the title of Frances Hodgson Burnett's popular novel for girls. The connection with maternal space (in Burnett's novel it is the dead mother's garden, lost and overgrown) may have come from her sense of writing as a forbidden joy. From childhood Wharton was possessed with what she called the "ecstasy" of "making up," almost a form of illicit sexual indulgence: "The call came regularly and imperiously and . . . I would struggle against it conscientiously."

The House of Mirth marks the point at which Wharton found herself able to give in to her creative jouissance, to assert her creative power as a woman artist, and to merge the male and female sides of her lineage into a mature fiction that could deal seriously with the sexual relationships of men and women in a modern society. Writing *The House of Mirth* had important professional, literary, and psychological consequences for Wharton's career, and it is clear that she herself thought of it as a turning point in her life as a writer. In her autobiography, Wharton described the process of writing *The House of Mirth* as a serial for *Scribner's Magazine* as one that taught her the work of writing, that transformed her "from a drifting amateur into a professional." Because she had agreed to complete the book within five months, Wharton was forced to exchange the leisurely rhythms of the lady novelist's routine, with its manifold "distractions of a busy and hospitable life, full of friends and travel, reading and gardening" for the "discipline of the daily task." The necessity for "systematic daily effort" also redefined and excused the pleasures of "making up" as part of her process of gaining "mastery over my tools."

Under the pressures of the deadline, Wharton also made tough choices about her narrative, choices that reflected her own transition to a more serious artistic professionalism, craftsmanship, and control. In choosing to have Lily die, Wharton was judging and rejecting the infantile aspects of her own self, the part that lacked confidence as a working writer, that longed for the escapism of the lady's world and feared the sexual consequences of creating rather than becoming art. Secondly, Wharton mastered her emotional conflicts as material for art, learning through the process that anger and other strong emotions, including sexual desire, could be safely expressed. The death of the lady is thus also the death of the lady novelist, the dutiful daughter who struggles to subdue her most powerful imaginative impulses. If Lily Bart, unable to change, gives way to the presence of a new generation of women, Edith Wharton survives the crisis of maturation at the turn of the century and becomes one of our American precursors of a literary history of female mastery and growth.

Chronology

1862   Edith Jones born in New York City on January 24 to George Jones and Lucretia Rhinelander Jones. She is the third of three children.

1866–72   Goes to Europe with her parents. Learns French, German, and Italian.

1876–77   Writes *Fast and Loose,* her first, unpublished novella.

1878   Lucretia Jones arranges a private printing of Edith's *Verses* (juvenilia).

1880–82   Trip to Europe with her parents. Death of her father in the south of France.

1885   Edith Jones marries Edward Wharton. From then on, she and her husband spend half the year in Europe, mainly in Italy, France, and England.

1890   Wharton publishes "Mrs. Manstey's View," her first short story.

1894–96   Wharton suffers a nervous breakdown, the first symptoms of which appeared in 1890.

1897–1900   Beginning of friendship with Walter Berry, whom she first met in 1883. Wharton publishes *The Decoration of Houses,* written in collaboration with Ogden Codman, Jr., as well as *The Greater Inclination,* her first collection of short stories, and *The Touchstone,* a novella.

1901–2   Wharton builds The Mount, which will be her home in the U.S. until its sale in 1911. She publishes *Crucial Instances,* a collection of short stories, and *The Valley of Decision,* her first novel. She translates *Es Lebe das Leben,* a play by Hermann Sudermann.

1903   Wharton meets Henry James. She publishes *Sanctuary,* a novella.

1904   Wharton publishes *The Descent of Man,* a collection of short stories, and *Italian Villas and Their Gardens.*

1905   Wharton publishes *Italian Backgrounds* and *The House of Mirth.*

1907   Wharton establishes her second home in Paris: she rents the Vanderbilt apartment at 58, rue de Varennes, in the heart of the Faubourg St-Germain. She motors through France with Henry James; publishes *The Fruit of the Tree,* a novel, and *Mme. de Treymes,* a novella.

1907–10   Affair with Morton Fullerton.

1908   Wharton publishes *A Motor-Flight through France.* Beginning of friendship with Henry Adams.

1909   Wharton moves to 53, rue de Varennes. Publishes *Artemis to Acteon and Other Verse.* Beginning of friendship with Bernard Berenson.

1910–12   Wharton publishes *Tales of Men and Ghosts,* a collection of short stories, *Ethan Frome,* and *The Reef.*

1913   Wharton divorces her husband. Publication of *The Custom of the Country.*

1914–18   Wharton does refugee work for which she will be made Chevalier of the Legion of Honor (1916). Visits the front lines and writes articles which are then collected as *Fighting France, from Dunkerque to Belfort.* Edits *The Book of the Homeless,* compiled for the benefit of the war relief. Travels to Algeria, Tunisia, and Morocco. Publishes *Xingu and Other Stories, Summer,* and *The Marne.* Beginning of friendship with André Gide.

1919   Wharton acquires two residences: Pavillon Colombe, near Paris, and Sainte-Claire, in the south of France. She publishes *French Ways and Their Meanings.*

1920   Wharton publishes *The Age of Innocence*, for which she receives the Pulitzer Prize. She also publishes *In Morocco*, travel sketches.

1921–23   Beginning of friendship with Paul Valéry. She publishes *The Glimpses of the Moon* and *A Son at the Front*, two novels. Wharton receives Doctor of Letters honorary degree from Yale University.

1924–26   Wharton publishes *Old New York*, a collection of four novellas; *The Mother's Recompense*, a novel; *The Writing of Fiction*; and *Here and Beyond*, a collection of short stories. She is elected to the National Institute of Arts and Letters.

1927–33   Wharton publishes four novels: *Twilight Sleep*, *The Children*, *Hudson River Bracketed*, and *The Gods Arrive*; and two collections of short stories: *Certain People* and *Human Nature*.

1934   Wharton publishes *A Backward Glance*, an autobiography.

1936   Publication of *The World Over*, a collection of short stories.

1937   Publishes *Ghosts*, a collection of short stories. Edith Wharton dies at Pavillon Colombe on August 11.

1938   Posthumous publication of *The Buccaneers*, her last, unfinished novel.

Contributors

HAROLD BLOOM, Sterling Professor of the Humanities at Yale University, is the author of *The Anxiety of Influence, Poetry and Repression,* and many other volumes of literary criticism. His forthcoming study, *Freud: Transference and Authority,* attempts a full-scale reading of all of Freud's major writings. A MacArthur Prize Fellow, he is general editor of five series of literary criticism published by Chelsea House.

R. W. B. LEWIS is Professor of English and American Studies at Yale University. His books include *The American Adam, The Poetry of Hart Crane,* and *Edith Wharton: A Biography,* for which he won a Pulitzer Prize. He is the editor and author of critical essays on writers such as Melville, Hawthorne, and Whitman.

RICHARD H. LAWSON is Professor of German Literature at the University of North Carolina, Chapel Hill. He is the author of *Edith Wharton and German Literature* and *Günter Grass.*

ELIZABETH AMMONS is Professor of English Literature at Tufts University. She is the editor of *Critical Essays on Harriet Beecher Stowe* and the author of *Edith Wharton's Argument with America.*

MARGARET B. McDOWELL is Professor of Rhetoric and Women's Studies at the University of Iowa. She is the author of *Carson McCullers* and *Edith Wharton.*

CYNTHIA GRIFFIN WOLFF is Professor of English and American Literature at M.I.T. She is the editor of *Classic American Women Writers* and the author of *Samuel Richardson and the Eighteenth Century Puritan Character* and *A Feast of Words: The Triumph of Edith Wharton.*

ALLAN GARDNER SMITH is Professor of American Literature at the University of East Anglia, England. He is the author of numerous essays on American writers, and his recent work includes "Edgar Allan Poe, the Will, and Horror Fiction" and "Stephen Crane, Impressionism, and William James."

JUDITH FRYER is Professor of English at Miami University, Oxford, Ohio. Her books include *The Faces of Eve: Women in the Nineteenth-Century American Novel.*

CAROL WERSHOVEN is Assistant Professor of English at Palm Beach Junior College of Boca Raton, Florida. She is the author of *The Female Intruder in the Novels of Edith Wharton.*

WAI-CHEE DIMOCK is Assistant Professor of English at Rutgers University and the author of critical essays on Melville.

ELAINE SHOWALTER is Professor of English at Princeton University. She is the author of *A Literature of Their Own: British Women Novelists from Brontë to Lessing,* and numerous essays of feminist criticism. She is the editor of *These Modern Women: Autobiographical Essays from the Twenties.*

Bibliography

Ammons, Elizabeth. "The Business of Marriage in Edith Wharton's *Custom of the Country.*" *Criticism* 16 (1974): 326–38.

———. "Cool Diana and the Blood-Red Muse: Edith Wharton on Innocence and Art." In *American Novelists Revisited: Essays in Feminist Criticism,* edited by Fritz Fleischmann, 209–24. Boston: G. K. Hall, 1982.

———. *Edith Wharton's Argument with America.* Athens: University of Georgia Press, 1980.

Auchincloss, Louis. *Edith Wharton: A Woman in Her Time.* New York: Viking Press, 1971.

Beach, Joseph Warren. *The Twentieth-Century Novel: Studies in Technique.* New York: Century Company, 1932.

Bell, Millicent. *Edith Wharton and Henry James: The Story of Their Friendship.* New York: George Braziller, 1965.

Bloom, Lynne G. Ethan Frome: *A Critical Commentary.* New York: American R. D. M. Corporation, 1964.

Coolidge, Olivia. *Edith Wharton: 1862–1937.* New York: Charles Scribner's Sons, 1965.

Crowley, John W. "The Unmastered Streak: Feminist Themes in Wharton's *Summer.*" *American Literary Realism* 15 (1982): 86–96.

Cuddy, Lois A. "Triangles of Defeat and Liberation: The Quest for Power in Edith Wharton's Fiction." *Perspectives in Contemporary Literature* 8 (1982): 18–26.

Eggenschwiler, David. "The Ordered Disorder of *Ethan Frome.*" *Studies in the Novel* 9 (1977): 237–46.

Fetterley, Judith. "The Temptation to Be a Beautiful Object: Double Standard and Double Bind in *The House of Mirth.*" *Studies in American Fiction* 5 (1977): 199–211.

Funston, Judith E. " 'Xingu': Edith Wharton's Velvet Gauntlet." *Studies in American Fiction* 12 (1984): 227–34.

Gargano, James W. "Edith Wharton's *The Reef:* The Genteel Woman's Quest for Knowledge." *Novel* 10 (1976): 40–48.

Gimbel, Wendy. *Edith Wharton: Orphancy and Survival.* New York: Praeger, 1984.

Howe, Irving, ed. *Edith Wharton: A Collection of Critical Essays.* Englewood Cliffs, N. J.: Prentice-Hall, 1962.

James, Henry. *Literary Criticism, Essays on Literature: American Writers, English Writers.* New York: Library of America, 1984.

Kekes, John. "The Great Guide of Human Life." *Philosophy and Literature* 8 (1984): 236–49.

Kellogg, Grace. *The Two Lives of Edith Wharton: The Woman and Her Work.* New York: Appleton-Century, 1965.

Lawson, Richard H. *Edith Wharton and German Literature.* Bonn: Bouvier Verlag Herbert Grundmann, 1974.

———. "Thematic Similarities in Edith Wharton and Thomas Mann." *Twentieth-Century Literature* 23 (1977): 289–98.

Leach, Nancy R. "Edith Wharton's Unpublished Novel." *American Literature* 25 (November 1953): 334–53.

Lewis, R. W. B. *Edith Wharton: A Biography.* New York: Harper & Row, 1975.

Lidoff, Joan. "Another Sleeping Beauty: Narcissism in *The House of Mirth.*" In *American Realism: New Essays,* edited by Eric J. Sundquist, 238–58. Baltimore: The Johns Hopkins University Press, 1980.

Lindberg, Gary H. *Edith Wharton and the Novel of Manners.* Charlottesville: University Press of Virginia, 1975.

Lubbock, Percy. *Portrait of Edith Wharton.* New York: D. Appleton-Century Company, 1947.

Lyde, Marilyn Jones. *Edith Wharton: Convention and Morality in the Work of a Novelist.* Norman: University of Oklahoma Press, 1959.

McDowell, Margaret B. *Edith Wharton.* Boston: Twayne Publishers, 1976.

Mansfield, Katherine. *Novels and Novelists.* New York: Alfred A. Knopf, 1930.

Maynard, Moira. "The Medusa's Face: A Study of Character and Behavior in the Fiction of Edith Wharton." Ph.D. diss., New York University, 1971.

Michelson, Bruce. "Edith Wharton's House Divided." *Studies in American Fiction* 12 (1984): 199–216.

Morrow, Nancy. "Games and Conflict in Edith Wharton's *The Custom of the Country.*" *American Literary Realism* 17 (1984): 32–39.

Nevius, Blake. *Edith Wharton: A Study of Her Fiction.* Berkeley: University of California Press, 1953.

Poirier, Richard. *A World Elsewhere: The Place of Style in American Literature.* New York: Oxford University Press, 1966.

Rae, Catherine M. *Edith Wharton's New York Quartet.* Foreword by R. W. B. Lewis. Lanham, Md.: University Press of America, 1984.

Rideout, Walter B. "Edith Wharton's *The House of Mirth.*" In *Twelve Original Essays on Great American Novels,* edited by Charles Shapiro, 148–76. Detroit: Wayne State University Press, 1958.

Rose, Alan Henry. "'Such Depths of Sad Initiation': Edith Wharton and New England." *New England Quarterly* 50 (1977): 423–39.

Schriber, Mary Suzanne. "Convention in the Fiction of Edith Wharton." *Studies in American Fiction* 11 (1983): 189–202.

Springer, Marlene. *Edith Wharton and Kate Chopin: A Reference Guide.* Boston: G. K. Hall, 1976.

Stein, Allen F. "Wharton's Blithedale: A New Reading of *The Fruit of the Tree.*" *American Literary Realism* 12 (1979): 330–37.

Strout, Cushing. "Complementary Portraits: James's Lady and Wharton's Age." *Hudson Review* 35 (1982): 405–15.

Tintner, Adeline R. "Jamesian Structures in *The Age of Innocence* and Related Stories." *Twentieth-Century Literature* 26 (1980): 332–47.

———. "Mothers, Daughters, and Incest in the Late Novels of Edith Wharton." In *The Lost Tradition: Mothers and Daughters in Literature,* edited by Cathy N. Davidson and E. M. Broner, 147–56. New York: Frederick Ungar Publishing Co., 1980.

Walton, Geoffrey. *Edith Wharton: A Critical Interpretation.* Rutherford, N. J.: Fairleigh Dickinson University Press, 1982.

Wershoven, Carol. "Edith Wharton's Final Vision: *The Buccaneers.*" *American Literary Realism* 15 (1982): 209–20.

———. *The Female Intruder in the Novels of Edith Wharton.* Rutherford, N. J.: Fairleigh Dickinson University Press, 1982.

Wolff, Cynthia Griffin. *A Feast of Words: The Triumph of Edith Wharton.* Oxford: Oxford University Press, 1977.

Worby, Diana Z. "The Ambiguity of Edith Wharton's 'Lurking Feminism.'" *Mid-Hudson Language Studies* 5 (1982): 81–90.

Acknowledgments

"A Writer of Short Stories" (originally entitled "Introduction") by R. W. B. Lewis from *The Collected Short Stories of Edith Wharton,* vol. 1, edited by R. W. B. Lewis, © 1968 by Charles Scribner's Sons. Reprinted by permission.

"Undine" by Richard H. Lawson from *Edith Wharton and German Literature* by Richard H. Lawson, © 1974 by Bouvier Verlag Herbert Grundmann. Reprinted by permission.

"Fairy-Tale Love and *The Reef*" by Elizabeth Ammons from *American Literature* 47, no. 4 (January 1976), © 1976 by Duke University Press. Reprinted by permission of the author and the publisher. To conform with this anthology, footnotes which appeared in the original publication have been omitted.

"*Hudson River Bracketed* and *The Gods Arrive*" by Margaret B. McDowell from *Edith Wharton* by Margaret B. McDowell, © 1976 by G. K. Hall and Co. Reprinted by permission of Twayne Publishers, a division of G. K. Hall and Co., Boston.

"*Ethan Frome:* 'This Vision of His Story'" (originally entitled "Landscapes of Desolation: The Fiction, 1889–1911") by Cynthia Griffin Wolff from *A Feast of Words: The Triumph of Edith Wharton* by Cynthia Griffin Wolff, © 1977 by Oxford University Press. Reprinted by permission.

"Edith Wharton and the Ghost Story" by Allan Gardner Smith from *Gender and Literary Voice* (Women and Literature, n.s. vol. 1), edited by Janet Todd, © 1980 by Holmes and Meier Publishers, Inc. Reprinted by permission.

"Purity and Power in *The Age of Innocence*" by Judith Fryer from *American Literary Realism 1870–1910* 17, no. 2 (Autumn 1984), © 1985 by The Department of English, The University of Texas at Arlington. Reprinted by permission.

"The Divided Conflict of Edith Wharton's *Summer*" by Carol Wershoven from *Colby Library Quarterly* 21, no. 1 (March 1985), © 1985 by Carol Wershoven. Reprinted by permission of the author.

"Debasing Exchange: Edith Wharton's *The House of Mirth*" by Wai-chee Dimock from *PMLA* 100, no. 5 (October 1985), © 1985 by The Modern Language Association of America. Reprinted by permission.

Index

Adams, Henry, 103; *The Education of Henry Adams,* 103
Aeschylus, 145
"After Holbein," 9; Anson Warley as character in, 26; Mrs. Jaspar as character in, 26; title of, 26
Age of Innocence, The, 9, 26, 142; and *The Ambassadors,* 113; and *A Backward Glance,* 101, 102; and *The Bostonians,* 113; discussed, 99–115; as a failed love story, 110, 111; and *The Golden Bough,* 106; and *The House of Mirth,* 111; individual vs. family in, 104; individual vs. society in, 103; passion in, 67; and *The Portrait of a Lady,* 100, 101; as a Pulitzer Prize-winning novel, 100; subject of, 100; as Wharton's pivotal novel, 104. *See also* Biographical Data; Elen Olenska; Newland Archer
Ahab (*Moby Dick*), 6
"All Souls," 18; discussed, 19–20, 90–91; eroticism in, 19; female suffering in, 97; and "The Looking Glass," 91–92; and masculine authority, 91; Mrs. Claymore as character in, 90–91; Sara Clayburn as character in, 19–20; sexual implications in, 90; as Wharton's last published story, 90; witchcraft in, 90, 91

Ammons, Elizabeth, vii, 39–50, 141, 153
Andrews, Wayne, 21
Anna Leath (*The Reef*), 41; and the double standard, 43; female dependency of, 44; as a Jamesian heroine, 39; and marriage, 40, 41, 42–45, 46; and romance, 40, 41, 42, 45; sexuality of, 43, 44, 47, 48; society's oppression of, 44; and Sophy Viner contrasted, 46, 48
Anthropology, cultural, 106
Artist: as portrayed in the fiction, 51, 53, 54–55, 56. *See also* Short stories: satirical
Artistic merit: in the novels, 4, 7, 39, 50, 51; in the short stories, 9–10, 11, 12, 13, 16, 17, 22, 23, 97
Art Nouveau, 145
Atlantic Monthly (periodical), 9
Austen, Jane, 11
"Autres Temps," 10–11; discussed, 16; divorce in, 12; social mores in, 16

Bahlman, Anna, 29
Balzac, Honoré de, 4; "La Grande Bretèche," 68
Bataille, Georges, 127
Beauvoir, Simone de, 49
Beinecke Library (Yale University), 67
Berenson, Bernard, 117
Berry, Walter, 12, 21–22, 23, 24

Bertha Dorset (*The House of Mirth*), 126, 127, 128, 130, 133, 134, 143, 145, 150
Bible (N.T.), 29; Luke 9:33, 30; Mark 9:15, 30; Matt. 17:4, 30
Biographical data: and *The Age of Innocence*, 101, 102, 104, 105; and *Ethan Frome*, 65, 66, 67, 87; and *The House of Mirth*, 153–54; and the short stories, 12, 20, 21, 22, 23, 24, 27–28
Bloomer, Amelia, 145
Brontë, Charlotte, *Wuthering Heights*, 70
Browning, Robert, 4; *The Ring and the Book*, 68–69
Burnett, Frances Hodgson, 153

Capitalist economy, 136, 148; alternative to, 135; and the bourgeoisie, 127; and financial transactions, 123, 124, 125, 126–27, 128, 130; in *The House of Mirth*, viii, 123–37; and justice, 125, 126, 127; and power, 122, 125–26; reductionism of, 125; and romance, 129; Wharton's critique of, 135; women in, 122, 147
Characterization: and dialogue, 55; and plot, 55; in the short stories, 10
Characters: and ability to confront reality, 117; female, 117; male, 117, 147–48, 149; as mirror images, 118, 119–20; names of, 1, 31, 41; and naturalism, 56; as outsiders, 117; in *Summer*, 120–21; and Wharton, biographical parallels to life of, 1–3, 4, 13, 101, 102, 108, 142. *See also* individual characters
Charity Royall (*Summer*): and Lawyer Royall compared, 118, 119–20; and marriage, vii, 121–22; masochism of, 119; and romantic love, 120
Chopin, Kate, 139; *The Awakening*, 139

Civil War (1861–65), 144
Cixous, Helen, 95
Clark, Sir Kenneth, 27
Coleridge, Samuel Taylor, 52, 57
Conrad, Joseph, 72
Convention: in *The Age of Innocence*, 110–11; in the short stories, 12, 13, 14; Wharton's attitude toward, 13
Cott, Nancy, 141
Coverdale (*The Blithedale Romance*), 69
Critics, 55, 152; on *Ethan Frome*, 66; on *The House of Mirth*, 152; on *The Reef*, 39; on *Summer*, 117; Wharton annoyed by, 55
Custom of the Country, The, 117; discussed, 1–3, 29–38; and Fouqué's *Undine* compared, 35, 36; materialism in, 113; passion in, 67; quoted from, 3; tragedy in, 32–33. *See also* Ralph Marvell; Undine Spragg

Darwin, Charles, 106, 140
Determinism, 55
Divorce: in *The Age of Innocence*, 110; in American life, 15; and the contemporary reader, 16; psychological consequences of, 16; and the sexual relation, 16; in the short stories, 12, 15, 16; social consequences of, 16. *See also* Marriage; Morality
Donovan, Josephine, 141
Dorian Gray (*The Picture of Dorian Gray*), 147
Dorothea Brooke (*Middlemarch*), 14
Double standard, society's, 43, 48
Douglas, Mary, 113
Du Bos, Charles, 14, 67

Edna Pontellier (*The Awakening*), 139, 140, 152
Edwards, Lee, 6, 104
Eliot, George, *Middlemarch*, 14

Ellen Olenska, 103, 106, 115; clothes of, 107, 108–9; divorce of, 110; and May Welland compared, 108; and Newland Archer compared, 109, 111, 112; as "outsider heroine," 114, 117; sexuality of, 109, 113–14; and Wharton, biographical parallels to life of, 101

Emerson, Ralph Waldo, 6

Ethan Brand ("Ethan Brand"), 69

Ethan Frome: aesthetic strength of, 7; apocalypse in, 85–86; and *A Backward Glance*, 66; and Balzac, 68; begun in French, 67–68; and "Bewitched," 92; and the "Black Book Ethan," 67–68, 69, 78; and Browning, 68–69; and Conrad, 72; discussed, 3–7, 65–87; dramatization of, 65; fatalism in, 6, 7; grotesqueness of, 85; and Hawthorne, 4, 69–70; imagery in, 6, 66, 81; irony in, 82; R. W. B. Lewis on, 4; and Melville, 70; and New England writers, 85–86; and Nietzsche, 4; as a Northern romance, 7; opening of, 70, 72; psychological perspective on, vii, 65–87; popularity of, 3; publishing history of, 3, 65–66; quoted from, 5–6, 70, 71, 73; and realism, 4, 7; structure of, 66, 68, 69, 70; suffering in, 4; threshold motif in, 77, 78, 79, 85; as a tragedy, 3–4, 7; visionary ethos of, 7, 81, 84; Wharton's Introduction to, 4, 5, 65–66, 68, 69; as Wharton's most American story, 3–4; Wharton's opinion of, 65, 66, 67, 87; and *Wuthering Heights*, 7, 70. *See also* Ethan Frome; Mattie Silver; Narrator; Zeena Frome

Ethan Frome (*Ethan Frome*), 5, 7, 75, 79–86; and the American Sublime, 6; character traits of, 6, 81, 82–83; and death, 6, 7, 81, 82, 84; and Melville's Ahab, 6; as a name, 69; and pathology, 80; sexuality of, 81, 82, 83; and silence, 79, 80, 81, 82; and suffering, 4; and Undine Spragg, 4; and Wharton, biographical parallels to character of, 4, 13, 101

Eumenides, the, 145

"Eyes, The," 10, 94; Alice Nowell as character in, 22, 23; Andrew Culwin as character in, 22, 23, 97; W. Berry on, 23; discussed, 22–23; and Freud, 97; and grotesqueness, 97; and Hawthorne, 69; homosexuality in, 22, 97; male sadism in, 97; moral significance of, 18; as the most powerful of Wharton's ghost stories, 97; quoted from, 97; title of, 22; and *The Turn of the Screw*, 18; virtuosity of, 22, 23, 97

Fairy-tale motif: and the American lifestyle, 49–50; de Beauvoir on, 49; and the Cinderella myth, 47, 48, 49; male rescuers in, 44, 47, 48; and masculine dominance, 48; and the Prince Charming fantasy, 40–41, 42, 43, 44, 45, 47, 48–49; and the Sleeping Beauty fantasy, 40, 42, 44, 45, 46, 47, 49. *See also The Reef*; Women

Fouqué, Friedrich von, 29; *Undine*, 29–38

Frazer, Sir James, *The Golden Bough*, 106

Freeman, Mary Wilkins: "A New England Nun," 146; "Old Woman Magoun," 146

Freud, Sigmund, 4, 19, 89, 94–95, 97, 140; "Femininity," 140

Fuller, Margaret, 153

George Darrow (*The Reef*), 41, 43–44; as Prince Charming, 43; as "savior" of women, 42, 43, 47, 49

Ghost stories, 10; biographical interest of, 12, 20; eroticism in, 18, 19,

Ghost stories (*continued*)
  20; and the fantastic, 19, 94; and
  feminism, vii, 89–97; grotesqueness in, 97; male sadism in, 97; origin of genre of, 18; and society,
  89–90; supernatural in, 94–95,
  97; and "Telling a Short Story,"
  18; violence in, 18; and Wharton
  on ghosts, 91; and Wharton's con-
  tribution to genre of, 97; women
  victims in, 96. *See also* individual
  ghost stories; Sexuality
Gissing, George, *The New Grub Street,*
  56
Gods Arrive, The: artistic merit of, 51;
  fiction discussed in, 54, 55–56;
  and the Great Depression, vii, 51,
  57; as a neglected novel, vii, 51;
  Wharton's views on literature in,
  51, 53–54. *See also* Artist; Halo
  Tarrant; Vance Weston
Goethe, Johann Wolfgang von, 11, 107
Grandmother Mingott (*The Age of Innocence*), 106, 111, 112, 113
Great Depression, the, vii, 51, 57
Guiney, Louise, 147
Gus Trenor (*The House of Mirth*), 124,
  125, 132, 143, 147, 148, 150

Hall, Edward, 104
Halo Tarrant (*The Gods Arrive*), 52,
  54, 55, 57, 59–63; and Lily Bart,
  59; as New Woman, 60; on
  Vance's writing, 60–63
Hardy, Thomas, 145; *Tess of the D'Ur-
  bervilles,* 145
Harrison, Constance Cary, 146; *The
  Anglomaniacs,* 146
Hawthorne, Nathaniel, 4, 7, 69–70;
  The Blithedale Romance, 69; *The
  Scarlet Letter,* 4
Heine, Heinrich, 29
Hemingway, Ernest, 10
"His Father's Son," incest in, 27;
  Wharton pleased with, 27; and
  Wharton's rumored illegitimacy, 27

Hoffmann, E. T. A., *Undine* (opera), 29
Holbein, Hans the Younger, 26
House of Mirth, The, 103; biographical
  interest of, 153–54; discussed,
  123–37, 139–54; ending of, 152–
  53; and female creativity, viii,
  143–44; and female solidarity in,
  153; Jews in, 149; as a Kunstlerroman, 142; and literary traditions,
  143–44; male characters in, 147–
  48, 149; and naturalism, 55; as a
  novel of transition, 140, 153; plot
  of, 144; quoted from, 129, 131–
  32, 135, 149; radical theme of,
  150; romanticism in, 137; translation of, 14; as Wharton's first
  great novel, 139; Wharton's views
  on society in, 135–36; and
  O. Wilde, 147; and the woman as
  novelist, viii, 139–54; women's relationships in, 144–45; writing of,
  153–54. *See also* Capitalist economy; Lily Bart; Morality; Women
Howells, William Dean, *A Modern Instance,* 15
Hudson River Bracketed: artistic merit
  of, 51; as a neglected novel, vii,
  51; provincial life in, 58; Wharton's views on literature in, 51,
  53–54. *See also* Artist; Great
  Depression, the; Vance Weston
Huxley, Thomas Henry, 106

Irony, in Wharton's fiction, 46, 48, 82,
  92

James, Henry: death of, 102; and literary theory, 10, 54; and the marriage theme, 11; on C. Nilsson,
  107; praising *The Reef,* 39, 40;
  and the short story genre, 10; and
  Wharton compared, 4, 10, 54,
  100, 113; Wharton's alleged apprenticeship to, 147; as Wharton's
  friend, 102; on Wharton's personality, 2; and Wharton praising *The*

Turn of the Screw, 18; as Wharton's rival, 11. Works: *The Bostonians,* 113; *The Golden Bowl,* 39; "The Jolly Corner," 95, 101; *The Turn of the Screw,* 18, 19; *The Tragic Muse,* 107
James, William, 93
Jessup, Josephine, *The Faith of Our Feminists,* 89
Jewett, Sarah Orne, 86
Jews, 149
Jones, George Frederick, 27
Jones, Lucretia Rhinelander (mother), 78, 153
Joyce, James, 10
Jung, Carl, 19
Jupiter, 18

Language, in the short stories, 25, 96
Lawrence, D. H., 10, 13; *Lady Chatterley's Lover,* 13; *A Study of Thomas Hardy,* 13; *Women in Love,* 13
Lawrence Selden (*The House of Mirth*), 117, 124, 146; and contemporary society, 149; as a negative hero, 130; as New Man, 142, 149; personal characteristics of, 127–30, 134
Lawyer Royall (*Summer*): and Charity Royall compared, 118, 119–20; importance of, as character, 117, 118; and male dominance, vii; marriage of, vii, 121–22
LeGuin, Ursula, *The Left Hand of Darkness,* 6
Lewis, R. W. B.: praising *Ethan Frome,* 4; publishing "Beatrice Palmato," 89; as Wharton's biographer, vii, 2; as Wharton's critic, vii; on Wharton's personality, 2–3; on Wharton's short stories, vii, 9–28
Lewis, Sinclair, *Elmer Gantry,* 58
Lily, The (periodical), 145
Lily Bart (*The House of Mirth*), 117, 125; and adulthood, 140; and the capitalist economy, 124, 128–29, 130, 132, 134; character traits of, 134; and K. Chopin's Edna Pontellier, 139, 140, 152; and death, 103, 130, 132, 135, 139, 153; deformed by society, 147; and Dorian Gray, 147; first name of, 145–46; and Freeman's Lily Dyer, 146; as a lady, 141–42, 149, 150–51; and marriage, 46, 133, 142; and morality, 135, 147; as New Woman, 149; and self-definition, 143; and spinsterhood, 144; and *Tess of the D'Urbervilles,* 145; and Wharton, biographical parallels to life of, 142. *See also* Working class
Lortzing, Albert, 29; *Undine* (opera), 29
Lovett, R. M., 90–91

McDowell, Margaret B., vii, 51–63, 95, 151
Marriage, theme of: and adultery, 12, 14; and Browning, 14; and children, 12, 15; and G. Eliot, 14; immorality of, 16; and love, 14, 40; and men, 148; and Russian writers, 11; in the short stories, 12, 13–14, 15, 16; and society, 12; as a stabilizing institution, 60; and Western fiction, 11–12; and Wharton, biographical parallels to life of, 12, 14, 60; and Wharton as first American writer on, 11; Wharton's critique of, 148. *See also* Divorce; individual characters; Women
Materialism, 113
Mattie Silver (*Ethan Frome*), 4, 7, 71, 77–78, 82, 83, 84
Maupassant, Guy de, 145
May Welland (*The Age of Innocence*), 106, 108, 110–11, 113, 114, 115. *See also* Ellen Olenska; Newland Archer

Melville, Herman, 6, 7; "Bartleby the Scrivener," 70; *Moby-Dick,* 6
Miriam Rooth (*The Tragic Muse*), 107
"Miss Mary Pask," discussed, 92–93; and female aging, 93; male attitudes in, 92, 93; sensuality in, 93
Morality: in *The Age of Innocence,* 13, 104; central theme of, 13; and divorce, 16; and extramarital sex, 21; in *The House of Mirth,* viii, 123–37; and the man-woman dilemma, 14; in *The Reef,* 39; and society, 13; and transcendence, 136–37; Wharton's view of, 13. *See also* Capitalist economy; Lawrence, Lily Bart

Narrative point of view: in *Ethan Frome,* 69, 70–77, 78; James on, 10; in *The Reef,* 39; in the short stories, 10, 27
Narrator: (*Ethan Frome*), 4–6, 68, 69, 70–77, 78; as Ethan Frome's shadow-self, 76, 81, 85, 87; and Hawthorne, 69–70; subjectivity of, 70, 71, 72, 74, 75, 77, 83; use of as a literary technique, 70; Wharton on, 68. *See also* Brontë; Hawthorne; Melville
Naturalism, 53, 55–56
Nettie Struther (*The House of Mirth*), 136–37, 151, 152, 153
Nevius, Blake, 24, 26, 53, 118
Newland Archer (*The Age of Innocence*), 106, 114; and Ellen Olenska compared, 109, 111, 112; and May Newland's world, 110–11, 115; and morality, 13; and society, vii, 104, 107, 110; as a weak male, 117; and Wharton, 108
New Testament. *See* Bible
New York City, historical: and Old New York society, 1, 3, 25–27, 107, 146, 151; as setting of Wharton's fiction, 26, 105, 106, 107, 110, 121

Nietzsche, Friedrich Wilhelm, 4; *The Genealogy of Morals,* 4
Nilsson, Christine, 107

"Other Two, The," 10, 12; comedy of manners in, 17; quoted from, 17; Waythorn as character in, 175; as Wharton's best short story, 17

Persephone, legend of, 18–19
Pluto, 18
"Pomegranate Seed," 18, 94; discussed, 18–19, 96–97; Elsie as character in, 19; Kenneth Ashby as character in, 18, 19; and Persephone, 18–19; quoted from, 96–97; sexuality in, 19; title of, 18–19
Pornography, 89–90
Pound, Ezra, 147
Pulitzer Prize, 100

Ralph Marvell (*The Custom of the Country*), 2, 31–32, 33, 36, 37, 38
Realism, 4, 7, 89
Reductiveness, as a literary technique, vii, 1, 3, 4, 7
Reef, The, 117, 142; artistic beauty of, 50; as a fairy tale, 40–41; female destiny in, 50; imagery in, 41; irony in, 46, 48; and James, vii, 39, 40, 50; manuscript of, 41; moral of, 39; as a neglected work, 50; quoted from, 42, 43; romance vs. reality in, 42; theme of, 39, 40, 49; and title, 43, 50; and woman's salvation, vii, 40, 47–48. *See also* Anna Leath; Fairy-tale motif; George Darrow; Sophy Viner; Women
"Roman Fever," 9; dialogue in, 27; discussed, 27–28; Grace Ansley as character in, 27–28; illegitimacy in, 12, 27, 28; and Wharton, 27–28

Romanticism, 86, 137; German, 31, 38

Rosaldo, Michelle Zimbalist, 106;
    Women, Culture and Society, 106

Rosedale (*The House of Mirth*), 133,
    147, 149

Satire, artistic life as subject of, 24; in
    The Gods Arrive, 56, 57, 58–59;
    in *Hudson River Bracketed,* 56–
    57, 58–59; of popular fiction, 56;
    in the short stories, 24–26

Schelling, Friedrich William Joseph von,
    89

Schopenhauer, Arthur, 4

Scribner's Magazine, 9, 154

Self: and dependency, 78–79; escape
    from, 118, 119; in *Ethan Frome,*
    76, 79; and fiction, 87; fragmenta-
    tion of, 104

Setting: in *The Age of Innocence,* 58,
    105, 106, 109, 111; in *Ethan
    Frome,* 5–6, 73, 74, 76, 85, 92; in
    The Gods Arrive, 54; in *Hudson
    River Bracketed,* 52, 56, 57–59; in
    The Reef, 41, 42, 43, 45, 54; in
    the short stories, 18, 23, 24, 27,
    92. *See also* New York City, his-
    torical

Sexuality: and "distancing" technique,
    19; and eroticism, 19, 20, 90; and
    fantasy, 19; and Freud, 89; and the
    ghost story, 19, 89; and homosex-
    uality, 22, 97; and incest, 27, 104;
    and mythology, 19; and pathology,
    89, 90; and realistic fiction, 19;
    and sadism, 18, 97; and society,
    89; and spirituality, 21; and the
    subconscious, 90; and the superna-
    tural, 90; and the Victorian era,
    19; and Wharton's writing, 67. *See
    also* Pornography

Short stories: and the classical tradition,
    10, 11; early, 9; and the ghost
    story, 10; illegitimacy in, 12, 27,
    28; and James as rival, 11; of later
    years, 9; number of produced, 9;

and Russian writers of, 11; satiri-
    cal, 24–26; situations in, 10–11;
    subject matter of, 10; and "Telling
    a Short Story," 10, 11; unpub-
    lished manuscripts of, 9; and
    Wharton as a writer of, 9. *See also*
    individual short stories

Sitwell, Osbert, 91

Smith, Elizabeth Oakes, 140, 146; *Ber-
    tha and Lily,* 146

Smith-Rosenberg, Carroll, 140

Society: in *The Age of Innocence,* 103,
    104, 106, 107, 113–14; in *The
    House of Mirth,* 135–36; and the
    realist novel, 89; and social mores,
    16; and "taste," 107, 108; Whar-
    ton on, 135–37

Sophy Viner (*The Reef*), 40, 46, 47.
    See also Anna Leath

"Souls Belated," 10, 14; adultery in,
    12; discussed, 12–14; flaws in, 13;
    Lydia Tillotson as character in, 12,
    14; marriage in, 12; Ralph Gan-
    nett as character in, 12

Spacks, Patricia Meyer, 152

Spencer, Herbert, 106

Starkfield, 5, 66, 85

Stendhal, 11

Stevens, Wallace, 1, 6

Stream-of-consciousness technique, 55–
    56

Sturgis, Howard, 102

Suicide, 4, 36

Summer, 142; concept of reality in,
    118, 119, 120–21; discussed,
    117–22; marriage in, 118, 121–
    22; patriarchy in, 119; praised by
    Berenson, 117; quoted from, 120;
    romantic love in, 67, 119, 120; as
    uncharacteristic of Wharton's nov-
    els, 118; Wharton on, 117;
    Wharton's favorite theme in, 120.
    See also Charity Royall; Lawyer
    Royall

Supernatural, genre of, 18, 90. *See also*
    Ghost stories

Tarpeia, 147
Thackeray, William, 1
Todorov, Tzvetan, 93, 94
Tolstoy, Lev, 11, 13
Trollope, Anthony, 11
Tyler, Elisina, 27

Undine (Fouqué), discussed, 29–38;
　　and German romanticism, 31;
　　Wharton's acquaintance with, 29,
　　30. *See also The Custom of the
　　Country*
Undine (*Undine*), as a water nymph,
　　30, 34, 37–38. *See also* Undine
　　Spragg
Undine Spragg (*The Custom of the
　　Country*): and Becky Sharp, 1; first
　　name of, 30, 31, 33; and Fouqué's
　　Undine compared, vii, 30, 32, 34–
　　35, 36, 37, 38; and marriage, 2,
　　35; and Mrs. Alfred Uruguay, 3;
　　as a reductionist, 1, 3; and Whar-
　　ton, parallels to personality of, 1–
　　3. *See also* Lewis, R. W. B.; Un-
　　dine

Vance Weston (*Hudson River Brack-
　　eted; The Gods Arrive*), 60–63;
　　and American education, 57–58;
　　Midwestern background of, 57–
　　58; romantic life of, 52–54; as a
　　spokesman for Wharton's literary
　　views, 53–57; and Wharton's
　　snobbishness, 57; and Words-
　　worth, 54; as writer, 51–52, 53,
　　54–56

Warren, Robert Penn, *World Enough
　　and Time,* 4
Wharton, Edith: as an adolescent, 78;
　　and adulthood, 78, 87; childhood
　　of, 2, 29, 100, 153; and cultural
　　anthropology, 106; death of, 9,
　　27; diary of, 21; divorce of, 15;

early fiction of, 9, 103; as an expa-
　　triate, 51, 101; favorite theme of,
　　120; fictional characters of (*see*
　　Characters); and financial success,
　　55; as Freud's contemporary, 4;
　　friends of, 2, 14, 27, 67, 102; gov-
　　erness of, 29; and history, 103; as
　　house-owner, 100; illegitimacy of,
　　rumor about, 27, 28; illness of,
　　78; and James (*see* James); lan-
　　guage facilities of, 29, 67; later fic-
　　tion of, 9, 90; at Lenox, 65, 69;
　　life crisis of, 27; marriage of, 12,
　　21, 24 (*see also* Wharton, Edward
　　Robbins); mother of, 78 (*see also*
　　Jones, Lucretia Rhinelander); as a
　　Nietzschean, 4; and the past, 102;
　　personal characteristics of, 1–3, 23,
　　25, 57, 86; politics of, 124, 135–
　　37; psychological concepts about,
　　2, 78, 87, 100, 101; as a reduc-
　　tionist, vii, 1, 3, 4, 7; romantic re-
　　lationships of, 12, 21–22, 23, 24,
　　66–67; sexuality of, 21, 67; social
　　background of, 142; views on the
　　family of, 103; views on literature
　　of, 4, 10, 11, 51, 53–57; and
　　World War I, experience of, 54,
　　101–2, 103, 104–5; as a writer, 9,
　　55, 65, 66, 87, 100, 142, 153,
　　154. Works: "Afterward," 94–95;
　　A Backward Glance, 66, 101, 102,
　　106, 113, 153, 154; "Beatrice Pal-
　　mato," 89, 104; *The Best Short
　　Stories of Edith Wharton,* 21; "Be-
　　witched," 19, 92; "A Bottle of
　　Perrier," 9, 11; *The Buccaneers,* 9;
　　The Children, 57, 104; "A Cup of
　　Cold Water," 10; "The Debt," 24;
　　The Decoration of Houses, 100;
　　"The Descent of Man," 24, 25;
　　"Diagnosis," 12; "Dieu d'Amour,"
　　21; "The Dilettante," 12; "The
　　Duchess at Prayer," 21; *Fighting
　　France,* 104; *French Ways and
　　Their Meanings,* 113; "The Full-
　　ness of Life," 12; *Ghosts,* 91;

"The Hermit and the Wild Woman," 20–22; "Her Son," 12, 27; "The House of the Dead Hand," 24; "The Introducers," 12; Introduction to *Ethan Frome,* 4, 5, 65–66, 68, 69; "A Journey," 9; "Kerfol," 18, 96; "The Lady's Maid's Bell," 19; "The Lamp of Psyche," 12; "The Last Asset," 12, 15; "The Letters," 12; *Literature,* 51, 54; "The Long Run," 12, 14, 23, 25–26; "The Looking Glass," 91–92; "The Mission of Jane," 15; *Mother's Recompense,* 103; "Mr. Jones," 18, 95–96; "The Muse's Tragedy," 23; *New Year's Day,* 118; *The Old Maid,* 27, 103; "The Pelican," 9, 24; *The Powers of Darkness,* 90; Preface to *Ghosts,* 91, 95; "The Quicksand," 12; "The Recovery," 9; *A Son at the Front,* 54, 60; "Telling a Short Story" (essay), 10, 11, 18; "That Good May Come," 10; "The Triumph of Night," 94; *Twilight Sleep,* 57, 60, 103; "The Valley of Childish Things and Other Emblems," 20, 99–100, 113; *The Valley of Decision,* 9, 118; *Verses,* 9; "Xingu," 24, 25. *See also* "After Holbein"; *The Age of Innocence;* "All Souls"; Artistic merit; Biographical data; Characters; *The Custom of the Country; Ethan Frome;* "The Eyes"; *The Gods Arrive;* "His Father's Son"; *The House of Mirth; Hudson River Bracketed;* Lewis, R. W. B.; "Miss Mary Pask"; "The Other Two"; "Pomegranate Seed"; *The Reef;* "Roman Fever"; "Souls Belated"; *Summer*

Wharton, Edward Robbins (Teddy), 12, 24

Wilde, Oscar, 147; *The Picture of Dorian Gray,* 147

Wilson, Edmund, 145, 149; "Justice to Edith Wharton," 145

Winthrop, Egerton, 102

Wolff, Cynthia Griffin, vii, 65–87, 127, 142, 152; *A Feast of Words,* 127

Women: vs. capitalist economy, 122, 147; and creativity, 143–44; as decorative objects, 100, 142; and the double standard, 43, 48; and economic security, 46, 122, 148; and the family, 103–4; and female destiny, 50; and female society, 107, 113–14; in fiction, as portrayed by male writers, 142, 147; and freedom, 46, 50; Freud on, 140; and ghosts, 96; and history, 103; and *The House of Mirth,* 125–26, 139–46, 147, 153; and identity, 140; and the life cycle, 92–93, 105, 139–40; and marriage, 40, 46; and men, 44, 48, 50, 92, 106, 140–41, 149; and the New Woman, 141; "nice," 48–49, 109; and power, 125–26; and relationships to other women, 92, 114, 147, 149, 150, 151; and society, 44, 106, 147; and "The Valley of Childish Things and Other Emblems," 113; and Victorian culture, 140, 141; and war, 104, 105; and Wharton's feminist contributions to fiction, 89; as whores, 48–49, 60; Woolf on, 104, 105; and the working class, 150, 151. *See also* Fairy-tale motif; Ghost stories; individual characters

Women's writing, American: and Wharton's fiction, 141, 145, 146, 153; and "woman's fiction," 139–40, 141, 144, 145

Woolf, Virginia, 104–5; and Wharton compared, 104

Wordsworth, William, 54

Working class: in *The House of Mirth,* 136–37, 150, 151–52; Wharton on, 136–37; and women, 150, 151

World (periodical), 9
World War I, 54, 101–2, 103, 104–5
Yeats, William Butler, 136; "A Prayer for My Daughter," 136

Zeena Frome (*Ethan Frome*), 71, 77, 80, 82
Zenobia (*The Blithedale Romance*), 69
Zenobia Frome. *See* Zeena Frome